IDENTITY, PRIVACY, AND PERSONAL FREEDOM

IDENTITY, PRIVACY, AND PERSONAL FREEDOM

BIG BROTHER vs. THE NEW RESISTANCE

SHELDON CHARRETT

PALADIN PRESS • BOULDER, COLORADO

Also by Sheldon Charrett:

The Modern Identity Changer
Electronic Circuits and Secrets of an Old-Fashioned Spy

Identity, Privacy, and Personal Freedom:
Big Brother v. The New Resistance
by Sheldon Charrett

ISBN 1-58160-042-9
Printed in the United States of America

Published by Paladin Press, a division of
Paladin Enterprises, Inc., P.O. Box 1307,
Boulder, Colorado 80306, USA.
(303) 443-7250

Direct inquiries and/or orders to the above address.

PALADIN, PALADIN PRESS, and the "horse head" design
are trademarks belonging to Paladin Enterprises and
registered in United States Patent and Trademark Office.

Visit our Web site at: www.paladin-press.com

Contents

SECTION TWO
ACQUIRING PRIVACY, PERSONAL FREEDOM, AND NEW ID

....

....

Acknowledgements

I would like to thank the following people for their contributions to this work:

The K-man for being a good kid and a good friend.

Pauline for her support, encouragement, and editorial assistance.

My mom for finally believing I would not be imprisoned for writing this.

Barb, Donna, Jon, Karen, and Tina for remembering me at Christmas and keeping me inspired though the darkness of winter.

PL and the whole Paladin gang of freedom fighters.

The thousands of people who read my first book and continue to support me. Thank you for all the comments, suggestions, and kind words.

Warning

Sorry folks, but I gotta do this.

This book is for academic study by free-thinking individuals. It contains suggestions, procedures, and ideas that, if acted upon, may be illegal in many jurisdictions of the United States and elsewhere. Under the current interpretation of the First Amendment to the Constitution of the United States of America, it is legal for authors to write, publishers to publish, and readers to buy and read books on topics about illegal activities. However, carrying out illegal activities, even those proposed or implied by a constitutionally protected book, is a crime and punishable by harsh fines, lengthy imprisonment, or both.

Some of the ideas in this book, such as constructing and using a novelty ID, may seem harmless or even quaint. But according to the law, you can be arrested, jailed, arraigned, indicted, tried, convicted, fined, and sentenced for doing just that. Being dragged through the system is not fun. It can ruin your life and preclude you from pursuing any occupational or political aspirations you may have (e.g., if you want to become a lawyer someday, being convicted of document fraud will probably preclude you from ever doing so).

Since the publisher and I have duly warned you, liability for any use or misuse of the information contained in this text is hereby disclaimed. The reader assumes *full responsibility* for his or her actions and the consequences resulting therefrom.

Now, let's have fun!

Preface

It's been a mere two years since the release of my first book, *The Modern Identity Changer*, yet so much has changed. Some of this change started while my spindly digits were still hammering away at the final chapters of that text. The net effect of those changes, such as the proposed "Know Your Customer" banking regulations and holographic security devices implemented in state drivers' licenses, are now taking a firm hold in our society. I'm sure that even as I type this line, some congressional representative somewhere is drafting a bill that will ultimately impose further restrictions on our liberties.

There were a few occasions when I thought *The Modern Identity Changer* would be my only book about privacy, personal freedom, and identity change. But then I would think back to a time when I was "pulled over" by the police just for walking after midnight. In fact, I had been "pulled over" for walking exactly three times in my youth. One time resulted in an arrest for an unpaid traffic ticket. On each of these occasions, I could have legally walked away and the officers would have had no legal recourse. But I did not know my rights.

I also did not know about police "profiles." If I knew then what I know now, I would've known that just the action of walking at night matches the police profile of a "potential" wrongdoer in many jurisdictions in the United States. I would also have known that stopping me solely on the basis of my matching a profile is a violation of my civil rights under the U.S. Constitution. Surely if such a thing ever happened to me today, I would ask for the officers' names and badge numbers, be filing papers in court the next day, and ruminating on the sizable settlement I'd be virtually assured of receiving.

I was one of the lucky ones. I grew up as a white, so-called "middle-class" American. I wonder today how many times less fortunate minorities were pulled over for walking at night because they matched a police profile. I wonder how many others were stopped during broad daylight for having the wrong color skin or for speaking the wrong language.

Then I think, *what's changed?* The same things are going on today. Less than before? Perhaps. But nonetheless, these civil injustices are committed by bureaucrats and police officers every day of the year a thousand times over, which is a thousand times 365 days too many.

If this book can save just one person from just one instance of civil injustice, then I am morally and philosophically obligated to write it. Therefore, I dedicate this book to anyone who has ever been taken advantage of by our government and its servants because they did not know, or feared to exercise, their civil rights. I further dedicate this book to those who will be spared from civil injustice because they have studied these pages and learned their options. I hope there will be many such people.

Introduction

Panem et circenses
(Bread and circuses)
Juvenal (c. 60–c. 130)

Individual freedom is evanescing at an alarming rate. What's more alarming is our complacency about its disappearance. Born into a society that places restrictions on our liberties from cradle to grave, too many of us are unfazed when Big Brother increases his stranglehold on our lives with new laws and regulations.

But the stranglehold on liberty is reaching a point of critical mass, a point beyond which even the most complacent citizens can't help but notice that something is seriously wrong. Big Government, which includes Corporate America, has become a paranoid, self-serving machine and, for the most part, is no longer controlled by We, The People.

Fueled by insiders desperately clinging to inherited sinecures, government exists to ensure its own perpetuation. Members of the "inner party" have a strong interest in protecting the status quo and expanding the power and authority of government to secure future employment for their offspring. They protect the status quo by offering bread and circuses to the masses while passing laws to restrict their movements.

To ensure that no one steps out of line, Big Government uses modern supercomputers to hoard ridiculous amounts of personal information on citizens, who are forcibly sucked into the imploding nucleus of an impending catastrophe. That catastrophe is the inevitable misuse of our personal information to strip us of our privacy, personal freedom, and identity. A free-thinking citizen is a bureaucrat's worst nightmare; a population of broken spirits is much less likely to throw monkey wrenches into the machine.

Fortunately, there are those among us who have seen the future. They have seen the nucleus of Big Brother undergo a radioactive decay, sparking a reaction that ultimately will cause its demise.

They are the members of the New Resistance. Those who have stood outside the machine, studied it, and seen it for what it was: an unloving foster parent that we never asked for yet does everything it can to control our lives under the threat of forceful reprisal.

Who is a part of the New Resistance?

It's the lone juror who refuses to indict a young girl on minor drug charges. The treasury cop who resigns after showing his superiors extensive research that proves the Internal Revenue Service (IRS) is unconstitutional. The lawyer who puts aside his disgust with an indicted racial separatist to win him an acquittal and expose the feds who lied and set him up. The U.S. soldier who refuses to recognize United Nation authority because that was not his oath when he joined the armed forces. The waitress who hides tips from the IRS, wondering why the hell they should get a cut of her hard-earned coins. The cop who looks the other way while some college kids smoke a joint. The man who duct-tapes his license plate and drives past a traffic speed-control surveillance camera.

The New Resistance gains new members every day. You may wish to become one after reading this book. Perhaps you already have.

WHAT THIS BOOK IS

This book is about privacy, personal freedom, and identity changing. The ideas expressed herein may be applicable to one or more of these topics, and applicability may vary depending on your current state of residence, your desired state of residence, your current situation, and your ultimate goals.

It is up to you, the reader, to decide how to apply these ideas and whether such ideas can legally be used in your personal pursuit of happiness. Where specific laws are known to me they will be identified, but in most instances legality is not discussed, and the reader is solely responsible for researching applicable laws and for accepting the consequences of breaking them.

The terms privacy, personal freedom, and identity changing may apply interchangeably to certain topics discussed in this book. In other instances, their true definitions may have distinct connotations. Therefore, it is best that I define them here.

Privacy. The privacy seeker is concerned with limiting access by bureaucrats and others to his or her personal thoughts, conversations, information, records, history, and environment.

Personal freedom. Freedom fighters are interested in unfettered speech, movement, and business transactions while limiting government interference, tracking, and control over the same.

Identity changing. The identity changer is concerned with altering one or more aspects of what society, government, and Corporate America deem his or her identity to be.

WHAT THIS BOOK ISN'T

This book is not speculative. You can feel secure knowing that all material presented inside these covers has been thoroughly researched. You will not be dragged down by theoretical suggestions and conjecture as to how you *might* deal with Big Brother. You will not see any, "You could do this," or "You might try that," or "I suppose it's possible to do something else." You will not be swamped by incredible anecdotes with histories firmly rooted solely in the author's imagination. This book is a compilation of privacy, personal freedom, and identity changing *facts* that were accurate at the time of its printing.

WHO THIS BOOK IS FOR

This book is for anybody who has ever felt the hand of government reach too far into their personal life, dig too deep into their pocket, or squeeze too tightly on their soul. It is for anyone who feels a twinge of annoyance whenever some bureaucrat demands a Social Security number or driver's license. If you've ever felt labeled, stamped, numbered, subdivided, or cast aside by the government that you've elected and paid for, then this book is for you.

Anybody who has read and enjoyed my first book, *The Modern Identity Changer*, will enjoy this book as well, perhaps even more. This book delves into the nuances of privacy and identity and explores the cracks in the pavement of civilized life, where freedom fighters can still sniff out some choice morsels now and then—occasional tidbits of information to help them stay on the better side of the sanity line and at least one giant step ahead of Big Brother.

If you are already living under a new identity, this book will be tremendously useful to you. For example, Chapter 8, "Freedom Of Employment and Income," lists many "no ID required" employment opportunities, and Chapter 12, "Freedom on the Road," will help keep the authorities off your back as you make your way around the country.

WHAT THIS BOOK WILL DO FOR YOU

As a privacy seeker, you will learn new tricks and new ways of thinking to help keep Big Government and Corporate America out of your personal affairs. Freedom fighters will learn the best techniques for turning the Bureaucratic Machine against itself and making the most out of life in a civilized society. The hard-core identity changer will find this text an invaluable supplement to *The Modern Identity Changer* and other books more strictly geared toward slipping out of your skin and into someone else's. Where appropriate, new wrinkles will be outlined and new loopholes exposed. When you are done with this book, you will be able to do the following:

- Open a bank account in any name you choose
- Provide for yourself financially in any situation, whatever your skills or limitations
- Recognize which *unassigned* Social Security numbers will pass the "High Group" charts used by banks, creditors, landlords, and employers
- Manufacture a hologram-secured state driver's license and ID card
- Duplicate repetitive lettering techniques used to secure state drivers' licenses
- Drive without a driver's license
- Make a college ID card with a hologram
- Obtain a library card under an alternate identity
- Maintain a residence and mailbox free from mailing list invasion
- Avoid bill collectors
- Effectively deal with bureaucrats and police
- Take over a condo association
- Obtain a legal, camouflage passport

You will finish this book knowing that the insanity of modern society is not merely your imagination. You will gain a sense of camaraderie with other privacy seekers, freedom fighters, and identity changers who have been appalled by our evanescing liberty and the disintegration of our civil rights. Ultimately you will become an empowered member of the New Resistance and do your part, however small, to help peel back the ever-tightening talons of Big Brother.

HOW THIS BOOK IS DIFFERENT

This book is different from others like it in that it does not solely address the single issue of privacy, the philosophies of personal freedom, or the specific methods of identity change. Rather, I've done my best to encompass all three, with the expectation that the finished product will be more complete and more universal and may be used as a broad reference to these closely linked, yet separate, subjects.

In this way, the reader who has come to this book with a vague sense of global injustice may learn the causes behind it but not be forced into a detailed description of how to get away from it. And those readers concerned specifically with privacy, personal freedom, or identity change will have their needs fulfilled and develop a better understanding of how all three subjects are intrinsically linked.

Finally, it must be noted that government bodies and the corporations that help them (such as those that manufacture security features for identity documents) will also get a broader view of the minds and habits of privacy seekers, freedom fighters, and identity changers.

HOW TO USE THIS BOOK

Privacy, personal freedom, and identity changing are perpetually evolving issues. Laws are changing constantly, and loopholes seem to open and close daily. What's more, these laws and loopholes vary considerably, not only from state to state but often from town to town. Gone are the days when you could pick up a book and reliably follow a step-by-step paradigm for attaining ultimate privacy or a foolproof identity.

Rather, privacy seekers, freedom fighters, and identity changers must be vigilant. Success in these endeavors will require careful consideration, research, and work. This book will clearly illustrate the essential issues and concerns of these subjects. But readers will need to discern for themselves what information is useful to their current needs and geographical location.

Use this book to increase your awareness and add to your arsenal of knowledge in the battle against Big Brother. When this book exposes for you a choice morsel from the cracked pavement in the road of bureaucratic life, dig it out carefully. Ask questions. Research recent laws and regulations. Where are they headed? Review your life goals. Where are you headed? With an up-to-date arsenal of knowledge at your disposal and a well-defined battle plan, you will be able to strategically structure your affairs in a manner advantageous to you and detrimental to Big Brother. Future generations may not be so lucky.

FINAL NOTES BEFORE WE GET TO THE GOOD STUFF

All original material presented in this book comes from my personal experience as a private detective, reader feedback, and thorough, up-to-date research of the topics presented. Information outside those sources has been verified, deemed reliable, and credited to appropriate authors and publishers.

Though many of this book's topics may have global implications and be useful worldwide, it is primarily written from and for the viewpoint of a United States resident. Therefore, references to Social Security, the federal government, taxing authorities, and phrases such as "throughout the country" and "our country," unless otherwise noted, refer to the United States of America.

This text was written under a strict, self-imposed "no-bullshit, no rehash" rule. If I've read it in another book or have reason to believe you did, you will not find it here. Privacy seekers, freedom fighters, and identity changers are in a battle against the Bureaucratic Machine, and I'm afraid there is simply no time for rehash. Surely, as you will see, it's time to march on.

For this reason and out of respect for the thousands of readers, the soldiers of personal liberty, who believed in me and my first book, the "no-bullshit, no rehash" rule also applies to topics covered in *The Modern Identity Changer*, which is the true introduction to this work. Where appropriate, vital references to that text will appear in parentheses, unobtrusively abbreviated as *MIC*, followed by the page or chapter reference.

So, if you are part of my previous constituency, you can revel in the security of knowing that I intend to keep you up to date and that you did not just blow your hard-earned cash to read a mere rewording of my previous book. You are about to be further enlightened by *new* information, *updated* caveats, and *additional* tips, tricks, angles, loopholes, and slam-dunks to help keep you from being sucked into the maw of the Bureaucratic Machine.

Now, let's get to work.

The Battle with Big Brother

Big Brother is Getting Bigger

They say there is strangeness too dangerous
In our theaters and bookstore shelves.
Neil Peart

In this alleged era of shrinking government and corporate downsizing (or "rightsizing" as is now the politically correct term), you might find it disappointing to learn that Big Brother is still getting bigger. It may be true that many jurisdictions and bureaus of the United States are successfully "trimming the fat" from government. But, with the exponential expansion of modern technology and computers, Big Brother is actually becoming streamlined and more efficient.

Because taxpayers are increasingly reluctant to support the hiring of new personnel for an already bloated system, modern bureaucrats are turning to technology to maintain and strengthen their stranglehold on the public's privacy. Every anomalous crime is sensationalized in the media, and anxious pols line up in front of the television cameras to call for more controls. I don't think it was a full two hours after the shootings of the two security guards at the Capitol Building in Washington, D.C., when government officials began stressing the importance of tighter security and recommended that computer "face scanners" be installed in all government buildings as soon as practicable. "Facecrime" has arrived, after all.

CORPORATE CONDITIONING

But not all of Big Brother's tentacles sprawl from Washington, D.C. There is another, perhaps more dangerous beast born of Big Brother. That beast is Corporate America.

From a very young age, we are told by Corporate America how we should look, how much we should weigh, and how we should act among our peers. Television, magazines, billboards, and now the Internet bombard us with images of "ideal people." They tell us that deviations from the ideal are unacceptable and that the more we deviate, the more we should hate ourselves and the harder we should try to conform.

Why does a nine-year-old girl call herself ugly? Because a tube tells her she's ugly. Why do teenage women become anorexic? Because a magazine tells them they're fat, and *all* fat is bad. Since they can never be like the images in the magazine, they hate themselves and punish themselves in an effort to be thin.

Why do men obsess for hours at the gym and lack confidence around women? Because a billboard tells them their body must look a certain way and because a magazine tells them their penis must be a certain size. But no matter how much time they spend in Big Stud's Gymnasium, there's always some guy at the beach with a more enviable physique and larger bulge in his swim trunks.

Because they believe they need to change themselves, people spend *billions* of dollars each year on makeup, diet books, exercise equipment and videos, health club memberships, alcohol, drugs, psychotherapy, prescriptions, diet pills, clothes, breast reductions, breast enlargements, liposuction, plastic surgery, face lifts, face creams, age creams, Gingko Biloba, DHEA, enzymes, hormones, silicone implants, vitamins, health magazines, etc., etc., etc.

People who become obsessed with attaining the unattainable ultimately become enslaved to Big Brother. They need Big Brother to provide for them, give them direction, and set for them new goals to strive for. So they can cast aside their past failures, so they can earn more money, so they can buy more stuff to distract them from their plight, so they can become disenchanted and unfulfilled. So they can again turn to Big Brother for direction . . .

Indeed, Corporate America has a high stake in keeping us unhappy with ourselves.

SOCIAL IDENTITIES

But people can't be walking around without identities! It simply wouldn't be American. When the controlled masses are beaten into forgoing their childhood dreams and ideals, when they finally turn to Big Brother and say, "I love you," they do not walk around as zombies. Big Brother wouldn't stand for it. He can't control zombies! Instead, the masses are channeled into acceptable roles and personalities. Ultimately, each becomes some malformed, crossbreed incarnation of what they once were and what they are now expected to be.

Corporate Drones

Drone (drōn) n. 1. A male bee, esp. a honeybee, characteristically stingless, and producing no honey. (Source: *American Heritage Dictionary*)

Corporate America has made it fashionable to be stressed out over your job, running late, and never having any time to yourself. At social gatherings, the drones speak proudly about how "busy" they are and how their jobs have them "on the run" and how "stressed out" they are. This is the new American identity. These people actually believe they are ingratiating themselves to others when they talk like this.

If you go to one of these social gatherings and look relaxed, you'll probably be shunned. If you happen to mention that you like your job and only work 30 hours a week, don't expect to be invited back.

The drones "make deals," say "good enough then, Jack," "alrighty then," and "let's do lunch." There is a lingo, a dress code, and a hierarchy. Hairstyles and eyeglasses must conform to currently acceptable standards. Any deviation from this narrow collective identity is suspect. Indeed, if two guys are equally qualified for the same promotion, the guy with the newer haircut will get it.

The corporate headset is not something that can be left at the company door. Even in their off hours, they must do all the things their co-workers are doing: take their turn at hosting social gatherings (i.e., shop-talk fests) and attend every recital, birthday party, wedding, wake, and funeral of even the most remote fellow drone. When they do get together to relax, it will be on Sunday to watch a football game or play golf. These are the acceptable pastimes of Droneworld.

In all their busyness, corporate drones, like honey bee drones, are ultimately ineffective and produce nothing.

Welfare Drones

Drone (drōn) n. 2. An idle person who lives off others; loafer.

In addition to an entire population of people accomplishing little more than shuffling little green pieces of paper, we have a parasite population dependent on the very flow of that paper. As long as the paper keeps flowing back and forth, there will be welfare drones who will live off it.

Let me say at this point that I have nothing but respect for disadvantaged people who utilize the welfare system, better themselves, and then move on. Unfortunately, these individuals are the exception rather than the rule. Most people on welfare in this country today are abusing the system, and you and I are paying for it.

But the system is insidious. Big Brother's bloated welfare bureaucracy, minimal life-sustaining handouts, and self-serving regulations strip the poor of all hope and human identity. Ultimately, it becomes easier for "beneficiaries" of the welfare program to accept free heroin money and hypodermic needles than to fight the Bureaucratic Machine.

Worker Bees

The drone population is counterbalanced by a population of noncorporate worker bees who provide the actual blood, sweat, and labor that keep this country going. It's the factory workers and farmers who are the backbone of this country and receive little or no recognition for it. They are steady, dependable workers who literally devote their lives to producing and processing raw materials for feeding, clothing, and sheltering our country. They are paid one-tenth of what the corporate drones are paid and must struggle every day just to survive. This leaves little time for self exploration and growth. Once they are trapped in the routine, most remain there for life.

STRANGLEHOLD

Big Brother chokes our liberty with a treacherous half-nelson hold. Then, when the referee is not looking, he slips the other hand behind our necks for full suffocation of our rights.

Once the masses are satisfactorily under control, the Big Machine does not downshift. Because there have been uprisings in the past—historic incidents and eras where free-thinking individuals rose up and monkey-wrenched the regime—the establishment is paranoid and peremptorily enacts laws and regulations to secure the status quo.

A good example of this is the current trend of states enacting mobile scanner laws. Big Brother is trying to restrict the use of police scanners because it fears these devices may undermine its quest for total control. Of course, the next step will be to make them illegal altogether.

A few states have reasonable mobile scanner laws that allow penalties only when the scanner is used in the commission of a crime. Such states include California, New Jersey, Oklahoma, Vermont, and Virginia. Other states have blanket laws that provide for fining and imprisonment of any citizen whose vehicle contains a scanner, even if the scanner is not connected or turned on. These states readily confess that such laws are aimed at criminals who use scanners to perpetrate a crime or evade apprehension by authorities after committing a crime. This is sloppy and dangerous legislation because it punishes the innocent with the guilty. It is a lazy solution to a relatively minor problem.

How are the innocent hurt, you ask?

I have a Radio Shack PRO-46 hand-held scanner that fits nicely in the cell phone pocket of my briefcase. That's where I keep it whether I'm at home, on the road, or in a motel. I've used it on the road to successfully route myself around traffic accidents and avoid closed roads during flooding. My scanner also receives NOAA Weather Radio. There has been more than one time where, based on NOAA storm warnings, I've decided to get off the road and spend the night in a safe motel. On other occasions NOAA reports have induced me to get the hell off the coast-hugging U.S. Route 1 during dangerously high storm tides.

Furthermore, because I use and depend on my scanner wherever I go, it sits, as I said, in my briefcase. When I go somewhere, my briefcase goes with me. If Kentucky authorities happen to discover my scanner as I'm passing though, they're authorized to confiscate it and arrest me. Am I supposed to leave my scanner at the border? Circumvent Kentucky out of fear? Excuse me? Is this the United States of America?

Unfortunately, many states have enacted mobile scanner laws that impose penalties of fines and imprisonment. Among them are Florida, Iowa, Kentucky, Michigan, Minnesota, New York, and South Dakota. The Third Reich of New York, as usual, takes first prize for the most dehumanizing scanner law. Possession of a police scanner without a permit is illegal in New York state. I guess only inner-party members get permits. Can you say *Adolph Hitler*?

Here's the egregious "law," with all the boring shit removed:

> New York State Vehicle and Traffic Law
> Section 397
> EQUIPPING MOTOR VEHICLES WITH RADIO RECEIVING SETS CAPABLE OF RECEIVING SIGNALS ON THE FREQUENCIES ALLOCATED FOR POLICE USE.
> A person . . . who equips a motor vehicle with a [police scanner] or knowingly uses a motor vehicle so equipped . . . without having first secured a permit to do so . . . is guilty of a misdemeanor, punishable by a fine . . . imprisonment . . . or both.

Other states exempt ham radio operators, "recognized" news services, and persons who have an "apparent need" to monitor NOAA Weather Radio, if the scanner is so equipped. The "apparent need" is at the sole discretion of some low-level bureaucrat who knows nothing about needs nor weather. As I said, lazy, sloppy legislation. Where do I sign up for Mars colonization?

POLICE POWER

> Although the courts have traditionally been conservative in extending the scope of police power, changing social and economic conditions have influenced the courts toward making broader interpretations of this power in recent years—and the trend is likely to continue. (*Real Estate Fundamentals*, Fourth Edition Revised, by Wade E. Gaddy, Jr. and Robert E. Hart, Dearborn Publishing Group, Chicago, 1996, page 261)

Bureaucrats and police use the growing population and the resulting changes in social and economic conditions as an excuse to impose more police power and government controls in our everyday life. This is easy for them to do. The population will always be growing, and the bureaucrats can always point to it as a "problem."

While this creates more jobs for the bureaucrats and their cronies, it only amounts to a Band-Aid on a fundamentally flawed system. As police power is allowed to increase, dissension in the ranks is the likely result. This will ultimately lead to a societal breakdown.

Aside from a well-worded sentence in the Gaddy-Hart real estate book, what evidence is there of increased police power? Oh, I don't know . . . perhaps a little something called "The Mandrake"?

The Mandrake is a face-scanning system developed by Software & Systems in Slough, England. Surveillance cameras are set out at strategic locations such as airport terminals, train depots, shopping centers, and busy streets. The cameras are hooked up to computers that rapidly compare facial snapshots against a database of known and wanted criminals.

The system is very accurate. Since the device looks for skeletal patterns, it is not fooled by weight gains, changes in facial hair, or sunglasses. Since the skeletal structure of a human face does not change from age 13 to age 70 or beyond, Mandrake will not be thrown even by considerable aging. If your face is recorded in the Mandrake database, whether rightfully so or not, you can be tracked by these devices well into your old age.

When Mandrake finds a match, it audibly alerts the system administrator and places the suspect's picture at the bottom of a computer screen along with the database match. After recording the suspect's location, Mandrake continues to scan for other "criminals." If the system administrator confirms Mandrake's match, authorities can be dispatched to the suspect's location and, presumably, "dragnet" the area until he or she is apprehended. Can you say *Orwellian nightmare*?

UNCONSTITUTIONAL LAWS

Sometimes, for their own needs or personal gain, our representatives in government pass laws that are marginally constitutional at best and all too often just flagrantly unconstitutional. Normal procedure in most legislatures is for a proposed bill to run though a committee that assesses its constitutionality. But when the pol's own interests are at stake, committees can be bypassed and legislation can be sandwiched into unrelated bills, such as the annual budget.

Many "laws" get on the books exactly this way. They remain there and are pointed to by bureaucrats a thousand times over to discourage citizens from doing something they have every right to do. Politicians and bureaucrats skate by on these "laws" for years and can legally do so until some brave citizen challenges the law in court. At this point, the pols and bureaucrats will do everything in their power to have the suit dropped. A lump sum settlement may be offered and, unfortunately, is usually accepted. And there the law sits for a few more years, remaining on the books until challenged by an organization such as the American Civil Liberties Union or by a stand-up citizen who refuses to be paid off. Then, only if the plaintiffs are successful, the law will finally be removed. (For a good example of this, see *Colorado v. Ro'mar* under "Our Final Hope: The Courts" below.)

MONOPOLISTIC MAIL

The U.S. Post Office, allegedly organized as a private corporation on July 1, 1971, resembles a private corporation about as much as a jackal resembles a squid.

Chapter four of *The Modern Identity Changer* explained that commercial mail-receiving agencies—known as "CMRAs" to postal cretins and as "mail drops" to the rest of us—were a great place to find privacy. The operative word, unfortunately, is "were."

For years, we citizens were "allowed" to lease private mailboxes (PMBs in cretin-speak) from mail drops and use natural-sounding address designations for our mailboxes. In other words, if you had mailbox 16 at your local mail drop, you could receive mail addressed to "Suite 16," "Apartment 16," or "Cubby Hole Sixteen" at the mail drop's street address. By using a mail drop as your address, you could keep your real address private.

What were some of the benefits of this? After meeting a love interest on the Internet who wanted to send his picture, a judicious young lady could give her mail drop address, thus shielding her from a potential fatal attraction. Similarly, registering an automobile to a mail drop could prevent unexpected visits from road ragers. A home-based business could give the appearance of having a separate office. The uses were endless.

Now the postal prigs have implemented a new federal regulation forcing CMRA users to designate their private mailboxes as "PMB." No longer can you use the "Suite" or "Apt." address designation at a mail drop. Rather, your correspondents must address letters to you as "PMB" or your mail will not be delivered.

But using the PMB designation, like using the P.O. Box designation, is like saying, "Okay axe murderers, I dare you to find my real address!" It immediately tips off potential nasties that you live somewhere other than where they are sending you mail. This is a lawsuit waiting to happen, my friends, and when some senator's daughter turns up dead because her private mailbox was taken away, you betcha there'll be hell to pay. Until then, the "masses" must put up with this outrage.

The ability to sell "Suite" and "Apt." designations was the bread and butter of the mail drop industry. It was the main reason people plopped down $30 a month for a mail drop rather than $3 a month for a P.O. Box. This "fedreg" will force many, many mail drop establishments out of business.

If any other "private corporation" enacted a policy that so severely affected its direct competition, that corporation would be brought up on antitrust violations and fined harshly. The government that enacted this regulation is the same government that investigated Microsoft Corporation for antitrust violations. Yet, this squelching of the mail drop industry is far worse and more far-reaching than anything Microsoft ever did. This is just another example of Big Brother's double standard of control.

BIG BROTHER BANKING

A long-standing rule (since 1970) of which few people are aware is that the IRS requires banks to file a report for each customer transaction involving more than $10,000. The report must include the customer's Social Security number (SSN). A similar but separate report is also required on any person involved in a trade or business who makes a cash transaction over $10,000.

This means any person who, for example, cashes out a certificate of deposit (CD) worth over $10,000 will have a record of that transaction not only at the bank but also at Big Brother Central, aka the IRS. If a businessperson, needing to move money between banks, withdraws $10,000 in cash to avoid paying $10 for a cashier's check or a $15 wire service fee, the IRS must be notified. If your parents give you a gift of over $10,000 and you deposit it into your account, the IRS will know about that, too.

Isn't it our right to privately avoid unnecessary and exorbitant bank fees? Not anymore. Remember to thank your congressional representative.

The Office of the Comptroller of Currency

There is a new animal born to the Office of the Comptroller of Currency (OCC) known as 12 CFR Part 21 or more commonly as the "Know Your Customer" law. It is a regulation that is so blatantly unconstitutional and so flagrantly Orwellian that I can't even believe my fingers are typing these words. But since it is a "regulation" rather than actual "law," the Department of the Treasury can, at least for the time being, get away with pissing on the Constitution.

What follows are excerpts from the *Federal Register* and explanations of how they affect banking privacy. Excerpts are indented, and I have added all italic emphasis of particularly salient language.

> DEPARTMENT OF THE TREASURY
> Office of the Comptroller of the Currency
> 12 CFR Part 21
> [Docket No. 96-02]
> RIN 1557-AB19
> Minimum Security Devices and Procedures, Reports of Suspicious Activities, and Bank Secrecy Act Compliance Program
> ACTION: Final rule.
>
> SUMMARY: The Office of the Comptroller of the Currency (OCC) is amending its regulations that require national banks to file criminal referral and suspicious transaction reports. This final rule *streamlines reporting requirements* by providing that national banks file a new Suspicious Activity Report (SAR) with the OCC and the appropriate Federal law enforcement agencies by sending SARs to the Financial Crimes Enforcement Network of the Department of the Treasury (FinCEN) to report a known or *suspected* criminal offense or a transaction that a bank *suspects* involves money laundering or violates the Bank Secrecy Act (BSA).
>
> EFFECTIVE DATE: April 1, 1996

Perhaps the most significant line of this excerpt is the last one pertaining to the effective date. Recognize it? Yes, it's April Fool's Day. Could the OCC have been any less sensitive to those of us concerned with privacy?

This is a regulation promulgated by an actual branch of the government of the United States of America, and, as of April Fool's Day 1996, it is a standing rule! If a bank representative "suspects" you have done or may do something wrong, a Suspicious Activity Report (SAR) is *required*. The ramifications of this alone are far reaching, but it doesn't stop there. The new regulation also:

- Eliminates the need to file supporting documentation with the SAR
- Allows the bank to keep "business copies" of the supporting documentation, which may be computer hard drive copies or photocopies (such copies are to have the same force as an original document)
- Mandates SAR filing for *suspected* "suspicious transactions"
- Defines "suspicious transaction" as "not the sort in which the particular customer would normally be expected to engage"
- Includes currency exchanges, loans, and sales of CDs under their definition of "transaction"
- Mandates reporting of "potential" crimes
- Mandates reporting of "violations that *may* occur"
- Establishes a database accessible to federal and state regulators and law enforcement agencies
- Emphasizes a "safe harbor" law, which exempts banks *and their employees* from civil liability for filing SARs (the regulation does not provide penalties even if an employee *knowingly* makes false statements)

Let's take a look at some of the language of this regulation and discuss its implications on privacy seekers. Subsections less relevant to our discussion have been omitted. Repetitious language and legal permutations within subsections have also been omitted as indicated by ellipses (. . .). Otherwise, the language follows in order.

Section 21.11 Suspicious Activity Report
(c) SARs required. A national bank shall file a SAR with the appropriate Federal law enforcement agencies and the Department of the Treasury in accordance with the form's instructions, by sending a completed SAR to FinCEN in the following circumstances:
(2) Violations aggregating $5,000 or more where a suspect can be identified. Whenever the national bank detects any known or suspected Federal criminal violation . . . against the bank . . . where the bank believes it was an actual victim or potential victim of a criminal violation . . . or that it was used to facilitate a criminal transaction . . . If it is determined . . . the suspect . . . has used an alias, then . . . identifiers such as drivers' license, social security numbers, addresses and telephone numbers, must be reported.

Privacy seekers must note the provision in subsection (2) that allows sums to be reported in the aggregate. That means if you make five $1,000 deposits of "suspected" drug money, the teller is required to file a SAR on you. Identity changers may wish to take note of the last 26 words of the excerpt.

Subsection (3) (not shown) calls for a threshold limit of $25,000 for instances where no suspect has been identified.

Let's review another section:

Section 21.11 Suspicious Activity Report
(c) SARs required. [Same language as above.]
(4) Transactions aggregating $5,000 or more that involve potential money laundering . . . Any transaction . . . means a deposit, withdrawal, transfer between accounts, exchange of currency, loan, extension of credit, or purchase or sale of any

stock, bond certificate of deposit, or other monetary instrument or investment security, or any other payment, transfer, or delivery by, through, or to a financial institution, by whatever means . . . if the bank knows, suspects, or has reason to suspect that:

(i) The transaction involves funds derived from illegal activities or is intended or conducted in order to hide or disguise funds or assets derived from illegal activities . . . as part of a plan to violate or evade any law or regulation or to avoid any transaction reporting requirement under Federal law;

(iii) The transaction has no business or apparent lawful purpose or is not the sort in which the particular customer would normally be expected to engage, and the institution knows of no reasonable explanation for the transaction . . .

In plain English, this leaves the door wide open for banks to file a SAR on anybody who makes two $5,000 deposits instead of one $10,000 deposit. For instance, Poor Jack was forgotten in his uncle's will but his two caring sisters each wrote him a check for $5,000 upon settlement of the estate. He received the checks on different days and deposited each the day he received it.

Since Jack has carried a balance of under $400 for the past 10 years and has never deposited more than $200 at a time, this transaction is "not the sort in which [he] would normally be expected to engage." Additionally, the teller would suspect that Jack made separate deposits to avoid the IRS $10,000 reporting requirement (see previous section). That's two demerits for poor Jack. The teller must file a SAR on Jack. Jack's life is about to become very complicated.

Another noteworthy aspect of subsections (i) and (iii) is that the bank is now authorized to determine our "intent," to decide what we have "business" to do, and to file a SAR on us if there is no "apparent lawful purpose" for the way we conduct our business. All of this is included in the language, while no provision is made to allow a potential suspect to defend himself or herself *or even to be told he or she is a suspect*. To the contrary. The *Federal Register*, Volume 61, Number 24, page 4336 (available on the Internet at wais.access.gpo.gov), paraphrases the U.S. Code as follows:

31 U.S.C 5318(g) (2)
[P]rohibits financial institutions and directors, officers, employees, or agents of financial institutions from notifying any person involved in suspicious transactions that the transaction has been reported.

If the suspect happens to be an "insider," the process is even more dehumanizing.

Section 21.11 Suspicious Activity Report
(h) (2) Suspect is a director or executive officer.
If the bank files a SAR . . . and the suspect is a director or executive officer, the bank may not notify the suspect . . . but shall notify all directors who are not suspects.

Isn't there something in a little document entitled the Constitution of the United States of America that states that every American citizen has a right to face his accusers? Gee, whatever happened to that? Can you say *Inquisition*?

This regulation is so unconstitutionally broad, far-reaching, and thoughtlessly prepared that it actually undermines our nation's court systems. By exploiting loopholes provided by this banking regulation, law enforcement officials need not obtain a subpoena to peruse our "private" financial records.

Federal Register, Volume 61, Number 24, page 4335
The final rule . . . means that subsequent requests from law enforcement authorities for the supporting documentation relating to a particular SAR do not require the service of a subpoena or other legal processes normally associated with

providing information to law enforcement agencies. [. . .] The Agencies [OCC, et al.] are therefore of the opinion that the final rule . . . does not give rise to RFPA liability.

RFPA stands for the Right to Financial Privacy Act, which, apparently, is a mother lode of bullshit.

If, after reading this, you still wish to have a bank account, Chapter 10, "Banking Privacy," contains suggestions, safety precautions, and countermeasures you can use to keep your banking private.

Ride 'em In—Rawhide!

Banking regulations allegedly designed to protect the public have ultimately been more beneficial to the banking industry. Banks are so railed to the regulatory inside track, they can effectively dictate monthly fees, ATM transaction fees, interest rates, and who can and cannot have an account.

Like cattle, we are channeled into the banking system and forced to feed on the falsified fodder of teaser introductory interest rates, "totally free checking" (except for the mandatory monthly ATM card fee), and introductory "account terms and conditions," which are "subject to change without notice at any time."

And we must comply.

The government leaves no opening for real competition in the industry. If a small bank does offer a little edge to the customer, it is invariably squeezed out and bought up by a big bank that doesn't.

Nor do banks give consumers a reliable set of rules by which to play. Open a bank account in any bank in any city of the United States. You will be given a brochure explaining your account, the interest rate and how it's calculated, and various transaction fees, penalties, and policies associated with your new account. I guarantee you that within three months, your monthly bank statement will include a pamphlet highlighting "some important changes to your account." If you have the time to read through the 10,000 words of fine print and untangle the legal jargon, you will inevitably find that these "changes" are indeed very "important"—for the bank! You will find that some small right you had was amended in the bank's favor, that your interest rate has been recalculated to the bank's advantage, and that penalties and fees have been increased.

Postscript

Just before this book went to press, the Federal Reserve, OCC, Office of Thrift Supervision (OTC), and Federal Deposit Insurance Corporation (FDIC) quietly withdrew their support of the Know Your Customer (KYC) proposal. The Federal Reserve (which originally proposed the rule), OCC, and OTC had already approved it; the FDIC was the last hurdle before this dragon became law. That's how close we came to 1984, folks.

Before KYC, the largest response ever drawn during an FDIC public comment period was 3,000 letters. The average response is about 150 letters. In response to KYC, the FDIC received *over a quarter-million* protests from outraged Americans.

In fairness to the FDIC, it should be noted that a whopping 71 of the 254,000 letters were in support of Know Your Customer. That's about .0002 percent, which the banking industry idiots probably see as a victory.

It looks like KYC is dead in the water at least for a few years. The animal slowly and silently curled its tail between its legs and skulked to a corner to cower and lick its wounds. Why? Because *you* spoke up and *you were heard*. This demonstrates that the people ultimately have the voice of power, even if it takes a quarter-million voices to awaken the sleeping bureaucrats.

Now, let's see what else we can do to keep Big Brother at bay.

OUR FINAL HOPE: THE COURTS

Corruption exists everywhere, and the courts, especially those in "independent republics" like Texas and Louisiana, are no exception. The good thing about the courts, though, is that they are required to at least have the appearance of righteousness. Anytime you feel you're being shafted by the court system, make a lot of noise, attract the press if possible, and make it clear that you intend to pursue all appeals and remedies available under the law.

Most corruption exists in the lower courts. If you fail there, you can appeal to a higher court, provided you can pinpoint a flaw in the way you were dealt your "justice." So long as you're not suing anybody backed by a powerful Washington lobby, you have one more shot at justice in the higher courts.

Colorado v. Ro'mar: **A Small Victory For Our Side**

To elucidate what I'm talking about and to encourage you to challenge unconstitutional laws whenever possible, I would like to share with you the case of The People of the State of Colorado v. Scott L. Ro'mar. I am partial to this case because it involves a security agency (Robert Arthur Schultz and Ro'mar Investigation and Security, Inc). This time it was actually the state that began the action, but the defendants alleged that the state was trying to enforce an unconstitutional law.

The State of Colorado charged the defendants were in violation of Section 16-13-306, CRS 1973, which declares that it is a nuisance to carry on without a license any business required by law to be licensed. The statute in question, Section 12-21-101, CRS 1973, provides, "No person, firm or corporation shall carry on a detective business within this state without having first obtained a license as provided in this article." Operating a detective business without a license is declared a misdemeanor by Section 12-21-109.

The defendants won the first round, and the case was eventually appealed to the Colorado Supreme Court. What follows is the higher court's opinion as given by Justice Jim R. Carrigan:

> The District Attorney commenced this civil action to abate a public nuisance. The nuisance alleged is that the defendants are conducting their security guard service without obtaining a license to carry on a "detective business." The district court granted the defendants' motion to dismiss the action, holding the detective licensing statute unconstitutionally vague. We affirm.
>
> Nowhere in the statutes does there appear any definition of the term "detective business." Nor are those charged with enforcing the licensing requirement afforded any statutory standards or guidelines for determining what activities fall within the statute. Thus the statute fails to identify the persons on whom it imposes the licensing requirement. It leaves the determination of what constitutes a detective business to those charged with enforcement, and to the courts, without legislative guidance. For example, in this case we are asked to decide, without any guidelines, whether or not the defendants, by operating a security guard service, were carrying on a "detective business."
>
> Similarly, neither the dictionary definition of "detective" nor common usage gives notice what conduct may be subject to the statute's licensing restrictions and criminal penalties. Thus one must engage at his peril in the business of credit checking, skip tracing, insurance adjusting, or providing private security services. There is no sufficient definitional basis in the statute, or its legislative history, on which to predicate a sound judicial interpretation of its meaning.
>
> Nor can certainty regarding the meaning of "detective business" be gleaned from the licensing statutes of our sister states. For example, California, Indiana, New York, and Texas distinguish industrial or plant guards from private detectives. But Illinois and Iowa do not.
>
> In short, Colorado's statute leaves the intended content of the term "detective business" unknown and unknowable not only from the standpoint of authorities charged with enforcement but also from the standpoint of businessmen charged with compliance.
>
> Fair notice is the essence of the substantive due process required of penal and regulatory statutes. Fundamental notions of fair play require that such a statute: "be

sufficiently explicit to inform those who are subject to it what conduct on their part will render them liable to its penalties . . . and a statute which either forbids or requires the doing of an act in terms so vague that men of common intelligence must necessarily guess at its meaning and differ as to its application, violates the first essential of due process of law." Connally v. General Construction Co., 269 U. S. 385, 391, 46 S.Ct. 126, 127, 70 L.Ed. 322, 328 (1926). Cf. Watson v. Board of Regents, 182 Colo. 307, 512 P.2d 1162 (1973) (regulation).

The General Assembly's authority, under the police power, to regulate certain business activities is not questioned. But when a regulatory statute imposes criminal or civil sanctions, due process requires that it make reasonably clear to those intended to be affected what conduct is within its scope. Fair notice of duty to comply is particularly essential where, as here, the value of an existing business or investment may be destroyed by injunction for failure to comply. Memorial Trusts, Inc. v. Beery, 144 Colo. 448, 356 P2d 884 (1960).

The statute in question is unconstitutional in that it denies the due process of law guaranteed by the Fourteenth Amendment to the United States Constitution and by Article II, section 25 of the Colorado Constitution.

The judgment of the district court is affirmed.

After the court's decision, Colorado's Secretary of State issued the following memorandum:

MEMORANDUM
TO: Private Detective Business, Agencies and Individual Operators
FROM: Department of State, Licensing Office
RE: Licensing of Private Detectives

On February 7, 1977, the Colorado Supreme Court in the case of The People of the State of Colorado v. Scott L. Ro'mar, 559 P 2d 710 (1977) declared the state statutes (secs 12-21-101 through 110, C.R.S. 1973) requiring a license as a prerequisite to carrying on a detective business to be unconstitutional. A new law has not been enacted by the legislature.

There is no statewide control over persons who seek to operate a detective business, nor any bonding requirements. If any detective business, agency or individual opens or operates a detective business, clearance should be obtained from the local government, county or city, regarding local licensing or regulation.

Persons opening or operating such businesses should avoid advertising, or otherwise describing the business as being licensed or bonded by the State of Colorado.

The representation by any detective business, agency or individual that the business is licensed or bonded may be deceptive within the meaning of the Colorado Consumer Protection Act. Section 6-1-105 of the ACT provides that a person engages in deceptive trade practice when he knowingly makes a false representation as to the approval, sponsorship or certification of his services.

I first read about this case in *Requirements To Become a P.I. in the 50 States and Elsewhere* by Joseph J. Culligan (Hallmark Press, Inc., Miami, 1992). I then had an attorney friend (an oxymoron, I know) pull the case off Westlaw for me.

The reasons I was drawn to this case are manifold. As mentioned, it involved a private detective firm and I am a private detective. Also, it has long been my belief that states enact private detective licensing laws not to protect the public but to protect their own interests and those of their "inner party" constituency. Most state licensing requirements allow retired police officers, retired members of

U.S. investigative services, and the like to qualify for P.I. and security agency licenses while making it difficult for the average guy to do so.

Some might say my suspicion is paranoid. I would tell them to turn to the "Investigators" section of certain big city yellow page directories and note the very first ad. It is usually sponsored by the Department of State Police and reads something like this: "Attention Citizens: Before contracting the services of a Private Detective, make sure they are licensed and bonded under the laws of our state. This ad is a public service of the Department of State Police."

Then turn to the "Physicians and Surgeons" section in the same directory. There is nothing to warn citizens of the dangers of unlicensed doctors. Turn to the "Lawyers" section or the same directory—again, no "public service" caveats for the consumer. Interesting.

The constitutional issues of this case also intrigue me. Above all, it demonstrates how states enact unconstitutional laws to better their own interests and the interests of their own. It shows how bureaucratic stagnation and overcrowded courts help unconstitutional laws stay on the books for years while the state's cronies reap the benefits. I can't even imagine how many people were forced to comply with this law, forced out of business because of it, or fined for noncompliance. The most important aspect of this case was, by their winning, the defendants removed the law from the books. It shows that ordinary citizens are *not* powerless against the state if they engage it with strong arguments based on solid facts, persistance, and courage.

The Battle Continues

You say you want a revolution . . .
The Beatles

As Big Brother gets bigger and more intrusive, free-thinking individuals get angrier. Even those who once tolerated an occasional piece of junk mail or unreasonable Social Security number request are now fighting back. For those just awakening to this Orwellian nightmare, as well as seasoned veterans of the freedom fight, there are information resources available to further acquaint you with Big Brother's attacks and the New Resistance against them.

THE NEW RESISTANCE

There are a growing number of books, magazines, reports, journals, newsletters, Internet sites, and television shows about privacy, personal freedom, and identity changing. In this chapter I have listed some of my favorites. The list is by no means exhaustive; I'm sure there are many others I've yet to discover and even more yet to be born.

Newsletters and Magazines

Newsletters and magazines are important information resources if you wish to remain up to date with privacy issues and laws in the United States and around the globe. Our privacy is under *constant* attack. Even if these attacks never bear fruit, it's important to know about all threats to our privacy. We learned this lesson from Know Your Customer—just because KYC didn't pass this time, it doesn't mean it won't be proposed again in the future. In fact, I would count on it. We must learn our history lessons, because those in power have demonstrated a stubborn willingness not to.

Books are important, of course, but some of the information found in them may become outdated shortly after publication. I therefore suggest supplementing your book diet with the information resources listed below.

The Freedom, Wealth, & Privacy Report

The *Freedom, Wealth, & Privacy Report* is published by Liberty Publishing. They are based in the Channel Islands, which are in Europe. The report deals primarily with citizenship, tax sheltering, and off-shore banking for United Kingdom mainlanders. It has subscribers in over 70 countries who offer diverse input through the "Subscriber's Forum" on a wide range of privacy and identity issues.

I subscribe to this report precisely because it's not a U.S. publication. It provides valuable insight into how other countries deal with wealth management, tax avoidance, and use of off-shore havens.

The *FW&P Report* is circulated every two months and available by subscription only at the annual rate of $270. Expensive? Yes. Worth it? Indubitably. The report contains no outside advertisements, double-spaced columns, or reissue rehash. It is cover-to-cover information. A must-have for the serious privacy seeker. Their address:

Night Sky LTD
P.O. Box 115
St. Helier, Jersey JE4 8QQ
Channel Island via Great Britain
The subscription rate includes air mail postage, and they do accept Visa and Mastercard.

Privacy Journal

Privacy Journal, published monthly, reports on legislation, legal trends, new technology, and public attitudes affecting the confidentiality of information and the individual's right to privacy. The annual subscription rate is $118, with discounts offered to students and certain others. For more information or to subscribe, write:

Privacy Journal
P.O. Box 28577
Providence, RI 02908
Email: privacyjournal@internet.mci.com
Web: www.townonline.com/privacyjournal
Visa and Mastercard are accepted.

Privacy Journal also publishes the *Compilation of State and Federal Privacy Laws*. The compilation has detailed information concerning the confidentiality (or lack thereof) of records kept on you ranging from arrest and conviction records to employment urinalysis tests. Privacy laws concerning bank, cable television, credit, insurance, schools, and the telephone company are also included.

I've read the compilation. It is thorough, accurate, and up to date. Supplements are published annually, so you need not be concerned about relying on outdated information.

ISPI Privacy Reporter

The *ISPI Privacy Reporter* is a bimonthly newsletter mailed complimentary to all members of the Institute for the Study of Privacy Issues. The minimum donation to become a member is $60 for a one-year membership. The material covered by the newsletter is timely and relevant. For information on becoming a member or to learn about their nonmember services, contact:

Institute for the Study of Privacy Issues
828 Elrick Place
Victoria, BC, Canada V9A 4T1
Email: ISPI4Privacy@ama-gi.com

For a free trial of ISPI privacy-related news clips, email ISPIClips@ama-gi.com and include the following sentence: Please enter [Your Name] into the ISPI Clips list: [youremail@address.com].

The Nation

The Nation reports weekly on issues of labor, national politics, business, consumer affairs, environmental politics, and civil liberties. While this publication is quick to voice outrage at civil liberties violations, its solutions to other societal problems tend to be more statist.

The Nation
P.O. Box 37072
Boone, IA 50037
Email: info@TheNation.com
Web: www.TheNation.com

Book Publishers

Aside from my all-time favorite, Paladin Press, other outfits like Loompanics Unlimited, CRB Research Books, Eden Press, and a new one called Javelin Press are putting out some excellent titles on privacy, personal freedom, identity changing, and general Big Brother bashing.

These book publishers should be commended for daring to publish bold, new assertions and nonmainstream literature. Certainly they could make much more money publishing traditionally accepted material. The privacy movement needs loyal advocates who are unwilling to sell out. These book publishers, among others, fill that need. Be sure to get on their mailing lists.

Paladin Press

In addition to their excellent privacy, personal freedom, and new ID sections, Paladin publishes extensively on topics such as street and knife fighting, martial arts, police science, and private investigations. Diverse knowledge in these fields may indeed come in handy in your fight to maintain your privacy and personal freedom.

Paladin Press
P.O. Box 1307
Boulder, CO 80306
Email: service@paladin-press.com
Web: www.paladin-press.com

Loompanics Unlimited

Loompanics has extensive sections on identity changing, tax avoision, and the underground economy. They offer a slew of outrageous yet well-written books, the topics of which are so original they can only fall under "miscellaneous." Their catalog in itself is a delight to read.

Loompanics Unlimited
P.O. Box 1197
Port Townsend, WA 98368
Email: loompanx@olympus.net
Web: www.loompanics.com

CRB Research Books

The police scanner was invented in 1968, but CRB Research was around before that, publishing guides to public safety radio frequencies so hobbyists with tunable receivers could watch the watchers.

In 1978, communications author Tom Kneitel came up with the idea of compiling a directory of federal government frequencies. A major electronics book publisher wanted the book, but would publish it only if the author agreed to remove FBI and Secret Service frequencies, among others. Tom refused and canceled his contract. He brought his book to CRB, who published *Top Secret Registry* without chopping a single frequency.

CRB Research Books, Inc.
P.O. Box 56
Commack, NY 11725

Email: sales@crbbooks.com
Web: www.crbbooks.com

Eden Press

Eden Press pioneered the *Paper Trip* books, spawning further research by dozens of authors, lawyers, and private detectives who discovered new loopholes, tricks, and tips for new IDers. Eden still publishes ID books today and has even released an updated *Paper Trip III.*

Eden Press
11623 Slater "E"
P.O. Box 8410
Fountain Valley, CA 92728

Javelin Press

Javelin publishes the work of renowned author Boston T. Party, whose books include *You and the Police!*, *Bulletproof Privacy*, *Hologram of Liberty*, *Boston on Guns and Courage*, and *Good-Bye April 15th!*

Javelin Press
P.O. Box 31W
Ignacio, CO 81137-0031
Web: www.javelinpress.com

Internet and Web Sites

We hope the dark day never comes, but it might: Big Brother wins a case in the U.S. Supreme Court and suddenly bookstores are dropping your favorite titles from the shelves faster than you can say "Goodnight, First Amendment." They can't risk their business by carrying banned books for the handful of customers who want them, so they stock up on Danielle Steele romances instead. Where does that leave you? This would certainly be a sad day, but while the lawyers are sorting it all out, you'll probably be able to locate and buy the banned books somewhere on the Internet.

As new bills are proposed daily calling for limitations on what the public should be "allowed" to read, Internet and Web access to freedom information becomes more important. When the local police chief shuts down a bookstore because it also shelves pornographic magazines, it's nice to know you can order your ID books from the Web while the storeowner fights for his rights in court.

Sometimes it's nice to deal over the Web anyway. You can order your books under an assumed name and pick them up at a mail drop. You will not chance meeting your boss in the bookstore checkout line holding *Be Your Own Boss* in your left hand while greeting him with your right.

If the dark day does arrive, bookstores will be easy enforcement targets. Contraband will be confiscated by the police, hauled out to the street, and ignited to a toasty 451° Fahrenheit.

Policemen cannot, however, march into a Web site. World Wide Web bookstore administrators can operate anywhere—from the back of a freezer truck to a bunker 20 stories underground—or they could divide their stock among hundreds of warehouses sprinkled around the globe. For the New Resistance cannot be quelled.

To learn what some freedom fighters are doing to ensure that the day of darkness never arrives, visit these Web sites:

Electronic Privacy Information Center (EPIC): www.epic.org
American Civil Liberties Union (ACLU): www.aclu.org

According to its Web site, EPIC is a public interest research center out of Washington, D.C. Established in 1994, its goal is "to focus public attention on emerging civil liberties issues and to protect privacy, the First Amendment, and constitutional values." EPIC works in association with Privacy International, a London-based human rights group, and is a member of the Global Internet Liberty Campaign, the Internet Free Expression Alliance, and the Internet Privacy Coalition.

The ACLU has a specific page that I like to encourage people to read. It is www.aclu.org/library/fighting_police_abuse. Great information on organizing your community to police the police.

Listed below are a few more privacy-related web sites. By checking out these sites and others like them, you will develop a better understanding of your privacy rights, how they might be infringed upon, and what you can do to prevent it from happening.

www.privacyrights.org
www.privacy.org
www.spycounterspy.com

YOU ARE NOT POWERLESS

Some fledgling freedom fighters might be intimidated by the foregoing roster of New Resistance members. After all, the ACLU has grown into a large and powerful adversary of the government, and the testicular fortitude of book publishers such as Paladin and Loompanics is indeed awe inspiring. But these organizations are meaningless without the individuals who believe in and support them: people just like you.

The simple process of staying informed and spreading the word means you are important to the freedom fight. Perhaps after reading this book you will be inspired to do more. I realize that many of you reading this, even if inspiration strikes, are limited in time and means. This may leave some of you frustrated: you'd like to do a bigger part, but you're still stuck in the gears of the Big Machine, working 60 to 80 hours a week and answering Big Brother's requests for paperwork (tax bills, census, license renewals, etc.) out of fear of losing your home, job, or freedom.

Many people are tied to their daily situations, their "home," in exactly this way. So, if your means are limited, perhaps this is exactly where your fight should start—your community, your home.

There are many ways to fight Big Brother on the fringe of his assault. You can show up at a town meeting with a group of neighbors and force the town council to come up with a more realistic budget for the upcoming fiscal year. Or it can be as simple as obtaining a full refund on every subpar product you buy rather than bending over and grabbing your ankles every time Corporate America tries to sell you a can of snake oil.

For it is the town council and the local superstore that are the very talons of the ubiquitous Big Brother animal. And Big Brother derives most of his power not from actual statute but by default. When citizens fail to exercise their own power, either out of ignorance or fear, Big Brother becomes empowered. Like the young Sheldon Charrett in this book's preface, most people unwittingly divest their power directly into Big Brother's avaricious claws.

A fortunate but often overlooked aspect of our society is that ordinary citizens have the most power where it can do the most good. It's true that the Constitution empowers us against the state, and when we are aggrieved we should invoke our rights. But such fights are lengthy and costly. For most people, time and money are scarce commodities, and they opt to leave such battles for the ACLU and other freedom-fighter organizations.

But there are many situations more local to us where we can immediately benefit from our power. Counties, towns, and even smaller governing bodies such as school districts and condominium associations pass unconstitutional laws daily. Often, one strongly worded letter can reverse the freedom-squelching trend of a particular local issue. Sometimes, all society needs is one person to stand up and eloquently state what everybody knows in their hearts to be true. You can be this person.

Counties, Towns, and Neighborhoods

Your county decides to impose a blanket 10 P.M. curfew on all minors, and your 17-year-old son is stopped on his way home from the closing shift at the local convenience store. Your city decides to impose a tax on all personal property held by you, either personally or in trust, and requires you to fill out a "Declaration of Personal Possessions." Your neighborhood association decides that all mailboxes will be white and placed only on the right side of the driveway. You have a blue mailbox already installed on the left side of your driveway.

Do any of these things sound fair? Well, my friends, I didn't make them up. They are real-life examples and, yes, they happened in the United States. Perhaps something similar has happened to you or someone you know.

When something like this happens, many people just assume the governing body has a right to do it; otherwise it wouldn't be happening. That is most definitely *not* the case. The governing body

FIGURE 2.1

LAW IS . . .
Unconstitutional Example

Narrower (more restrictive) than state law

State law says a tenancy at will may be terminated with 30 days' notice. Local housing project requires 60 days notice.

Unconstitutionally broad

Town passes "blanket" 10 P.M. curfew on all minors. No provision is made for minors traveling to and from work, school banquets, family Christmas parties, etc.

Has been enacted "ex post facto," or after the fact

Town rezones your storefront location for residential use only and tries to close your store. Since you established your store when the zoning law clearly allowed for business storefronts, the town must allow your store to remain as a "nonconforming use." Since the town cannot be more restrictive than the state, attempting to close your store on the basis of a new law violates the Constitutional provision barring states from enacting *ex post facto* laws.

Unconstitutionally vague

Town says street people are not allowed engage in unwanted solicitation of money on public property. Town fails to define what a street person is, what constitutes an unwanted solicitation, and what penalty may be imposed.

Specifically Unconstitutional

State passes contractor registration law and says owners need not obey contracts with unregistered home improvement contractors. Under the Constitution, this law cannot apply to existing contracts, even of lengthy duration. If provision is not made for existing contracts, the courts may deem the entire law unconstitutional.

Identity, Privacy, and Personal Freedom

certainly has a right to *try* and impose these restrictions, but you also have the right to oppose them. All it takes is one person willing to see justice done. All of the above incidents, for example, were eventually deemed unconstitutional and the laws stricken.

The best advice I can give you? Know the Constitution and know your state law. The biggest legislative mistake made by most small governing bodies is to enact laws that are either unconstitutional or more restrictive than state law, neither of which is enforceable.

Figure 2.1 shows the most common reasons why local laws are rendered effete along with some real-life examples.

Some fights are even closer to home than your state or town government. This is especially true for those of you who have chosen to make your home in a condominium. Because of their widespread and increasing popularity, I've chosen a condominium takeover as a case study in freedom fighting.

CASE STUDY:
HOW TO TAKE OVER A CONDO ASSOCIATION

Nothing is more disheartening than to move into your new "dream home" only to discover that an undersexed retired civil servant is president of your condo association and intends for all residents to adhere strictly to the association rules that he and his cronies invent and then quibble over in their trustee meetings. Rules like "all cars must be parked facing the building for easy parking sticker inspection" and "$25 per day late fee on condo fees received after the first of the month" and other minutia to keep people tense.

Condos enact more unenforceable laws than any other governing body you'll ever encounter. If you live in a condominium or plan to, your life will be much easier after reading this section. When you're done, the trustees of your association will see you as a force to be reckoned with and as the potential undoer of all their tedious regulations. They will ultimately go out of their way to keep the hell away from you.

If it should ever become necessary, you will have the tools of knowledge necessary to oust the trustees and management company, vote in new trustees, and have the association manage itself. To take over a condo association or become a trustee yourself, however, means donating a lot of time for no compensation and thus should be avoided. Follow the suggestions below and, in most cases, things should never progress to the point of a takeover attempt.

First you must obtain current copies of the association rules, bylaws, and master deed. The rules should be available for free or you don't have to obey them. The bylaws are usually available for free, too, and the master deed should be available for a nominal charge. If the management company tries to charge you too much for the bylaws and master deed copies, you have the right to review them in their office provided you give them reasonable notice. You can also find them at the local registry of deeds. You may be able to photocopy them there for less than it costs to buy them from the management company.

Once, when I was monetarily forced by management to obtain the information on my own, I inveigled a clerk at the deeds registry to give me the information on disk. I told her about the management company and she became enraged. I told her if I could have the information on a disk, I would make printouts and floppies available for the whole association of 360 units, one of which was owned by her daughter.

At the next condo meeting I let everybody know that the rules, bylaws, and master deed were available from me at cost. Over the next two years I saved people hundreds of dollars, and the management company was eventually dismissed.

However you obtain your documents, make sure they are the most updated versions, then read through and know them well.

Understanding The Hierarchy

The condominium government hierarchy is regrettably understood by few people. Most owners believe they are powerless over the management company or that the management company *is* the condo association. This is definitely not the case. It is imperative to understand that *you* control the management company and not the other way around. *You* hire them through the trustees that *you* elect. You and your co-owners can fire them at any time. Moreover, once they know you know this, they will do what it takes to make you happy.

Few condo owners understand the concept of condo trust. Most don't even know their association is governed by trustees, and the ones who do don't know that *they elect the trustees.*

Assert Your Rights

Most management companies and condo trustees feel inadequately equipped to handle the responsibilities bestowed upon them. Sometimes a simple assertion of your rights is all it takes to get them to back off. For instance, the trustees decide that owners' dogs are destroying the property, so they make a bylaw stating that owners can no longer have dogs. You get a scary, professional-looking letter citing the new bylaw and telling you to get rid of your dog. Simply respond in kind:

Dear Board:

The provision of your recent bylaw affecting current dog owners violates Article I, Section 10, of the U.S. Constitution, which prohibits the passing of ex post facto *laws. Therefore, I will not abide by it, and any further requests for me to do so will be deemed harassment and forwarded to the Secretary of State's office for investigation.*

Sincerely,

Acon Doe Owner

The *ex post facto* assertion works against a great number of condominium bylaws. Basically, anytime they ask you to change or remove something that was previously allowed, you should assert it.

When It's Time for Revolt

If you're upset with the way your condo is being managed, it's a good bet that most other owners are likewise upset. But how do you talk to the other owners? Wait for the next annual meeting? But most owners don't show up! Besides, it would be very stressful to take on the trustees and the management company during a meeting organized by them. Should you just give up? Definitely not! Nor should you wait for the next meeting, because few things are ever accomplished during annual meetings.

Once you've decided it's time to get rid of the management company and replace the board of trustees, go down to the county assessor's office and ask for a computer printout of all owners at your condo association. If they are helpful they'll do this for you right off. If not, they will require the address of each unit. If your condo is at 500 Main Street, tell them you want a printout of 500 Main Street, Units 1 through 360 (or whatever). There will be a nominal charge.

The printout will contain the billing address of all unit owners. This is important because not all owners live at the condo; some are out-of-town or out-of-state investors who are probably the most disenchanted of all because they feel they have no control over what's happening in the association. Your job is to change that attitude.

You will write each owner, explaining the problems of the association and proposing a solution. You will tell each owner to show up at a special meeting that you are organizing or to sign their vote over to you in a proxy statement. You are under no obligation whatsoever to inform the management company of your special meeting. It is your right as a condo owner to call such a meeting, and it is also your right to not allow the management company's representative in the door if one should try to come in and take over. In fact, you can call the police and have the slick-talking rep removed.

You must realize that some of the owners are also the trustees of the condo association. This is not too much of a problem. You'll be surprised at how many of the trustees are unhappy with what's going on but feel controlled by the management company. But there's bound to be at least one trustee in the management company's pocket. For this reason, you may want to sort all trustee letters to the end of your mailing and accidentally run out of stamps when you get to them. You still have to send the letters, of course, but it may take you a couple days to get down to the post office to buy those gosh-darned stamps. The unfortunate consequence of this mistake means the trustees will be the last ones informed, leaving them and the management company little time to develop a counterplan. Oh well, what can you do?

Though you can do all your letter writing by hand, it's preferable to enter the owner's addresses into a database and merge it with a word processor file on a computer. The word processor file contains an overview of why you're writing to them and a proxy statement and introduces the enclosed pamphlet. The pamphlet outlines the proposed changes.

Rather than enter a lengthy discussion of all the possible things that can go wrong in a condo association, I've included an actual pamphlet from an actual condo takeover I helped a friend with (Figure 2.2, pages 28-29). To protect her identity, certain names and references have been changed.

Special Notes Regarding Proxies

Some association rules state that a single unit owner cannot hold more than a certain number of proxy votes or a certain percentage of the total vote. This varies from association to association. It is therefore necessary for you to review your master deed and bylaws to see whether such a provision exists. If so, you may need other unit owners to help you hold proxy votes. For example, if you are limited to holding no more than 10 percent of the vote, you will need at least five other unit owners to help you hold proxies. Between the six of you, you'll have 60 percent of the vote.

Also be aware that certain items, usually capital expenditures, often require a larger percent of the vote in order to be enacted. This varies either by association or state law. Sometimes this can be as much as 75 percent, so you may need other "conspirators" in certain situations. Dissolution of a condominium usually requires 100 percent of the vote. Oftentimes, however, a single person can hold by proxy all the voting power necessary to effect significant changes in how a condo association is run.

The fact that many meetings barely have 50 percent of the vote present, which is usually just enough for a quorum, will work in your favor. Because only half of the voting power is present, any proxies you collect act as double votes (i.e., 30 percent proxy votes at a meeting where only 50 percent of the total vote is present equals 60 percent of the meeting vote).

• • • • •

Well, I've certainly given you enough fodder to handle any ugliness that might rear its head in your private condominium home. Bear in mind that all of the above is perfectly legal, and you are well within your rights to tame the condo association if it ever drives you to it. But this is a chapter in a Sheldon Charrett book, and as such would not be complete without a few tips and tricks landing in the gray areas of Big Brother's law. Thus, I present to you . . .

VOTE EARLY, VOTE OFTEN

There are 513,200 elected officials in this country as this sentence is written. Most of them are low-level officials who most certainly *do* need your vote. These offices are sometimes won by only *one* vote, and winning an office by less than a hundred votes is more the rule than the exception. A typical election outcome for a school committee chair in a midsize town may be 123 to 101 for a two-candidate race. What would happen if all 10,000 registered voters actually voted? It would indeed be a very different race.

The problem is most people don't consider these small elections important. Yet at least half of all registered voters usually get out and vote for the presidential races. I find this ironic. The office of the president has become all but titular in this country, and almost nothing significant ever happens quickly in Washington. Yet people flock to the polls because the tube tells them they must go. But company acted deceptively by mis-stating this law. We believe this is a good example of the lengths the board will go to in order to keep tabs on, and invade the privacy of, individual unit owners.

FAIR ACCESS TO INFORMATION:

We also believe that the current charge of $25.00 each for a copies of the bylaws and master deed is unreasonable. We will use your proxy vote to amend the by-laws to make this information available to all unit owners at cost, rather than at a profit.

If you can't attend this meeting, please be sure to return your pre-addressed proxy!

For additional information contact:

Mia Thisaddress

500 Main Street, Unit #315

Anytown, USA 99999

PROXY

I, <<OWNER's NAME>>, owner of King's Court Condominium Unit(s) <<UNIT #'s>> located at 500 Main Street, Anytown, USA 99999, hereby grant Mia Thisaddress my proxy vote in a special meeting of unit owners to be held on December 16, 1996, or such other date as may be rescheduled, for the purpose of voting in all matters brought forth at that meeting.

Signatures*

_____

_____

_____

_____

* All person listed on the unit deed must sign in order for your vote to be counted. If unit is held in trust, a majority of the trustees must sign.

This proxy will be returned to you if you decide to show up at the meeting.

YOU ARE NOT POWERLESS!

Special Meeting

OF

King's Court

Condominium Association

Proposed Amendments

Eliminate Special Assessments:

At the 1995 Annual Meeting for King's Court, a number of unit owners were present protesting a proposed increase of Condo Fees.

Due to the number of protestors, the board was in no position to follow through with the proposed increase. However, in 1996, the board approved a special assessment as well as a mandatory $25.00 payment for pest extermination. This amounts to a 6% increase in condo fees and the year is not yet over.

In 1981, the condo fees and the annual budget were roughly half of what they are now. Even when economic inflation is factored in, this increase over a period of 15 years is unjustified. As a community, King's Court should become more efficient in handling its finances. We should not be heading down hill.

---

when some crooked bastard is trying to oust their local selectman who has a long-standing favorable record, most voters don't even know about it.

Typically, local election issues are not well publicized. When they are, they are too convoluted to understand. When I vote, if I am uncertain of the difference between two candidates (all too often there is none), I simply vote for the underdog. If successful, the underdog will have to work hard to secure the public trust and, ultimately, reelection. Conversely, if the favorite gets in, the race will be that much closer (assuming there are others who vote like I do). The incumbent or favorite will not feel as though reelection is necessarily "in the bag" and thus will be put on notice to actually do something over the next two years.

If you are a dual resident, then by all means register and vote in both jurisdictions. If you happen

Budget Restructuring:

There are certain areas of the King's Court budget which need to be addressed by the unit owners. Of major concern is the awarding of contracts. With your meeting participation or proxy vote, we, the unit owners, independent of the board and independent of the management company will offer the following contracts up for bid. We're confident that we can significantly reduce the 1997 annual budget and condo fees.

Contract	1996 Proposed	1995 Actual
Property Management	$27,000	$21,000
Cleaning	$13,000	$8,930
Landscape	$11,000	$7,995
Pest Control	$8,550	$4,296
Snow Removal	$12,500	$6,423
Trash Pickup	$13,500	$9,074
Maintenance	$26,000	$17,945

This represents a 36.2% increase in one year!

We are taking bids from three new contractors for each above item. Your proxy vote will allow us to award the contract to local, established contractors who will appreciate our business! There is no need to pay top dollar to larger businesses who are no longer connected to our community. There are plenty of reputable, small businesspersons eager to please us!

CURRENT CONTRACTORS

Wetake Property Management is located in Padville and is owned by a man who lives in 50 miles away. Why are we paying for their toll calls and travel time to our city?

Weinfest Pest Control has offices in Timbuktu, Tibet and Siberia. Why not use a smaller, local contractor who would appreciate the business and guarantee his work?

Halfload Container Services' nearest office is 40 miles away and they subcontract to a dumpsite over 150 miles away. Again, why are we paying for their extended travels?

Snow Removal: If the 1995 actual budget for snow removal was $6,423, why did we need to budget over $12,000 for 1996? Certainly there are contractors willing to offer a substantial discount if it doesn't snow. In any case, we are confident that we will find a reputable contractor to contract for well under $10,000 per year.

Other Unreasonable Budget Increases

We can also find nothing to account for the expected $9,000 increase in our water bill nor the $16,000 increase in our heating bill.

With 1995 actual water expenses at 21,090 and the implementation of water saving devices, why are we budgeting an additional $9,000? With 1995 actual gas expenses of $54,427, why are we again budgeting $70,000?

POWER AND CONTROL:

Perhaps more serious than the budget is the board's continued effort to get "control" over the citizens of King's Court.

Parking Stickers

Though the parking sticker program may be a good idea, the board goes way beyond its jurisdiction by requiring residents to show a valid state driver's license and registration. Certainly this will present many problems for people just moving to the area, for teenagers who'd like to purchase a vehicle before they are licensed and for individuals who are residing at King's Court on a temporary basis (such as students).

We believe a resident only needs to state that he/she has a motor vehicle and requires a sticker. Tag numbers may be written down for snow removal purposes but there is no need to keep license information on file. Especially where our state uses the Social Security Number as a driver's license number.

Notice of Delinquency to Mortgagees

Recently, the board sent a flyer, citing state law, demanding all unit owners furnish the association with mortgage holder, tenant, child, pet & automobile make, model and plate information.

We have found NO SUCH LAW ON THE BOOKS! The closest relevant statute states that the organization of unit owners is required to mail a notice of delinquency to first mortgage holders ONLY IF THE FIRST MORTGAGE HOLDER HAS NOTIFIED THE ASSOCIATION OF ITS NAME AND ADDRESS and only if the unit owner has been delinquent for more than 60 days in his or her common area expenses (condo fees). There is no stipulation authorizing the association to collect mortgagee information from the individual unit owners.

Certainly the board as well as the management

to have a few different identities or a self-inflicted multiple personality disorder, well, you'll have to decide how to handle that. But here are a few things to keep in mind.

Voter Registration Requirements

To register to vote in any U.S. federal election, an applicant must:

- be at least 18 years old
- be a U.S. citizen
- attest to the above by signing under the penalties of perjury

However, a voter registration agency may *not*:

- require identification
- require your SSN
- require notarization of your signature

Here is an excerpt from the controlling statute (italic emphasis is mine):

> U.S.C. TITLE 42—THE PUBLIC HEALTH AND WELFARE
> CHAPTER 20—ELECTIVE FRANCHISE
> § 1973gg-7. Federal coordination and regulations
>
> (b) Contents of mail voter registration form
>
> The mail voter registration form developed under subsection (a)(2) of this section—
>
> (1) may require only such identifying information (including the signature of the applicant) and other information (including data relating to previous registration by the applicant), as is necessary to enable the appropriate State election official to assess the eligibility of the applicant and to administer voter registration and other parts of the election process;
> (2) shall include a statement that—
> (A) specifies each eligibility requirement (including citizenship);
> (B) contains an attestation that the applicant meets each such requirement; and
> (C) requires the signature of the applicant, under penalty of perjury;
> *(3) may not include any requirement for notarization or other formal authentication;*

Since neither a driver's license nor SSN provides proof of U.S. citizenship, neither may be requested as proof of the same. In fact, the voter registration system has no effective way of keeping an invented person, or your dog, Rover, from voting in federal elections. It is a well-known fact that many nonpersons have voted over the years. In fact, it is widely believed that JFK could very possibly have become president thanks to the dead voters of Chicago.

Of course, election fraud carries with it serious penalties. Anybody considering a delve into the legal gray area of voting as a dual resident must first understand how some people are caught casting multiple votes. Here are some of the more common mistakes:

- Registering the same first name but different last name at the same address, especially if female, may give rise to inquiry.
- Voting in person, rather than by mail, under two or more identities. Some people, especially bureaucrats, never forget a face!
- In most cases, voting as a dead person is no longer effective. Voter registration entries are cross-checked against city death records.

The best method of establishing multiple voting identities is to use a different name and address for each one and always vote by mail.

One Roadblock

Under federal law, states are granted the power to request that mail-in registrants vote in person their first time. After that, they may vote by mail for the rest of their lives. For a state to enforce this, it must first pass a law, which few states have done. In any event, the state is still not allowed to request identification from you. Therefore, the man of a thousand faces may vote under a thousand identities. A man of one face may vote in a thousand cities.

Acquiring Privacy, Personal Freedom, and New ID

3

How to Manufacture Professional-Quality Identity Documents

Papers!
Hitler's SS

Many of you have expressed an interest in seeing the topic of ID manufacture greatly expanded. The overwhelming consensus is that more information on making novelty drivers' licenses is needed. Mostly, people seem to be having difficulty with security devices (such as holograms), lamination techniques, and getting their licenses to appear as a single piece rather than a card with a picture glued to it.

In the first part of this chapter you'll learn to recognize security devices and construction methods used in government-issued identity documents. In the second part, you'll learn various techniques to replicate them.

Since everyone seems to be interested in reproducing state drivers' licenses, I've organized this chapter around doing exactly that. Of course, the construction methods described herein can also be used to create other identity documents such as student IDs, work badges, and state-issued identity cards.

Since manufacturing state drivers' licenses may be illegal, we will concern ourselves with making novelty versions of these and other documents. But be advised: in many cases, the novelty versions will look remarkably—if not exactly—like the real thing. If you are depicted on a novelty drivers' license under the name of Jane Doe and the cop that stops you happens to know you by another name, you will be detained, hassled, and subject to harsh fines, lengthy imprisonment, or both.

If, despite this warning, you still want your novelty ID to look exactly like a real drivers' license, you will have to know what the real version looks like. Keep reading.

KNOW THE ID

In order to make a novelty version of any document, it is best to have an actual up-to-date example as a reference. This is not always possible, especially with state driver's licenses. People don't readily part with them, and states won't issue one to you unless you have proper supporting documentation (in which case you wouldn't need to manufacture the license!). If you don't have an actual example, you will need to research the ID in order to produce a believable replica.

A good resource for is *The ID Checking Guide*. This guide has examples of valid driver's licenses from all 50 U.S. states, the Canadian provinces, Puerto Rico, and Mexico. It includes full-color, actual-size photographs of current, former, and "under 21" versions of each license and state ID card. Because the guide is produced in cooperation with several jurisdictions, it lists the security features, license number format, term of license, and potential variations between issuing bodies.

The guide also has sections on military, federal and Department of State IDs, bank cards, and automobile registration plates. Obviously, such information is an invaluable reference for bankers, nightclub owners, and employers.

Document forgers can use the guide to learn which security features have been designed into the document they intend to reproduce. This is important because, as you will see, security features are not always readily evident. The document forger can thus include subtle details such as proper soundex license numbers and camera station ID numbers.

The ID Checking Guide is published by:

The Drivers License Guide Company
P.O. Box 5305, Dept. 98
Redwood City, CA 94063

It is available from the Florida Banker's Association for $18.95 at the time of this writing. They can be reached at:

Florida Bankers Association
1001 Thomasville Road, Suite 201
Tallahassee, FL 32303

You can also order it online at www.webbanker.com.

I've heard that some people have had trouble buying this guide because they couldn't prove they were nightclub owners, bankers, or someone else with a "need to know." If this is the case, it's a simple matter to establish a business (*MIC*, Chapter 5) and order your guide through it. If your business is refused a copy of the guide, send a copy of your refusal letter back to the company's legal department along with the following cover letter:

Dear Legal Department:

On September 1, 2000, I received a letter from your company explaining why you are refusing to sell me a copy of your ID guide.

The ID Checking Guide is a monopoly, and by selling only to certain businesses you are limiting open competition in a free marketplace. This is a direct violation of United States antitrust laws, under which prosecution could provide serious civil and criminal penalties against you.

Again, I have enclosed a properly filled out order form and full payment. If I do not receive a copy of the guide by September 15, 2000, I will refer the matter to your state secretary's office for criminal prosecution and seek the advice of an attorney for a possible civil action against your company.

Respectfully,

Sally Noguide

Federal antitrust laws prohibit businesses from conspiring to give one or the other of them an unfair advantage over other businesses in a similar marketplace. If you claim to be a business that could benefit from using an ID guide, then you have a case under the antitrust laws and the legal department should respond in your favor. Even if you are a landlord, this should entitle you to the guide in order to be on a fair playing field with other landlords who may have the guide (i.e., landlords who also own banks or nightclubs).

Identity, Privacy, and Personal Freedom

Document Security Devices

A security feature is a device that hinders the alteration, reproduction, or misuse of a given identity document. As you will see by the list below, the device is not always physical, tangible, readily apparent, or widely understood. To be successful, counterfeiters must be able to recognize and replicate document security features.

The information below will enable a novelty ID builder or a businessperson designing employee identification to produce a document that is more believable and secure. It is also my firm belief that if bureaucracies are going to implement these devices to track and control the population, then the population should be as informed as possible about them.

The older and more popular schemes are listed first.

One-Piece ID

This is something that is no longer included in typical discussions and texts about identity document security. For years, special cameras have enabled state motor vehicle bureaus, college registrar offices, and corporate human resources departments to issue one-piece identification documents. Instead of a photograph being glued to the ID card, the photograph and identifying information make up one card, which is then laminated. The days of simply slipping your picture onto another's ID and relaminating are gone. In today's society, the bump caused by an inserted picture is the mark of a sure fake.

State Registration System

Another thing not commonly thought of as a security feature is the fact that all states have a central registry of the drivers' licenses they issue. They share this information with other states. A police officer's ability to "call in" your license number for verification offers an apparently ultimate level of document security.

That said, I can recall three occasions when a police officer told me he could not find me in the state's computer. On one occasion I had handed him my actual driver's license; on another, I had left my license at home (more on this later). The first time, when the police officer informed me that he couldn't find me in the computer, I said, "Okay . . ." and that was the end of his inquiry. The time I forgot my license, I was issued a ticket for exactly that reason. One other time, the cop wrote me a ticket because I had gone through a red light (my own fault). The point is, on each occasion I drove away.

Lamination

This is probably the first roadblock most fledgling forgers run into. It's also the first thing most of us recognize as a security feature. The simple and common technique of lamination is measure enough to keep 95 percent of the population from pursuing the idea of document manipulation. Lamination is cheap, easy to implement, and effective—a bureaucrat's fantasy. Of course, there is still that 5 percent who realize you can give Kinko's $0.75 and they'll happily laminate your novelty artwork. And if your local Kinko's happens to be owned by a crabby, resentful ex-bureaucrat who refuses to laminate your masterpiece, an office supply store will sell you a laminator for as little as $50, though I do recommend a slightly more expensive model.

You can get laminators and lamination pouches from USI, Inc. USI's FX400 Pouch Laminator sells for $164.95, and its FX1200 Pouch Laminator goes for $199.95. The address is:

USI, Inc.
33 Business Park Drive, Suite 5
Branford, CT 06405-2944

A better place price-wise is Lamination Station. They have a personal laminator (H410) for $59. It won't accept pouches larger than 4 1/2 inches in width or 5 mil thick, which might be a consideration.

Their commercial laminators CT400 and PL4A both accept pouches up to 4 inches wide and 10 mil thick. They sell for $99 and $129 respectively. Still, much better than USI. The address is:

Lamination Station
837 Miramar Street
Cape Coral, FL 33904
E-mail: sales@laminationstation.com
Web: www.laminationstation.com

I've never used any Lamination Station products, so I can't vouch for their quality. But with satisfied customers such as MTV, Lockheed Martin, Boeing, Harlem Globetrotters, Eastman Kodak, John Deere, Kansas City Chiefs, USA Hockey, and numerous other Fortune 500 companies, they appear to be on firm ground in their field.

USI is more expensive, but I've never had a problem with their products. I can't say the same about their service, however.

Both establishments have a wide variety of 3, 5, and 10 mil lamination pouches in business card, credit card, employment badge, and military ID styles. Chances are, one of these will exactly match that used by your state. If not, trimming is a simple matter.

State Seal & Signature Overlap

This security measure implements a registrar's signature, state seal, or other graphic that partially overlaps the photograph on a picture ID. It's a holdover from the days when people would simply slip their picture onto another's license and use it to drive or get into bars. Today, slipping your picture onto an overlap-protected license will chop off half of the graphic, leaving the other half plainly visible to the bureaucrat inspecting your license. All except the most exceptionally stupid bureaucrats will immediately see that something is awry and call a supervisor.

Security overlaps are used today mostly for the purpose of adding another level of difficulty for would-be forgers but also to benefit exceptionally stupid bureaucrats. As security features go, and as you will see, overlaps are not too difficult to replicate.

Background Design: Color, Pattern, Line

These measures are usually reserved for bank checks and credit card signature boxes. They are the funny squiggles you see where you sign on the back of your American Express card, and they are meant to expose erasures. Erase the signature, the squiggles disappear with it. The same thing happens when you try to erase the dollar amount or payee on a bank check. Once erased, the elaborate design is very difficult to redraw—even for an accomplished artist with all the right tools. One trick for AMEX: erase the *whole* area, then write in your new signature.

Soundex

Soundex is a method of encoding the driver's name and other identifying data into the driver's license number. Classified by sound, consonants are assigned a numeral from 1 to 6. Vowels are not coded. Here's the scheme:

1. b, f, p, v
2. c, g, j, k, q, s, x, z
3. d, t
4. l
5. m, n
6. r

A few states encode license numbers with this system. They usually implement an encoding scheme similar to that illustrated below, which is used by Florida.

First Character = First letter of last name
Next three digits = Next nonrepeating consonants of
last name, soundex encoded

Don't encode the first letter, as it's already been used. Since W and H are not encoded, ignore them altogether. If a consonant shares the same soundex code as the decoded one immediately before it, go to the next consonant. If there are not enough qualifying consonants, fill the remaining spaces with zeroes.

For example, Charrett would be encoded as follows:

C630
C for the first letter
H is skipped
6 for R (skip the next R)
3 for T (skip the next T)
0 (Since there are no more letters, add a zero to make three digits)

Florida then encodes an internal code followed by the birth year, birth date, and sex. Other states go on to encode the first name, etc. This extra coding is done to ensure there are no duplicate license numbers. Sometimes, by sheer coincidence, the soundex scheme will encode two licensees the same way. When this happens, a computer catches the problem and adds -1, -2, -3, etc. The scheme varies, and it's important to know whether your state uses one and, if so, how to decode it. At the time of this writing, the following states use some form of soundex encoding: Florida, Illinois, Maryland, Michigan, Minnesota, and Wisconsin.

The states in Figure 3.1 use non-soundex encoding:

FIGURE 3.1
State License Number Encoding

Connecticut
First two digits encode driver's birth month. If birth year is odd, digits appear normally as 01-12 for January to December. If birth year is even, digits are encoded 13-24. The months fall in order with January at 13, December at 24.

Kansas
Beginning November 1995, first digit is first letter of last name. Next two digits are the year issued.

New Hampshire
First two digits are the birth month followed by first letter of last name, last letter of last name, then first letter of first name. Sheldon Charrett would be CTS.

New Jersey
First letter of last name followed by nine digits of internal codes. Last five digits are month, year of birth, and eye color. Females have a 5 or 6 in the first position for month. For example, May would be 55 or 65 instead of 05.

Nevada
12-digit number only: SSN-based number followed by year of birth.

New York
19-digit number only: first digit is first letter of last name, last two digits are year of birth.

Rhode Island
First two digits are year of issue.

Washington
First five letters of last name followed by first and middle initial. Next two digits are the birth year subtracted from 100 followed by internal codes.

UV Ink

This ink is invisible until held under an ultraviolet (UV) light. Presently, states that have UV printing on the front or back are Florida, Michigan, New York, and Texas. If your favorite bank or state bureau does not have a UV light handy, then it really doesn't matter if the state wrote "Please don't drink and drive" all over your license in invisible ink.

Of course, distilled lemon juice, liquid Tide, and a number of highlighter-type pens have been known to effectively reproduce invisible, UV-readable ink. You can also purchase UV-sensitive fluid from engineering blueprint supply shops or from several sources on the Internet. It is then a simple matter to have a stamp made up in the desired shape for easy license "validation."

Incite Technologies has UV ink available in liquid and crayon form. Their address is:

Incite Technologies Corporation
10059 East Washington Street
Indianapolis, IN 46229
Web: www.my-secret.com

I've never tried either product, so I can't say how effective they are.

Hologram

Many readers have written asking about holograms. What are they? Colloquially, the term hologram is used to describe various optical effects, including those seen in document security devices. Technically, a hologram is a laser-generated recording of an object onto a light-sensitive material. Unlike standard photography, it is the interference pattern of light waves caused by the object that is stored rather than a picture of the object itself. A hologram is, in essence, an optical record of an object's three-dimensionality, which can be played back by shining another laser through it (transmission hologram) or by allowing ambient light to pass though it (rainbow hologram).

So bureaucrats don't have to tote around heavy lasers, document security holograms are rainbow holograms.

What we call holograms on state driver's licenses are not always true holograms. Sometimes metalized translucent paint applied to a layer of laminate and other light-refracting techniques are referred to as holograms. The term has also been used to encompass the old "blue" New York IDs, which use a semireflective image press technique.

For our purposes, a hologram is a transparent graphical overlay that appears three dimensional and changes color as it is held at different angles to a given light source. Typical state license holograms range in transparency from almost clear to a nearly opaque bright green when turned to the light.

Holograms used in state drivers' licenses may be an image of the state's seal (Massachusetts, Illinois, Mississippi), outline (West Virginia), slogan (Hawaii), bird (Minnesota), registry logo (North Carolina), or name (Georgia, Pennsylvania). Personally, I like the plain and simple rectangle holograms (Connecticut, Kansas, South Dakota, Virginia) because they are easily reproduced with the iridescent tissue method (see below). Many states have some combination of holograms, such as state seal and name (Alabama, Oregon, Wisconsin) or some other combination (Arizona, California, New Mexico, North Dakota, Ohio).

Holograms are a hot topic among novelty ID makers. We'll greatly expand our discussion of them under the section "More on Holograms" below.

Machine-Readable Technologies

Machine-readable technologies such as bar codes and magnetic swipe cards simplify the lives of bureaucrats and complicate the lives of document forgers. Fortunately for now, bar codes and magnetic swipes are only read by police officers and registry bureaucrats. An invented bar code and properly laminated length of recording tape is still sufficient for bank tellers, employers, and stock brokers.

The fact that these technologies are implemented on credit-card-style (PVC) licenses is more of a problem than the security devices themselves. Printing on PVC requires the use of an expensive printer, and the lamination process is also more involved. More on this under the subheading "More on PVC" below.

Ghost Image

A ghost image is a halftone duplication of the main photograph moved to some other area of the license, such as over the birth date or other vital information. They are the stupidest and most unattractive security devices ever conceived since bureaucrats (*homo bureaucraticus*) came down from the trees and began walking erect. I wouldn't be so offended by them if they actually performed some measure of added security, but they don't. They are easily reproduced on a home computer. The method for doing this will be covered below under the subheading "Getting Your Picture on the Template."

Optically Variable Device

Strictly speaking, an optically variable device (OVD) is an image that shifts position, changes into another object, or appears to be moving as you hold it at different angles to the light. An example of this is the hologram from American Banknote Holographics, which appears in the appendix of *Optical Document Security* (Artech House Publishing, Boston/London, 1998, edited by Rudolf L. van Renesse). The image is a multiplane hologram of an eagle's head. As you tilt the image, the eagle's beak opens and closes.

Michigan uses an OVD in its newest license. As you tilt the license, the state name alternates with the state outline.

Security Device Miscellany

Below is a short list of other security devices you may come across. Hearing their names will help you watch for them in your daily life.

*   Microline printing
*   Rainbow printing
*   Guilloche pattern/design
*   Opacity mark
*   Out-of-gamut colors (pastel print)
*   Optical variable ultrahigh-resolution lines
*   Block graphics
*   Security fonts
*   Graphics with known hidden flaws
*   Card stock layer with colors

- Micrographics
- Retroflective security logos

The common factor of all these being, of course, difficulty in reproduction.

MAKING AN ID

Now that you know what your target ID looks like and what, if any, security features it contains, you can move on to the next step of making the sucker.

Using Templates

The quickest and most effective way to make a novelty driver's license is to use a template. A template is a picture, photocopy, or computer image of an actual driver's license that can be manipulated, usually by a computer, to produce a very believable novelty ID. Some state driver's licenses are easier to manipulate than others.

Templates seem all fine and dandy, but how do you get them? Here are a few ways that immediately come to mind:

- Scanning your own license
- Scanning someone else's license
- Looking in the *ID Checking Guide*
- Finding one over the Internet

Scanning: Connect a color scanner to your PC and scan every license and ID card you can get your hands on.

ID Checking Guide: The illustrations in the *ID Checking Guide* are actual full-size photographs, any one of which can be scanned into a computer and edited with Photoshop 5.0 or other graphics software to make a template. Unfortunately, the *ID Checking Guide* mentions nothing about the backs of the licenses. If you have access to an actual sample of the license you intend to copy, you can determine what is printed on the back.

The Internet: Internet sites are a great place to get driver's license templates. FakeID.net has some nice templates for not too much money *(for novelty purposes only)*, and the site is updated regularly. Other sites are free, but watch for quality. Some sites include template backs, others don't. There are friendly people in the discussion groups who will help you and even send you an ID back if you need one or have something to trade.

There are also Usenet newsgroups dedicated to the subject of identity documents as well as discussion groups on various Web sites. These groups often pop up, disappear, and reappear under a different name. If none of the ones listed below are still in business when you read this, a simple Internet search using the keywords "New ID" or "ID AND Fake" will dig up many sites you can access for information. Here are the ones available at the time of this writing:

fakeid.net
idcentral.com
promasteridcards.mcmail.com
mod-source.com/fake-id (good templates here)
geocities.com/MadisonAvenue/Boardroom/2229/main.htm
angelfire.com
belvine.com.uk

I strongly advise you to *not* send any money to anybody on the Internet. Get the product first if possible. If you do decide you trust someone enough to send money, get their bank's name and account number first. Send them a personal check and write, "For Deposit To [Bank's Name] Account of [Business Name] # [Account Number] ONLY."

Sites with their own domain name (such as fakeid.net) are generally safer than sites set up at places like Geocities, Angelfire, and other Web hosting services. Make sure you know the site well and have visited it a number of times over several months before considering it legitimate.

Getting Your Picture on the Template

A template with someone else's picture and identifying information is no good to you. Although you can, in many cases, use the techniques found in the section "Making a One-Piece ID," this section deals mostly with altering the template by computer.

You will first need to get a recent (or not so recent, depending on your purposes) picture of yourself. Passport photos are probably the best, but you can also take photos of yourself against varied backdrops. Either way, you'll need to scan your lovely visage into your PC. Unless . . .

The charm of the ages, my friends, is a digital camera. You can get a refurbished one for under $100 and throw all your film canisters away. These little devils allow you to take snapshots of yourself and then upload them to your PC—no scanning necessary! The results are instant, and you can make necessary refinements without waiting for your local pharmacist to develop the film. You also eliminate the chance of some clerky film developer seeing your artwork and alerting the authorities. If you do decide on a digital camera, get one with a high dpi (dots per inch) rating (resolutions of 1536 x 1024 are common at the time of this writing).

Once you have your picture and template on your PC, open them in a decent graphics-editing program. The crème de la crème is Photoshop 5.0, which also works nicely with digital cameras. It's pretty obvious what to do from here: cut and paste your picture on the template.

Background not quite right? No problem. Use the "color replace" function to change it to a better shade of blue, a new color, or to eliminate the background altogether, depending on your needs. Need a ghost image? Try setting your brightness between 10 percent and 50 percent or adjust your opacity setting until the image matches your state's.

Match the template's fonts and type in your new information. At this point I must stress that you be exacting in your work. There's no excuse not to be. You have the wonder of modern technology at your fingertips, and you should use it to produce professional results. If you feel yourself rushing, take a break or go for a walk and come back to it later. Keep all your edits to within a one pixel or .1mm specification.

When you are done, print it out. Use the paper recommended by your printer's manufacturer for best results. You won't be disappointed.

This is a New Jersey template taken from the Internet and edited with graphics software to remove the picture and vital information. Use your computer to insert your picture. Match fonts and put in your own vital stats.

Fading and Blurring

Sometimes a nice new ID will begin to fade a few days after you've printed it out or get blurry after lamination. Fading happens because you used the wrong type of paper (i.e., nonphoto paper). Blurring happens because photo-quality papers have a plastic-like coating that breaks down during lamination. It seems we have a catch-22 here!

To reduce fading, use the right type of print paper. Read your printer manual as well as the inserts that came with your print cartridge (if applicable) and use the paper recommended as best for photo-quality printing. Some companies make their own paper for this very purpose. If you don't feel like searching through manuals, a good high-gloss paper is Hammermill Ultra-Jet 1440. To reduce the blurring that can occur with these papers, laminate with lower heat. Use the lowest setting that will do the job.

If you still have fading problems, get a transparent "page protector" from an office supply store. Cut it to the exact size of the printed template you are using and round the corners the same way. Essentially you are making a custom-fit page protector for the printed template. Once it's done, place the printed template into the page protector and then place that whole assembly into the lamination pouch. Laminate as usual. Because the lamination pouch does not fuse to the paper, the plastic-like coating does not break down.

More On Holograms

I decided to do an in-depth hologram discussion under a separate heading because it is a popular topic and, as I'd mentioned, I've received numerous inquiries as to their use. More and more states are using them with varying degrees of effectiveness. As a novelty document maker, you have a few ways of dealing with holograms. You can procure one by stealing, finding, or bribing somebody for one, reusing an existing one, or making your own.

Obtaining A Hologram

Originally, this subheading was entitled "Haa, Ha, Ha, Ha, Hee, Hee, Tee, Hee, Bubble, Giggle," because the idea of actually getting your hands on one of these babies is that laughable. But it is a possibility and therefore must be discussed.

If you know somebody at the Department of Motor Vehicles who's repaying a large student loan or is just in need of some love and affection, you may be able to obtain a hologram with a large sum of money or a roll in the hay. Perhaps the night janitor has a glum expression that might be brightened upon seeing Ben Franklin's Mona Lisa-like smirk? Maybe a careless clerk turns around at an opportune moment? Is the DMV advertising for help by any chance?

A better bet is to peruse the Dumpster behind the DMV. Holograms found here will likely be ripped, torn, melted, or otherwise deemed useless by some registry clerk. Or, if it was at all usable, it probably got sliced in half before being dumped. But remember what you learned in math class? Two halves make a whole. Happy diving.

Reusing a Holo

Slightly more sophisticated than Dumpster diving for holograms is to reuse one. Here's the procedure:

1. Go to your friendly Department of Motor Vehicles.
2. Get a license, state ID card, or replacement license. The hologram will be there, a tenth of a millimeter below the laminate, teasing you 'til you just can't take it anymore.
3. Resist the temptation for as long as it takes to get to the privacy of your own home.
4. Peel back the corners of the laminate using your fingernail, a letter opener, stencil knife, or whatever it takes.
5. Using a cotton swab (Q-tip), gently work some lighter fluid (e.g., Zippo, Ronsonol), nail polish remover, acetone, or Goof Off! compound into the peeled corner.
6. Working slowly, gently peel the corner as the laminate softens.
7. DON'T RUSH!

8. If you do this too fast, you will damage the hologram, which will require another trip to the DMV with another pretext. Does that sound like fun? Didn't think so. Please, take your time.

More of a concern than direct hologram damage is damage caused by yet another security device. If you peel the hologram too fast, it becomes checkered to prevent reuse. Why? Because the DMV knows there are subversive bastards like us out there!

Once you have your hologram, set it aside for use in manufacturing a novelty version of your state's driver's license. Because checkers are actually caused by the glue from the heat-fused layer, a few checkers—sometimes even a moderate amount—are okay. The glue-based checks will often disappear upon relamination.

NOTE: Some people soak their entire license in lighter fluid or acetone. If you do this with a magnetic swipe card, you will damage the magnetic material.

Making Your Own Holo (Happy Holo-ween)

There are some sophisticated techniques for counterfeiting security holograms in common use at the time of this writing. If you have the money to spend on lasers, sandbag tables, and dichromated gelatin, you may wish to check out *Optical Document Security* (Artech House Publishing, Boston/London, 1998, edited by Rudolf L. van Renesse).

Optical Document Security covers in detail the forensics of document forgery and the various optical methods of securing identity documents, checks, and credit cards. Holograms and optically variable devices, among others, are covered in detail. In addition to some great examples of holograms and OVDs, the book comes with a searchable CD database, which I found to be quite informative.

Hologram Compromise

Okay. So you're not a world-renowned physicist like Mr. van Renesse. Nor can you afford lasers, sandbag tables, and dichromated gelatin. Well, as mentioned earlier, there is a difference between true holograms and what most people consider to be holograms. Because our eyes don't see true holograms on a regular basis, nonholographic security devices made from iridescent and optically variable material, when done well, can easily pass casual—and quite often moderate—scrutiny by bureaucrats.

Homemade Hologram: The Poor Man's (Iridescent Tissue) Method

This method should only be used to replicate iridescent, color-shifting holograms such as those used in Connecticutt, Georgia, Massachusetts, South Dakota, and Virgina. If you use this method to reproduce plain metallic, non-color-shifting holos such as those used in New Jersey (more on this below), you will end up with the wrong effect on your finished product. Although this has still fooled many an out-of-state bureaucrat, we are going for accuracy here.

There is a cellophane-type gift-wrapping tissue available from craft shops and party stores that has a rather nice quality to it. If you look straight through it, it appears roughly transparent. If you turn it at different angles to the light, you will see colors shift from iridescent green to a pastel reddish pink. Sound familiar? Yeah, it's kinda like a hologram, innit?

If you live in a state like Connecticutt, Georgia, South Dakota, or Virgina where the drivers' license hologram is a simple rectangle, the technique below may indeed have its benefits. Know a kindly predisposed, farsighted bank teller? Or a similar personality at the Social Security Administration office? They will quite readily accept your iridescent-tissue holograms, as will many others. And if you read on, you will learn how to combine this method with others to replicate more intricate holograms such as your state's seal.

Materials and Supplies

Iridescent tissue/gift wrap. Forget-Me-Not makes one that can be found in card shops, gift shops, party stores, or the gift wrap section of many department stores. You can get a small package of the stuff for about $3 at the time of this writing. Don't be disappointed if it doesn't have quite the effect you thought it would. Once it is held flat by the lamination and mounted with the appropriate background, the holographic effect will increase tenfold.

Glue stick. Make sure it's water soluble.

Glass mounting surface. Smooth, slightly rounded glass jar. My preference is an almost square jelly jar that is slightly rounded on all sides. If you have a cheap, 8-inch novelty crystal ball, this will be even better. But don't use anything valuable because you'll be cutting on it later.

Stencil knife. If you plan on doing a lot of this sort of thing, you may wish to pick up some extra blades. You may even try various blade types to see which one you can most easily control.

Lamination. 10 mil lamination pouches of appropriate size. "Credit Card" size is common.

Procedure

1. Get a template of the hologram.

Design or otherwise acquire a template of the hologram you wish to make. For example, if your state's hologram is the state seal, you will need a copy of the state seal. Some sources are:

- *State letterhead.* Correspond with any bureau of your state. The letterhead they respond on will have a copy of the state seal. Be sure your correspondence requires a response! Photocopy the seal, scaling it to the appropriate size, or scan it into your computer for easy manipulation in a good graphics program. If the seal already happens to be the correct size, you can work directly from the letterhead.
- *Internet.* Visit your state's homepage on the Internet. Click on the state seal with your right mouse button and save the image to your hard disk for easy resizing, editing, and printing.

Wherever you find your state's seal, chances are it will not be the correct size (i.e., the same size as the license's hologram). You will need a photocopier to scale the image to proper size, or you can adjust the image with your computer. Unless you find the image on the Internet or have it on a disk, you will need a scanner to scan the image into your computer before you can edit it. You will also need a graphics program capable of manipulating (i.e., resizing) the image. Even the cheapest black and white hand-held scanner should come with a decent graphics manipulation program.

There are a few advantages to using a computer. Your state may use its official seal as a security device in more than one identity document or even more than once in the same document. Each time, the image will be a different size. Once you have the image stored on your hard drive, you can print it out any size you like as often as you like. What's more, you can do this in the privacy of your own home instead of running down to Kinkos, Copy Cops, or Mail Boxes Etc.

2. Paste it up.

Once you have a template of the correct size, you will need to paste it up in order to stencil it well enough to make a believable replica. Refer to the series of photos on page 45.

(a) Cut a square of the iridescent cellophane big enough to cover the entire template and then some. For example, if your state seal is 1″ by 1″, make the square 2″ by 2″.
(b) Dab a small amount of glue on your finger and spread a thin, even layer onto the cellophane. Cover enough area to accommodate the template. If applying glue directly to the template, don't overwork it or you may cause the ink to run or the paper to disintegrate.
(c) Place the square of cellophane on the template glue-side down, smoothing it in all directions before the glue dries. We'll call this the "template assembly."
(d) Cut a triangle around the template assembly. Refer to the photo series on page 45. This will help you keep the design flat in later steps.
(e) Spread a thin layer of glue on the curved glass cutting surface. Cover enough area to accommodate the template assembly.
(f) Place the template assembly onto the glued area of glass and smooth in all directions.
(g) Tape the template assembly in place with scotch tape, starting with the points of the triangle.

While taping, pull the triangle just tight enough to eliminate wrinkles. The tape should be as close to the design as possible without overlapping it.

3. Trace the image.

Template assembly. Template printout does not have to be high quality since it's only used as a guide. Place glue on cellophane to reduce ink running.

Glue template assembly to glass. Cut a triangle around the template assembly and then glue it to a piece of (preferably rounded) glass. Ink, especially ink from an ink-jet printer, will run somewhat, but do not be concerned.

Stencil around template assembly. Trace along the edges of the template with a stencil knife. Be careful to cut in such a way that the finished product will be a single unit. Do not try to stencil around letters and symbols unless you are an unusually gifted artist. Use a blade that you're comfortable with and take your time. If you find yourself rushing, take a break!

Removing the hologram. Rinse the template assembly under warm water to separate it from the paper. To remove all traces of glue and ink, keep water flowing over it while gently massaging it between your fingers.

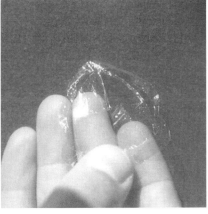

Completed hologram. After completing the process, the iridescent tissue will resemble a floppy hologram.

Store the hologram. Store the hologram in a lamination pouch to keep it safe and flat until it is needed.

Working comfortably with sufficient light, trace the design with your stencil knife. Take frequent breaks, especially if the design is intricate. Check a copy of the actual hologram to verify which sections of the design are holographic and which are completely transparent cutaways. Make your design as close as possible to the original without getting into details that are impossible to replicate (thereby resulting in hacks). Don't attempt to trace around any small print.

4. Separate the holo.

When you have completely traced around all edges with your stencil knife, do it again, making sure all corners are completely cut and all edges have been cut through to the glass. When you're sure of your work, carefully lift the cutout from the glass working area with the tip of your stencil knife. Run the cutout under warm water while gently massaging it between your thumb and fingers.

The iridescent cellophane will begin to separate from the paper you glued it to in step 2c. Take your time and allow this to happen naturally to avoid damage to the hologram.

5. Using the holo.

This hologram is most effectively used as a graphical overlay for a driver's license or identity card of your own creation. Some people laminate the holo first for easier control. I don't. I just lay it over my ID card and laminate using a 10 mil lamination pouch. If you do laminate the holo separately, I would suggest using a 3 or 5 mil pouch and then a 10 mil pouch for the final lamination.

In any case, be sure you have laid the hologram flat before laminating, because sometimes the cellophane tends to curl under itself, resulting in a hack and a redo. Once complete, you will have a very realistic, iridescent, color-shifting hologram incorporated into your ID.

Handling Letters and Symbols

When making the "Poor Man's Iridescent Tissue" hologram, certain states may present a problem. State seals, coats of arms, and even simple rectangle holograms often have letters or other symbols inside them, which are extremely difficult to stencil around. It most cases, it is best to not even attempt to reproduce such details. It's easier to get away with omitting them altogether rather than creating an obvious hack.

Omitting the print may not be an alternative in all cases, especially if the print is well known and expected to be there. There are several things you can do in these situations:

- Only use the ID out of state.
- Use a watermark to allude to the printing.
- Combine iridescent and metallic printing techniques.

Staying out of state. A nicely drafted rectangle or state seal hologram has a good chance of working in other states. The farther away the better. Even places that use an *ID Checking Guide* may not catch omissions of print, as the guide only mentions that there is a hologram. Even if the guide specifies the shape of the hologram, you will have satisfied that criterion. There are exceptions, of course, and this is why you should buy a guide of your own. For example, the guide mentions that the Georgia hologram says "Georgia."

Watermarks. By watermarking the unstencilable details onto iridescent tissue before stenciling, your finished product will have the illusion of entirety. A banker or librarian giving it a quick glance will have the suggestion of print. Of course, watermarks work like a charm on the farsighted and out-of-state checker.

To print a watermark on iridescent tissue, first tape an appropriate size square of it centered on an 8 1/2″ by 11″ sheet of paper. Load the paper into your printer. Assuming you already have your hologram on your PC's hard drive, open the image up in a word processor file such as Word 97. Center the image on the page, turn it into a watermark, then print—voila!

To do this in Word 97, you would open a new document and follow these steps:

1. Click View from the main menu and choose Page Layout.
2. Click View from the main menu and choose Header and Footer.
3. Click Insert from the main menu.
4. Select Picture.
5. Select From File.
6. Find the file you saved your hologram in and double-click it or click Insert.
7. Use the mouse to position the file center page.
8. Click Format from the main menu.
9. Select Picture.
10. Click the Color drop-down box and choose "watermark."
11. Click anywhere outside the picture frame to exit back to page layout view.

That should get you started. Experiment with different brightness and contrast in steps 9 and 10 to achieve the desired results. Write down what you do, and save all your work for future refinements.

Combining techniques. The quality resulting from combining hologram techniques is so good it'll scare you. It can only be done with the microdry printing method provided by ALPS MD series printers or their equivalents.

Print the state seal directly on some iridescent tissue using metallic ink (see the section "Metallic Holos" below) of a suitable color for your state. Stencil the appropriate areas without getting into too much detail. Sometimes just tracing out the perimeter will work fine. The less stenciling, the fewer hacks.

Once laminated over a template, you will have a beautiful (quite striking, actually), color-shifting hologram.

Tools of the poor man's trade. The poor man must make do with common household items. Shown here: glue stick, scissors, tape, iridescent tissue, credit card, nail clippers, some lamination pouches and an iron to seal them, an old inexpensive macro lens for shooting down IDs, film, paper cutter, jelly jar as a cutting surface for hologram templates, stencil knife kit, and a couple of in-process novelty IDs.

The Poor Man's New Jersey Holo

The New Jersey hologram is one that belongs under the loose street definition, rather than the technical definition, of a hologram. When you look at the Jersey hologram straight on in indirect light, it looks transparent and virtually invisible. When you turn it to the light, it turns gold. The paint used to accomplish this effect is called interference gold.

Procedure

1. Go to an art supply store and buy interference gold paint manufactured by Golden Acrylics, paint number 4040-2, series 7, also known as Interference Gold (fine).
2. While you are at the art store, pick up some tracing paper and a stencil knife.

3. Go to the hardware store and buy a foam applicator. This is a blackish gray stick-type thingy made of foam. Ask the proprietor.

4. Go home, get a picture of an appropriately sized New Jersey hologram, and trace it onto the tracing paper with a fine-point pen or marker. If you can print the holo from your computer, you can skip this step.

5. Tape the design to a piece of white poster board.

6. Use your stencil knife to cut the design into the poster board. You can use your index finger on the dull side of the blade for a smoother cut. If you have trouble doing this, hire an art student to do it for you.

7. If you are making a novelty New Jersey driver's license, you should have your altered template (see "Using Templates" above on computer-altered templates) already printed out and laminated with a 5 mil lamination pouch (available through USI). If you are using this holo technique for another ID of your own design, you should have it all set and laminated with a 5 mil lamination pouch.

8. Tape the stenciled poster board in the proper location on the ID.

9. Using a fine paint brush, place a thin, evenly spread amount of interference gold on the flat side of the foam applicator. Use a minuscule amount. More is *not* better.

10. Beginning at the top right of the stencil, jackhammer the applicator into the ID. You should barely see the paint going on. Work the paint down to the bottom left of the stencil.

11. Reapply another minuscule amount of paint and jackhammer it into the ID, working now from the bottom left to top right.

12. Check your work. You should have a very realistic-looking old-style (but still in use) New Jersey hologram. Looking at it straight on, it should be transparent; holding it in direct light, it should appear gold and glittery. If you did not achieve this effect, try again using (in most cases) less paint and hammering harder.

13. Once you have the desired result, allow your work of art to dry.

14. Once completely dry, laminate it with a 10 mil matte finish lamination pouch.

15. Congratulations. You now own one of the most realistic-looking novelty state driver's licenses in existence. Go to the bank before Jersey removes them all from circulation.

Metallic Holos

A metallic hologram is almost transparent when looked at straight on but turns gold, silver, metallic blue, or metallic magenta when shifted at angles to the light. The New Jersey hologram above is, in reality, a metallic hologram.

Aside from using the "poor man's" technique, holograms of this style can be printed directly onto the laminate, a transparency insert, or a template (see "Using Templates" above) with metallic ink of the right color. Unfortunately, printers commonly sold in PC packages cannot handle metallic ink. So if you've yet to buy a PC, don't bother getting a package deal that includes a printer. Save your money and buy an ALPS MD-1300 separately. This printer is the best in its price range for handling metallic ink. It will do New Jersey-style and other metallic holograms well enough to pass close scrutiny.

The Web site www.buy.com has an ALPS MD-1300 in its "buycomp" section currently selling for $353.95. You can also e-lease one for $12.51 per month. While you're there, pick up a metallic gold ink cartridge (106030-00) for $5.95 or $0.21 per month e-lease. You won't regret it! Other ALPS alternatives include the older 2010 model, which has the same output for metallic ink (600 x 600), or the 2030, which has the best photo quality output in its price range. Avoid the MD-1000, though, because it does not offer continuous tone output, and your novelty IDs will be less believable.

If you want to perform some real magic, buy all four metallic-ink cartridges (gold, silver, blue, and magenta). By combining colors, you can produce some really dazzling effects. Here are some combinations that work well:

• Print the hologram in gold using 40 to 60 percent opacity. Run this though the printer again, printing *only the lettering* in metallic blue using a slightly lower opacity. You will need two hologram files to do this; one regular file and one with everything removed except the lettering.

- Print the hologram in metallic blue and the outline and lettering in silver.
- Print the hologram in metallic blue, symbols and lettering in magenta, and outline in gold.
- This one's tricky but worth it. Divide your hologram into 1mm horizontal strips. Set up four computer files—graphics, watermark, or whatever you prefer. The first file will contain every first strip of the hologram. The second file will contain every second strip, the third file every third strip, and the fourth file every fourth strip. Print out the first strip in silver, the second in magenta, the third in gold, and the last in blue. This effect works particularly well for state seal holograms, especially ones that already contain horizontal lines such as the Massachusetts seal.

NOTE: Anytime you're printing in metallic ink, you will want to adjust the "opacity" of the object you're printing to achieve the holographic effect. Experiment with opacity settings from 20 to 80 percent until you have a successful result. Photoshop 5.0 has an opacity setting. If your software doesn't, use the watermark feature of your word processor and vary the brightness and contrast (see "Handling Letters and Symbols" above). Graphics-related software should also have a brightness adjustment, if not one for opacity.

Metallic Lettering

Some states print an obnoxious repeating metallic gold insignia across their license's lamination as a security feature. The ALPS MD-1300 will handle this "problem" easily. Write an appropriate word processor document such as . . .

STATE OF RHODE ISLAND
STATE OF RHODE ISLAND
STATE OF RHODE ISLAND
STATE OF RHODE ISLAND
STATE OF RHODE ISLAND
STATE OF RHODE ISLAND
STATE OF RHODE ISLAND
STATE OF RHODE ISLAND
STATE OF RHODE ISLAND
STATE OF RHODE ISLAND
STATE OF RHODE ISLAND
STATE OF RHODE ISLAND
STATE OF RHODE ISLAND
STATE OF RHODE ISLAND

- or -

INDIANA • INDIANA
INDIANA • INDIANA
INDIANA • INDIANA
INDIANA • INDIANA
INDIANA • INDIANA
INDIANA • INDIANA
INDIANA • INDIANA
INDIANA • INDIANA
INDIANA • INDIANA
INDIANA • INDIANA
INDIANA • INDIANA
INDIANA • INDIANA
INDIANA • INDIANA
INDIANA • INDIANA
INDIANA • INDIANA
INDIANA • INDIANA
INDIANA • INDIANA

. . . and print onto a lamination pouch in metallic gold a flawless novelty ID to fool your friends. What settings did I use for the Rhode Island effect? Arial 11 point font with a line spacing of 10.85 point.

There are 15 lines in all. Most of the top and bottom lines are meant to hang off the edges of the lamination. The letter "S" in "State" must hang halfway off the template's left side. Thus, some forethought and alignment is required.

If you don't like the idea of feeding lamination pouches through your brand new printer, you can also use the self-stick prelamination hologram printing technique (see below).

If you have Microsoft Word 97, the click sequence for changing line spacing is as follows:

- Highlight all 15 lines.
- Click Format from the main menu bar.
- Click Paragraph.
- Under Line Spacing, choose Exactly.
- Then type 10.85 in the At box next to it.
- Click Okay.

This'll get you to within .1mm of exact specs. If you want to be real technical, I suppose you could change the character spacing under Format, Font, and Character Spacing and throw a hard space between the words RHODE and ISLAND.

You can, of course, amend the Rhode Island method for other states that use the same technique. For Indiana there are 19 lines in all, and the top and bottom ones should appear clipped. Use these settings:

Font:	Arial 8 point for letters
	Symbol 8 point for dot (In Word 97 click on Insert,
	Symbol—the dot is the twelfth column over,
	third row up. Double click it.)
Line Spacing:	8.25pt

Watch your font style and size as well as character and line spacing as you experiment with other states. All modern word processors allow you to edit the typesetting. Take advantage of such features for a more believable novelty ID.

Self-Stick Prelamination Printing Technique

For repetitive lettering, this method is better than direct template printing or using transparency inserts. This is because most repetitive lettering patterns are meant to be on the laminate and therefore extend beyond the template area.

Although it's possible to print metallic rectangles and state seals directly to a template, the method below gives the hologram an added measure of dimensionality. The procedure assumes your template already has a backing. It can only be used with microdry printers (ALPS MD-1300).

For Holograms (Seals, Rectangles, etc.)
1. Print out your state's template, edited with your photo and identifying information.
2. Laminate it with a sheet of press-apply lamination, also known as contact lamination or self-stick lamination. Stationery and office supply stores sell it in sheet form.
3. Print your metallic hologram as you normally would. At this point you should know all the necessary opacity and brightness settings because you will have experimented on plain paper first. Due to the new printing medium (the press-apply laminate), you may need to slightly refine these settings.

4. Use a paper trimmer to cut out the printed product. Cut all edges evenly.
5. Using fingernail clippers and the rounded corner of a credit card as a guide, round the corners of your ID.
6. Laminate as usual.

For Repetitive Lettering

1. Experiment on paper until you have found the correct font, font size, character spacing, line spacing, opacity, and brightness. Add several extra lines, as they will be cut off later anyway.
2. Print out the pattern onto a self-stick lamination sheet.
3. Peel back the laminate and gently slide your completed template under it.
4. Line up the repetitive pattern with your template. When you are sure you've done this correctly, press the two together. Be careful not to leave fingerprints on the laminate.
5. Cut the template out, leaving the lamination overhangs intact.
6. Tear the binding of a lamination pouch enough to accommodate the overhanging prelaminate of repetitive lettering (so it appears to fall right off the top and bottom edges).
7. Once everything is lined up, stick the template to the bottom of the lamination pouch by pressing on the overhanging prelaminate.
8. Trim the excess off the edges.
9. Close the lamination pouch, put it in a guide, and laminate as usual.

Hologram Miscellany

For the most part, our extended discussion of holograms centered around light-refracting holograms (or at least reasonable facsimiles thereof). You should also be aware of light-*reflecting* holograms, such as those used by Visa and MasterCard. These types of holograms cause light to reflect back to your eye in all the colors of the rainbow.

Some book covers, magazine jackets, floppy disk labels, CD labels, wrapping paper, and gift bags use light refraction or reflection for effect. Small pieces of this material cut in the shape of a shield or logo are useful when creating novelty student and work IDs as well as credit cards (for ID purposes only).

For some good holo material that can be used in novelty student IDs and credit cards, check out the Volume 174, Number 6 (December 1988) issue of *National Geographic*. The whole cover is one of the best holograms I've ever seen. There are plenty of generic (no picture) areas that you can cut out for use in novelty IDs. Other special issues use holograms, too, but I just happen to have the December '88 issue next to me.

Gold eye shadow over a stencil will make a reasonably effective novelty (non-color-shifting) hologram. One advantage to this technique is that you can wipe it off and start over if you make a mistake.

Pearl nail polish, especially if sprinkled with gold eye shadow or iridescent sparkle dust from a craft store, will also produce some interesting results when applied *sparingly* over a stencil.

More on PVC

Printing on PVC has advantages and disadvantages. Unfortunately, the main disadvantage is the excessive cost of a PVC-capable printer. The biggest advantage, however, is that such printers do an excellent job. Some even laminate the card and encode the magnetic stripe while printing to produce a very believable document.

Where do you get them? How much do they cost?

Fargo Presto ® Quatro ID Card Printer. Regular price: $2,995. Will produce a full-color ID card in about 40 seconds.

Fargo PRO Printer. Regular price: $5,495. Has four megabytes of on-board memory to produce a full-color ID card in 25 seconds.

Fargo PRO-L Printer. Regular price: $7,495. The Pro-L has a built-in lamination station and can print and laminate a full-color card in 40 seconds. In batch-printing mode, it can produce up to 180 full-color, laminated cards per hour.

Sources for these printers:

NewMarket Solutions
9263 Ravenna Road
Twinsburg, OH 44087
E-mail: sales@cardsolutions.com

Smart ID Card, Ltd.
2160 8th Street, Suite B
Mandeville, LA 70471
Sales: sales@smartidcard.com
Info: info@smartidcard.com
Technical Support: support@smartidcard.com

Keep in mind that all dye sublimation printer manufacturers use the same Japanese company to make their print heads. They are all 300 dpi and capable of printing 16.7 million colors. Don't spend more money for higher resolution. You won't get it. The more expensive machines are meant for commercial use: they are the ones bought by the motor vehicle registries. This means that your bottom-of-the-line printer will have the same resolution as registry printers. This may change in the future.

Hacking the Magnetic Strip
There may be times when you wish to damage the magnetic strip on your driver's license or credit card. Here's how to do it.

Go to Radio Shack and buy a tape head demagnetizer, also known as a degausser. For your reference, the catalog number is 44-215. Go home, put your ID card on an iron or steel surface such as a frying pan, plug in the degausser, and make several close passes over the magnetic stripe. Pass the pencil-like tip of the degausser over the stripe *slowly* at various angles. Make a few passes with the side of the "pencil," too, and move the card while you move the degausser, preferably at 90-degree angles.

The degausser is made for demagnetizing tape heads, not tapes. This is why you must have something steel or iron behind the card. It interacts with the steel to create a magnetic field, which then passes through the magnetic stripe. The process is not perfect, but all you need is one small section "zapped" and the card will become unreadable. If you have a powerful magnet, it can also be used to degauss the stripe.

Degaussing will cause permanent damage to the magnetic stripe and force police officers to rely on the license's printed information. This is by no means foolproof, but when your new identity doesn't show up in the state's computer, you have a better chance of being sent on your way (see "Driving Without A License" below).

Making a One-Piece ID (The Old-Fashioned Way)
Making a one-piece ID without a special camera requires a lot of skill, knowledge, and extra effort. Most people constructing novelty IDs do not have access to, and cannot afford, special ID cameras. Computer manipulation of scanned templates (see above) is one way around this problem. But any photographer will tell you there is another way that can produce very pleasing results.

In Chapter 6 of *The Modern Identity Changer*, I outlined a perfectly acceptable method of constructing a one-piece ID. I still use that method today. In strict observance of the no rehash rule, I do not intend to repeat the procedure here. Rather, I will elaborate on it by showing you a permanent rig I made to enhance the procedure.

The purpose of the rig is to evenly illuminate the ID assembly (see *MIC*, Chapter 6, "Shooting Down the ID"), which consists of a 3″ x 5″ ID card, 2-inch passport photo, and transparency overlay pressed together by a pane of glass.

I'd always had problems with uneven illumination and unwanted reflections when shooting down the ID to a standard one-piece, license-size card. Traditionally I compensated for this by taking various exposures with different light and camera settings. This would usually yield a few usable pictures.

I've since found a way to eliminate reflections and evenly illuminate the ID assembly for photographing. I call it my one-piece ID rig.

Building Your Own Rig

Don't worry, we're not going to build an actual ID camera from scratch. That would be more expensive than buying one, which would defeat the purpose. Rather, we are going to enhance a camera you already have or can easily (and cheaply) obtain. No harm will come to the camera, as the device we'll be building is completely external to it.

You will need the following:

- A 35mm SLR camera
- Macro lens, or a telephoto lens with macro capabilities
- A 16″ open-top box made of light wood or heavy cardboard
- A translucent, drop-ceiling light cover or other translucent material
- A 30″ square of black felt, velvet, or similar material
- Flat white ceiling paint

The procedure:

1. Paint the inside of the box flat white. Do not use satin or gloss finish. Flat, latex, bright white ceiling paint is best. Texture or sand paint is even better because it helps to scatter the light, thereby eliminating reflections. You only need to paint three sides because the fourth side will be removed.
2. Remove the unpainted fourth side of the box and replace it with a 16″ square of translucent (not transparent) material, such as a drop ceiling light cover.
3. Cut a hole in the center of the velvet material. It should be big enough so your macro lens can fit through it (usually 50 to 55 mms).
4. You are done building the rig.

When you're ready to shoot down, place the ID assembly at the bottom of the box and shine a light through the translucent material at a 45-degree angle from above. Put your macro lens through the hole in the velvet material and hold it in place with an elastic. Set up your camera as usual and droop the black material over the box opening to prevent reflections. Adjust the light intensity as needed.

You will have a nice, evenly lighted ID with no unwanted reflections. Because of this, you will not need to take as many exposures to get an acceptable result. When you get your pictures back from the processing plant, trim out your favorite one, add a backing and hologram, and laminate it to produce a very believable student or employment ID. With some forethought and experimentation, state driver's licenses can also be made this way. To do this, you'll need to enlarge the template so that it will shoot down to the correct size.

Some state licenses and college IDs have a slight hue to them. You can use colored cellophane taped to the outside of the translucent material to achieve this effect. For more intense color, buy canister "gels" from a theatrical supplier.

Extension and Renewal Stickers

So you've gone through all the trouble of finding a "doable" template with security features that

Right: A college or fraternity ID template can be made with a word processor such as Word 97. The organizations' "official" seal can then be imported as a watermark for an added touch of class. Print out the template on a laser printer and enter your identifying info with a typewriter, as would happen in the real world.

Place your 2" passport photo in the upper left corner, then overlay the assembly with a transparency containing the security signature, which overlaps the bottom edge of the photo.

Press it all together with a small square of heavy glass and shoot down the 3-1/2" by 5" template to a 1-3/4" by 2-7/8" one-piece ID ready for a backing, hologram, and lamination.

Right: Here is the one piece ID being trimmed with a pair of fingernail clippers. A credit card or lamination pouch is a ready-made guide for making perfectly rounded corners.

Middle: After you've added your backing, hologram and laminate, you'll indeed have a very convincing ID. This photo was shot dead-on. Notice how the hologram is nearly transparent at this angle. In actual usage, the hologram will seem even more transparent, if not completely invisible.

Bottom: Turning the ID at a slight angle to the light, you'll notice it suddenly becomes quite visible. This effect was accomplished by using the "Poor Man's (Iridescent Tissue) Method."

Delta Pi Psi
FRATERNITY MEMBER
2220 COLLEGE ST. OWYHEE, NV 89832

THIS CARD ALLOWS YOU NATIONWIDE ACCESS TO ANY DELTA PI PSI HOUSE, FUNCTION OR EVENT. REPORT ITS LOSS TO THE MAIN OFFICE IN OWYHEE, NV. IF FOUND, PLEASE MAIL TO THE ABOVE ADDRESS. THIS CARD IS VALID FOR LIFE. IF YOU ARE ASKED TO WITHDRAW FROM DELTA PI PSI, THIS CARD MUST BE RETURNED IMMEDIATELY TO THE OWYHEE OFFICE.

REGISTRAR

728-14-9987	9/12/86
MEMBER ID	MEMBER SINCE

SIGNATURE

Sheldon X. Charrett	9/12/98
NAME	ISSUE DATE

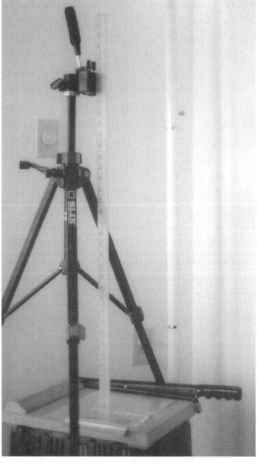

Above right: Although I recommend my "One-Piece ID Rig," an inexpensive SLR camera with macro lens can be set on a tripod directly above the template assembly (template, passport photo, and transparency). A halogen lamp placed in the corner provides sufficient and diffuse light. The yardstick is used to measure the lens' distance from the assembly. I recommend making several exposures from distances of 16 to 30 inches.

Identity, Privacy, and Personal Freedom

are easy enough to replicate. One problem: the frikkin' thing expires at the end of the year! Frustrating isn't it? Fortunately, there are many states that extend the term of a license simply by affixing a sticker to the back. There are several states whose prior-issue (nonhologram) licenses may be extended this way. This has certain advantages for the privacy seeker:

- You do not necessarily need to manufacture a state's most current (read: hologram-secured) license. You can use an older version that is easier to replicate.
- The extension sticker, in many cases, solves the problem of making an ID back.

Some states that use extension or renewal stickers are Alaska, Arizona, California, Colorado, Florida, Georgia (if honorary veteran), Idaho, Illinois, Iowa, Kansas, Louisiana, Massachusetts, Nevada, North Dakota, Oregon, Tennessee, Texas, and Utah. The stickers are valid from 30 days to six years, depending on the type of sticker and the state.

You could also choose a state whose license has a long expiration date to begin with and eliminate the need for a sticker. Since July 1993, an Arizona driver's license expires on the licensee's 60th birthday

When making a novelty driver's license or renewal sticker, it is important to heed all of the template and photograph warnings given below under the heading "State ID Cards."

Temporary Driver's License

After your relaxing and enjoyable visit to the Department of Motor Vehicles, some states, such as New York, issue you a temporary driver's license while you wait for your real one to arrive in the mail. Often, these states require that you hand over your current driver's license, leaving you without that piece of ID. At any given time in the United States, there are several thousand people walking around with only a temporary paper driver's license while they wait for their real driver's license in the mail. Therefore, there are times when a temporary driver's license is acceptable to bureaucrats as identification (although they'll still whine about it).

These paper documents are very easy to manufacture on a personal computer and, used properly with other supporting identification, privacy seekers and identity changers can sweet-talk bank tellers, mail drop clerks, and others into accepting a novelty "temporary driver's license" in lieu of a real one.

My home state of New York has always done it this way. Minnesota does it, and I've heard that Massachusetts has begun to as well. There are a couple of reasons why it's done. The first is practicality. Some states hire third parties to manufacture their IDs. The DMV does the verification process, collects current information (new address, name change, etc.), and takes a new photograph. The information and photograph are then sent to a third party, usually a private company, which manufactures the actual license.

The state saves money by not having to purchase new equipment and retrain hundreds of employees every time new technology is implemented, which seems to be every other year. Another benefit, perhaps more important to Big Brother, is that this process virtually eliminates the loophole described below under the heading "Borrowing a Driver's License." The disadvantage, of course, it that it opens the loophole described above.

GOOD NONLICENSE IDs

As promised, this chapter dealt mostly with document manufacture as it relates to state driver's licenses. This was appropriate because the driver's license is the most coveted form of picture identification among identity changers. There are still a few other forms of identification that I'd like to touch on, as well as a couple of points I feel are important to the subject of document manufacture in general.

State ID Cards

This loophole is so sweet I hate to tip off the bureaucrats by publishing it. But I'd feel remiss if I didn't share it with you. So, here goes.

Certain states either currently issue or have issued in the past state ID cards that are valid indefinitely. Some are stamped "lifetime," and some simply omit an expiration date altogether.

Maybe you suffer from epilepsy or some other ailment that has precluded your eligibility to drive. Perhaps you just don't want to be one of 40,000 people who die on U.S. roadways each year. It's possible you're an alcoholic and therefore thought it best to not obtain your driver's license. Could it be that you keep flunking that %#$!^& road test! There are countless reasons why people don't or can't drive, and there is no law that forces people to become licensed drivers.

For these reasons, most states issue ID cards so its nondriver citizens can cash checks, open bank accounts, get into bars, purchase liquor, write checks, and so forth. Establishments in the state have to accept these cards as identification or subject themselves to liability under discrimination laws.

It follows, therefore, that a well-constructed state ID card with no expiration date can be used indefinitely in your quest for privacy and personal freedom. Most states have caught on to this and now issue cards that expire. Their older issues, however, are still valid. The biggest problems for someone constructing a novelty state ID card are:

- Finding a template of the ID card
- Finding a suitable self-portrait

Finding a Template

You can find some templates in the *ID Checking Guide*. You may be able to find more templates in older issues of the *Guide* and other books like it. A better bet is to get on the Web and visit the sites I've listed. Get involved in the discussion groups and make friends. Find out who has (or has a friend that has) a state ID card. Ask them to upload a "scan" to the board's database or e-mail a scan to you. Some people will be glad to help out; others will want information, products, or service in exchange.

States that issue or have issued lifetime state ID cards include Alabama, Colorado, Georgia, Maine, Massachusetts, Missouri, Nevada, South Dakota, and Wyoming. Happy hunting.

Finding a Photo

When you do find a template of a state ID card, it's important to learn in which years your particular format was issued. For example, Nevada has many state ID card formats, all of which are valid indefinitely. However, making the mistake of putting your current photograph on a format that was last issued in 1980 would be a dead giveaway to most bureaucrats that the ID is a fake.

Colorado's "over 21" ID cards issued before 1996 are valid indefinitely. If you're old enough, you may be able to paste (with a computer) a recent picture of yourself onto a 1996 template, since an older person's appearance does not change too drastically even over 5 or 10 years. When you have your photo taken, wear some of your old clothes, change your hairdo and, if you're male, grow or remove your beard and/or mustache (whichever is opposite your current appearance).

If the template you've acquired requires an older picture, you will have to look through your old pictures or your high school and college yearbooks. Unless you've saved your old high school/college ID or happen to have retained your old driver's license or other ID, your chances of finding a picture with the appropriate color background are about nil. Even if you do have some old IDs, chances are the background won't be quite right.

What's the answer? Photoshop 5 is one. Any "true color" graphics editing software should suffice to help you erase your college sweetheart and paint in an appropriate backdrop. The software's "color replace" function will change the backdrop to any of more than 1.7 million colors. Chances are, though, you'll be using some shade of blue.

College ID Cards

A well-crafted (or otherwise obtained) college ID can serve many useful purposes. Most important, perhaps, is as a great secondary ID. Many identity changers also like to have the notoriety and prestige associated with a college education. College ID cards are also a great way to show your claim to temporary residency. Happen to be really good at making New Jersey driver's licenses but desire to live in California? Well, a nice University of Southern California ID card would explain why you're using a New Jersey driver's license to open a California bank account.

In Indiana, people with out-of-state licenses who get a traffic citation face one of the two following scenarios:

- If the other state has an agreement with Indiana, the license is taken from the violator and the ticket serves as a receipt. The other state will act to collect the fine if the driver doesn't pay the ticket.
- If the other state has no such agreement, the alleged violator must cough up the fine on the spot as a "security deposit" or be hauled downtown immediately.

Fortunately, Indiana cops will usually treat out-of-state students as Indiana residents if the alleged violator can provide a local address. This is such a scenario where having a college ID can come in very handy.

Business Cards

Yeah, I know: business cards—how lame can ID get? If you're like me, you're probably sick of hearing authors say, "Print up some business cards with various names and grab up business cards wherever you go!" Well, printing up business cards isn't exactly cheap, and using other people's cards often leads to danger. So, here are some novel thoughts to spice up this drab form of identification.

Easy to Make

With the explosion of computer technology, privacy seekers and identity changers now have the option of easily manufacturing their own business cards, which can include watermarks, holograms, and photographs. And you can manufacture different business cards for different situations and uses almost free (if you already own the computer equipment, which is recommended).

There's no longer any need to pay hundreds of dollars to a printer—whom you don't know and probably can't trust—to print thousands of cards you'll never use.

Realtor® Business Card

My favorite ID business cards are those used by the National Association of Realtors (other cards associated with the professional sales industry may be used in the same way). These cards are expected to contain a photograph of the bearer, thus they are more believable when presented as supporting ID or accidentally left in just the right place as subliminal ID.

Another great advantage: when you present a Realtor business card to somebody, they are so busy loathing you for being a Realtor they don't consider that your ID may be false.

Parking Stickers

The methods in this chapter can be used to manufacture parking decals. Cheap laminate sheets at Best Buy and office suppliers can be printed on with dry ink. Use a microdry (Alps MD) or dye-sublimation printer. Have fun.

NOTE: Selling parking stickers in a big city, while extremely profitable, is also extremely dangerous. You never know who you're selling to. Getting caught forging official documents will probably land you before the courts and, quite possibly, in prison.

Using The Correct Typewriter For Old Documents

If you're going to use a typewriter to produce a novelty historical document, you should at least know which typewriters were in wide use when the document was supposedly issued. You could not, for instance, produce a believable birth certificate from 1920 using an IBM Selectric II.

When visiting yard sales, flea markets, and salvage outlets, Table 3.1 will help you select an appropriate typewriter for whatever document project you may be working on.

TABLE 3.1
Typewriter Histories and Characteristics

YEAR	TYPEWRITER	NOTES
1873	Sholes & Glidden	
1878	Remington No. 2	
1879	The Stenograph	United States Stenograph Company. Shorthand characters. Ink ribbon.
1879	Crandall, Remington No. 3	
1880	Caligraph, Hall, Hammond, Remington No. 4	
1881	Crandall	Manufactured by the Crandall Machine Co., Groton, NY. Ornate design, ink ribbon, square keys, two-row keyboard.
1881	Hall	Brooklyn, NY. Walnut case.
1882	Caligraph	Model No. 1 was an uppercase-only version, soon replaced by Model No. 2, an upper and lowercase version during its first production year. This was Remington's first serious competition.
1882	Caligraph No. 2	
1883	Caligraph No. 3, Columbia, Horton	
1884	Hammonia	
1885	Sun Index	
1885	Morris, Sun	
1886	Lambert Lasar Type-Writer	Lasar Type-Writer Co., St. Louis. Uppercase only.
1886	The Morris	Hoggson & Pettis Manufacturing Co., New Haven, CT.

YEAR	TYPEWRITER	NOTES
1886	World Type-Writer	Many manufactured.
1886	Velograph, World	
1887	Yost, Brooks, Cash	
1888	Boston, Burns, Dictatype, Kosmopolit, Royal Bar-Lock, Smith-Premier	
1889	Barlock	By having the type bars mounted vertically between the keyboard and the carriage, the typist could see what he was typing.
1889	Munson	Munson Typewriter Co., Chicago. Predecessor of the Chicago. Nickel plated.
1889	National	National Typewriter Co., Philadelphia, PA. Ribbon inking, shift key, gold scrollwork.
1889	Odell Typewriter	Odell Typewriter Co. Early models uppercase only.
1889	Victor Type Writer	Tilton Manufacturing Co., Boston, MA. Probably the first daisy wheel.
1889	Barlock, International, National, Odell, Stenograph.	
1890	Ingersoll	
1890	Smith Premier	L.C. Smith Gun Co., Syracuse, NY
1890	Williams Typewriter	
1890	Daugherty, International, Merritt, Munson, Rapid, World No. 2	
1891	Edland	Primitive daisy wheel by Liberty Manufacturing Co., NY. Inexpensive, fragile design. Few remaining.
1891	The Franklin	
1891	Granville Automatic	Carriage return controlled from keyboard.

YEAR	TYPEWRITER	NOTES
1891	Densmore, Fitch, Franklin, Hall Braille	
1892	Wellington	Also appeared as Wannamaker, Davis, Empire, and Adler.
1892	American-Standard, Dennis Duplex, Frister & Rossman, Jewett, Williams	
1893	American Visible Typewriter	Manufactured by the American Typewriter Co. Rubber typefaces on a sliding mechanism.
1893	Universal Crandall	Later versions incorporated a "qwerty" keyboard.
1893	American Visible, Blickensderfer, Universal Crandall No. 3, Hammond No. 2, International, Maskelyne, Peoples, Remington-Sholes	
1894	Oliver Typewriter	Nickel plated. Back keys.
1894	Crary, Crown, Edison-Mimeograph, Elliott-Fisher, Hartford No. 1, Remington No. 6, Victor	
1895	Edison Mimeograph	A.B. Dick Co., Chicago. Slow, inefficient design. Blind typing.
1895	Travis Typewriter	Philadelphia Typewriter Co. Type wheel. Four-row keyboard.
1895	Blickensderfer No. 5, Ford, Graphic, Jewett No. 2, Smith-Premier Nos. 2 & 3, Travis, Underwood	
1896	Smith-Premier No. 4, Williams No. 2, Blickensderfer No. 6, Elliott-Hatch, Granville Automatic, Lambert, Oliver, Remington No. 7, Wellington	
1897	Blickensderfer No. 7, Densmore No. 2, Edelman, Munson No. 3, Oliver No. 2, Remington No. 8, Williams No. 3	

Identity, Privacy, and Personal Freedom

YEAR	TYPEWRITER	NOTES
1898	The Chicago	Succeeded the Munson with its closed-cover design. Very successful typewriter marketed until 1917 under the names Baltimore, Competitor, Conover, Draper, Galesburg, Ohio, and Yale, among others.
1898	Fox	Fox Typewriter Co., Grand Rapids, MI. Ornate design. Fox decal. Gold scrollwork on both sides. Later marketed as a portable under the name Sterling.
1898	Keystone Typewriter	Red and yellow Keystone decal
1898	Manhattan	Clone of Remington's No. 2. Ornate design. Wooden feed roller.
1898	Adler, Champion, Chicago, Commercial Visible, Jackson, Manhattan, Pittsburgh	
1899	Commercial Visible	An early "type ball" model where the ball was struck from behind with a hammer. Although it had a beautifully curved design, few were ever sold.
1899	American, Empire, Keystone, Saturn	
1900	Columbia Bar Lock, Conover, Draper, Ideal, New Century. Caligraph, Remington-Sholes No. 6, Smith-Premier No. 5, Williams No. 4	
1901	Underwood	First modern typewriter. Models 4 & 5 sales were nearly 4,000,000 from 1901 to 1931. Are by no means rare and are perfect for reproducing documents made between 1901 and 1940. Keep your eyes peeled at yard sales, flea markets, etc.
1901	Sun	
1902	Pittsburg Visible	Daugherty Typewriter Co., Kittanning, PA. Sold under the name Daugherty.

YEAR	TYPEWRITER	NOTES
1902	Densmore No. 4, Fox, Moya, Oliver No. 3, Pittsburg No. 10, Postal, Remington No. 10	
1903	Elliot-Fisher	Later merged with the Underwood Typewriter Co.
1903	Chicago No. 3, Coffman, Kanzler, Stoewer Record, Yetman	
1904	McCool, Mignon, Monarch, L. C. Smith & Bros.	
1905	Fay-Sholes, Hammond No. 12, Hartford No. 3, Remington-Sholes Visible, Secor, Sholes Visible, Stearns, Williams No. 5	
1906	Fox Visible, Molle, Monarch No. 2, Monarch No. 3, Royal, Williams No. 6	
1907	Junior	Junior Typewriter Company, NY. Ball type. Spacebar at top of keyboard. Ribbon ink mechanism introduced in 1910 and marketed as the Bennett.
1907	Blickensderfer No. 8, Densmore No. 5, Densmore No. 6, Emerson, Hanson, Imperial Visible, Junior, Oliver No. 5, Standard Folding	
1908	Postal	Postal Typewriter Co., New York, NY and Norwalk, CT. Ink ribbon.
1908	Burnett, Defi, Imperial, Mercantile, Smith-Premier Visible, Stearns No. 4, Victor, Yost Visible, Pullman No. 8	
1909	Empire No. 2, Japy, Mentor, Olivetti, Nickerson, Remington No. 9, Smith Premier Visible	
1910	McCool	Ribbon inking. Type wheel. Pre-patent models as early as 1904.

YEAR	TYPEWRITER	NOTES
1910	Bennet, Bijou, Columbia Barlock #14, Erika, Hammond Multiplex, Smith-Premier, Linowriter, Picht, Sterling, Titania Triumph, Victor #2, Visagraph	
1911	Crown Portable, Harris, Pittsburg No. 12, Stenotype, Royal No. 5	
1912	Corona	One of the biggest all-time sellers, this model, which fit neatly in its travel case, was in production for nearly 30 years, ceasing production around 1941. Was mass produced and thus can often be found at flea markets and yard sales for next to nothing! A great choice for replicating novelty documents produced between 1912 and 1950.
1912	Corona, Hooven Automatic, Imperial #1, Moon-Hopkins, Pierce Accounting, Underwood Std. Bookkeeping, Victor No. 3, Yost Visible No. 20	
1913	Harry A. Smith	
1914	Alexander, Annell, Century, Continental, Demountable, Halda, Harris Visible No. 4, Kappel, Oliver 7, Rex Visible, Senta, Shortwriter, Royal No. 10	
1915	Hammond Multiplex, Nippon, Reliance Visible, Woodstock	
1916	Autocrat, Blick Bar, Oliver No. 9	
1917	Portex No. 5, Reliance Premier, Blickensderfer No. 9	
1918	Molle	Molle Typewriter Co., Oshkosh, WI. Also marketed under the name Liberty.
1918	Fox Baby Portable, National Portable, New American, Oliver No. 11, Yu Ess.	

YEAR	TYPEWRITER	NOTES
1919	Allen, Blick Ninety, Garbell, Roberts Ninety, Underwood Portable	
1920	Gourland, Monarch Pioneer	
1921	The Noiseless	Noiseless Typewriter Co., Middletown, CT. Portable, three-bank design. Company purchased by Remington in 1924, which then issued the Remington Noiseless with a four-bank keyboard.
1921	Bar-Lock, Fox Sterling, Hammond Folding, Mercedes Electra, Noiseless Portable, Rofa, Shilling	
1922	Woodstock No. 5	
1923	Alexander, Diamond, Hermes, Liberty, Smith Premier No. 30	
1924	Dayton, Frolio, Geniatus, Gundka, M-W, Remington Scout	
1925	Bing, Remington Electric, Remington Noiseless, Woodstock Electrite	
1926	Barr, Merz, Underwood Fanfold, American Pocket	
1927	Bing No. 2, Imperial, Varityper, Victor Portable	
1928	Bijou, Oliver Portable, Rem-Blick	
1932	Masspro, Remington Bantam	
1933	Electromatic	
1934	Carissima.	
1935	Porto-Rite, Remington No. 11	
1938	Remington Rem-ette	
1939	Remington No. 17	

Of course you must also be careful to note whether your document-issuing body used typewriters at all during the year of your document's issue. This is especially important in the early years of typewriters, before they were in wide use. For example, in 1915 many governing bodies still issued birth, marriage, and death certificates in pen and ink.

Also note that some of the earlier typewriters printed only in all capital letters. If you ever look through old records and indices, you will note that, in fact, the typeface is all caps. There were also crossover years where many governing bodies still owned all-cap typewriters even though upper/lowercase versions were in wide use. You must always take care to note what was going on typewriter-wise in your jurisdiction during the year your document was allegedly issued.

One final note of interest. You can find companies on the Internet that produce vintage typeface fonts for personal computers. I've never tried them, but I'm sure free-thinking individuals can find a use for them.

Notarize That Document!

It's always a bummer when you spend countless hours constructing a fine-looking ancillary document only to have the whole ploy fail when some bank manager, border agent, or county clerk writes back to tell you said document must first be notarized. Notarized? How the hell am I going to do that? I'm not really Thomas Alva Edison! How can I forge a notary seal? Even if I could, can't they tell? Isn't there some log book they keep? Help!

The answers are: several ways; sometimes; yes, but it doesn't usually matter; and, okay I'll help.

Let's start with the last question first. I've already said I'll help, so the next question is one many people have asked me over the years: don't notaries keep a log book that precludes forgery? It's true that notaries keep a record of all documents they notarize. It's also true that if states wanted to, they could database these records and compare them with notarized documents, such as title transfers and articles or incorporation, to catch would-be forgers. But the truth is that states don't yet do this. A notary's log book is only checked long after allegations have been raised and some bureaucrat has reason to believe a certain document has been falsified. The notary process is at best a loose security measure that, for now at least, can be easily violated. And, to answer the preceding question: no, in most circumstances, the person receiving the falsely notarized document has no ready way of knowing he's been duped.

Can notary seals be forged? They most certainly can. There are many ways to do this. The best way is not a forgery at all but rather a mere fraud. You present false identification to a notary and he or she, in turn, notarizes your document with a valid stamp and seal. Even if the document is called into question or the feds implement computer checking some years down the road, the notarization has been duly recorded. Certain unscrupulous people might even be tempted to use the techniques in this chapter to make a driver's license, student ID, or employment badge to effect such a fraud against the local notary. Of course, this is not recommended. Neither is the somewhat simpler task of having the document notarized by a bored clerk at Comp USA or Kinko's.

Perchance you are of the squeamish variety and prefer not to pull such a stunt in person? Well, others much like yourself have been known to order a notary stamp, seal, and embosser from companies that supply them. You can find such companies on the Worldwide Web using the keywords: Notary AND Seal. Many of these companies will not ask for proof of your notary status. Simply fill out an order form and send payment. To make your stamp or seal believable, you must first study those used in your state. Pay close attention to font style and layout, license numbers, expiry dates, and whether state logos are used.

To use your stamp and seal effectively, you'll need to review your state laws. Some states do not require a notary's seal—a stamp with commission expiry date and signature will suffice. Other states require a stamp and seal, and a few require the seal to be placed on the document in a certain manner (such as directly over the notarized signature).

The best way to find out what's official is to go around to various notaries and have them notarize documents for you. A city clerk's office will only charge you one or two dollars for this service. Go to different cities for various examples of what practices are accepted in your target state.

Certain bad people have been known to put an erasable ink cartridge in a regular pen and visit the notary. When the notary tells them to sign on the dotted line, they do so quickly and with a light hand. The notary then seals the document, collects payment, and sends the bad guy on his way. Occasionally, one can spot such a bad guy sitting in the town hall parking lot erasing the very signature that was just notarized and writing in a new and altogether better signature in its place—or so I've heard.

WELL, THAT ABOUT COVERS IT

This chapter detailed every aspect I could think of regarding the manufacture of identity documents in the United States today. Of course Big Brother will find new ways to secure identity documents, and these will be fodder for future books on the subject. Although the above methods should prove useful for many years to come, be sure to keep your eye out for the latest technological developments in the field of document security. Even as this is written, new process patents are being filed with the U.S. Patent Office that may become the wave of the future. It's a wave I'm sure we'll be able to ride, but to do so we must first see it coming. So keep your eye to the horizon and be sure to share what you discover with other freedom fighters.

4

Obtaining Officially Issued Documents Under A New Identity

Deus ex Machina
"A god from the machine"
Plato

What if a being could simply spring from the Bureaucratic Machine? This is exactly what happens when a witness is relocated under the Federal Witness Protection Program, which is the neatest and most efficient method of creating a new identity. The feds have the golden key to every records office in the United States, and it's a simple matter (for them) to fill out and stamp a few forms.

Short of ratting out an organized crime leader, there is little chance the feds will ever give you a new identity. But this is no big loss for identity changers. Although the Witness Protection Program is the most efficient method of creating a new identity, it is certainly not the most desirable. After all, the *feds* will still know where you are, won't they? So you can pretty much forget about any creative tax financing or secret bank accounts if you go this route. Not to mention the fact that you'll have Vinnie Notso Molto-Generoso to think about every night as you try to sleep. No thank you, Big Brother.

The traditional method used by identity changers to get "real" documents is called "ghosting." This is the old standby of using a deceased person's birth certificate. A less common but equally valid method is to borrow another's identity. This often happens when somebody has a friend or relative who becomes incapacitated, leaving behind a clean driver's history, good credit, enviable bank account, real estate holdings, and no criminal record. We can't let all that go to waste now, can we? A less complete example of identity borrowing is when somebody adopts just enough of another identity to obtain credit.

After reading this, you're probably thinking that the feds' method of identity creation is the best. If only you could work their magic yourself and make a perfect identity, a god, rise from the machine. This is not necessarily impossible. I'll warn you up front that such wizardry is no easy feat, but there are a few tricks that can cause birth certificates, drivers' licenses, and whatnot to spring forth from Big Brother's Bureaucratic Machine.

DEUS EX MACHINA

The main problem with manufacturing effective public identity documents has nothing to do with obtaining blank forms, state seals, official signatures, notarization, or embossed templates. All of these things can be manufactured, acquired, or forged. The main problem is having the document entered into the public record. Only then does it become foolproof. This applies to Social Security numbers, drivers' licenses, professional licenses, employment IDs, college IDs, school records, and all vital records. For the purposes of this section, we will use the birth certificate as an example. Aside from entering the Witness Protection Program, the cold, hard fact is that there are only two ways to enter your document into the public record:

- Bribe a clerk to do it for you.
- Do the job yourself.

At first glance, both of these options seem pretty hopeless. But it's the truth, and the truth is not pretty. I won't lie to you: there are no simple answers here. But in the history of identity changing, both have been done many, many times. Let's examine our options.

Bribing a Clerk

If you decide to approach a clerk, you will either have to know somebody who works in the target office or have intestines of steel to pull it off. The chances of your knowing somebody are pretty slim. If you are friendly and creative, you could certainly plant yourself in the right place at the right time and get to know somebody.

This is the tack I took, albeit quite unintentionally. During my years as a full-time heir finder, I visited the vital statistics registry at least once a week, every week. I got to know a lot of the kids who worked there pulling records for me as I needed them. A couple of the kids worked out together a few times a week at a nearby gym. I was into working out at the time as well, and inevitably we fell into a pattern of discussing exercise routines. When the two were comfortable with me, they invited me to work out with them.

All sorts of happy opportunistic bells and whistles went off in my head. Now, I don't want to get anybody in trouble, 'cuz these guys ended up being pretty cool friends. Let me just say up front that I never took advantage of the situation (that time). But once we were in the gym, it was pretty easy for me to get these guys to talk about their work. I even shared with them some "hypothetical" ID change situations and, to my surprise, they were quite comfortable talking openly about it. In fact, it soon became clear that it was not the first time they had done so. They had discussed ideas of their own long before I ever entered the picture. I learned a *lot*.

A few quick points of interest. These guys did not have "official" access to the state's computer database, as I had assumed. However, as in many work environments, the password necessary to access that level of the computer system was taped to the supervisor's terminal. This was back when state records were first becoming computerized. Therefore, at that time all I would have needed was for these guys to enter a birth certificate from a defunct hospital into the public record. Had I asked, and had I something to offer in return, they would have done it, guaranteed. I had planned to offer one of the gents a nice Weider barbell set and a mountain bike, but ultimately I decided it was not worth risking their jobs.

Why a Defunct Hospital?

Let me just clear this up. The safest birth record to enter into the state's computer is from a hospital that cannot be easily contacted for verification. In other words, one that no longer exists or one that has had its records destroyed or lost.

But you can't just pick any defunct hospital. You must do some research. First you must determine whether the hospital had a maternity ward during the year you intend to be born. You must then find out what the hospital did with the birth records when they went belly up. Were they thrown out, returned to the families, transferred to a city or state hospital, put in storage, or transferred to the state vital statistics registry? If the latter, it's probably not the best hospital to be born at.

Hospitals don't catch on fire too often. Nor do they often get flooded, since most of them are built on hilltops. But if you happen to know of a hospital that has for some reason lost its records, it would probably be a good birthplace for you.

The loss or damage of city records, while still not overly common, does happen more often than the loss of hospital records. The ultimate birthplace for a new identity is at a hospital that has no record of your birth in a city that has permanently lost all birth records from your birth year. Your research may reveal only a one-month period where records were lost and, for whatever reason, could not be recovered from the hospital. That month would be a good birth month.

It's important to note that not all vital statistics registries have the same rules. Some require that all births be registered immediately with the state, while others require that local registrars transmit these records to the state every two years. Also, vital statistics registries may exclude certain areas from their reporting requirements. For example, in New York the state office does not maintain vital records from any of the five boroughs of New York City. There is a separate office for that.

Some states only house records going back to a certain year. The Colorado vital statistics office only has birth records back to 1958. For births before that date, one must contact the city or county where the birth occurred. Therefore it is vital that identity changers understand the record-keeping policies of the state they wish to be born in.

Amnesia

A seldom used but noteworthy method of obtaining new ID is to become an amnesiac. This requires a great deal of time and effort as well as considerable acting skills. Personally I don't recommend this method, but it has on several occasions helped many an embezzler or other police target drop out, start over, and acquire a new set of identification.

The basic plot is to get yourself "found" at some odd location (a highway median seems to be the current preference) and then let the authorities try and determine who you are. It's best to dress right on the border of street person and dressed-down businessman having a really bad vacation. This keeps the authorities interested, friendly, and guessing. A bump on the head or scratches near your left temple adds a nice touch.

Eventually you will be assigned to some social program and given some type of menial job. From both of these you will receive some low-level ID made out in the name of "X" Doe, where "X" is the name you mutter during your vague "flashbacks" or "accidentally" scream out in your sleep. This may all sound quite comical, but it's pretty much how it happens. I would not be able to keep a straight face while pulling off such an involved and silly stunt.

One final note: real amnesia is very, very rare. You will have to do a lot of reading up on it to convince an expert that you are truly an amnesiac. The upside is that the rarity of the condition means there are very few experts on it. Chances are, you will not run into one unless you beg the authorities to take you to one. Your average general practitioner will say, "Yeah, looks like amnesia, all right. First case I've ever seen."

Whatever you do, don't get yourself booked on *Unsolved Mysteries* or *The Today Show*. That's a dead giveaway you're faking it, not to mention the fact that cousin Jake or your old bookie will call in to collect the reward for "solving" the mystery if they happen to be watching.

Now let's introduce ourselves to some minor deities that may also rise from the machine . . .

DRIVER'S LICENSES

As pointed out in most books on identity documents, the driver's license has become the de facto national ID card in the United States (*MIC*, Chapter 3). But how often do we really *need* to present our driver's license? Let's take a look at some common instances where we may be asked to produce one. While we're at it, we'll also look at ways around having to do so, too.

Cashing a Check

If someone gives you a check and you run to their bank to cash it, you will need a driver's license. Occasionally, you can produce 17 other forms of ID in lieu of a driver's license and, if the check isn't for more than $100, you can get it cashed.

But in this country, there really is no need for anybody to put themselves through this wringer of check-cashing tyranny. Simply deposit the check in your own account, preferably through an ATM. If you actually need it cashed for some reason, most banks will let you take up to $100 of your uncleared deposits. So make the deposit and take back up to $100. If your account has overdraft protection, even better. Take up to your overdraft limit plus $100. You have, in effect, just "cashed" the check, right?

Using Credit Cards

Hardly ever happens. If a particular store insists on your license to use a credit card, just take your business elsewhere.

Driving

You can drive forever without a driver's license. Absolutely nothing will happen to you if you don't get pulled over. When you get pulled over, however, you will absolutely need to present a valid driver's license or your car will be towed and impounded and you will be walking home—if you're lucky. If you're not lucky you'll be headed for a jail cell. Ultimately you'll have a lot of explaining to do before a judge.

Rarely can you get away with presenting a phony driver's license to a police officer who pulls you over. For this to work, you will need a *perfect* forgery. You will also need to hope that one of the following circumstances is true:

- The officer is in a hurry (and decides not to run your license).
- The dispatcher's computer terminal is down (so your license can't be run).
- The officer believes the state's computer is wrong when it says your license does not exist.

Chances of those things happening? Not in your favor, to say the least. Therefore this is, for all practical purposes, not an option.

But remember what I said earlier: if you get pulled over, you will need "a" valid driver's license. I didn't say you will need "your" valid driver's license. Before I explain, let's take a look at the chart below to see where we stand.

TABLE 4.1
When a Driver's License is Needed

Occasion	Valid License Needed?	Alternative
Cashing a check	NO	Deposit all checks into your own bank account via ATM.
Using a credit card	NO	Not usually required. Change stores. Deal in cash.
Purchasing alcohol	NO	Don't drink. Use fake ID. Change stores.
Applying for a loan	NO	Apply over telephone or internet. Use owner financing for real estate purchases.
Pulled over	YES	Jail

Identity, Privacy, and Personal Freedom

As its name implies, the only time you're required to have a valid driver's license is *when you're driving!* And then only if you're pulled over. So if you're an identity changer who happens to get pulled over, what then do you present to the waiting officer?

You present a valid driver's license, that's what.

Borrowing a Driver's License

Maybe you have a goody-two-shoes cousin who's approximately your age, weight, and height. Does this cousin also have your hair and eye color? Does this cousin have a driver's license? Yes? Good.

So you go to the Department of Motor Vehicles and present yourself as your cousin saying you've lost your driver's license and need a duplicate. You'll be asked for your Social Security number, your date of birth, and possibly your mother's maiden name. In each case you'll supply your cousin's information. If you are asked for your old driver's license number, you will confess that you've never committed it to memory. The clerk will pull your cousin's information up on the computer and ask if you live at such and such address. Verify that you do (see WARNING below).

An on-the-ball clerk may check your physical description, which will not be a problem because you look so much like your cousin. Be careful in states that store licensees' pictures in their computer, however. Unless you and your cousin (or whoever) are close lookalikes, verify beforehand that your state does not record photos in their computer system.

You will be asked to fill out a card, and then you'll be given a duplicate license. Now you have a valid driver's license to present to police officers when you get stopped. But do yourself (and your cousin) a favor: don't get stopped (see Chapter 12, "Freedom On The Road"). Getting stopped could result in a ticket, which would blow your whole cover as well as your relationship with your cousin and probably your aunt and uncle, too. (If you do get stopped in this situation, you may be best off using the techniques presented later under "Driving Without a License" and risk a traffic ticket rather than surrendering the duplicate license.)

No cousin? Or you just don't have the heart to do that to kin? Neither would I, I must admit. Well, this method also works with total strangers, but you will need to do thorough research to verify physical features, address, SSN, mother's maiden name, etc. Also, you will want to verify their goody-two-shoes status. Why? Because you don't want the person whose license you've borrowed to have or acquire a criminal history. He or she must not even have unpaid parking or traffic tickets. Failure to verify these things could be disastrous.

WARNING: As mentioned above under "Temporary Driver's License," some states issue you a temporary driver's license and mail the actual one to your address. If you fail to do proper research, you will walk away from the DMV with an ultimately useless temporary driver's license, and your cousin will be mailed a duplicate driver's license with—guess what?—your picture on it! You will probably receive an irate and frantic phone call shortly thereafter. If your state mails the license after the fact, you will need to perform the following step before undertaking the above procedure.

Changing Your Address

Go to the DMV same as above and present yourself as your cousin. Tell the clerk you recently moved (to a mail drop) and you'd like to update your address information so you will receive your renewal notice and other correspondence. You will look like a goody-two-shoes yourself because most people don't do this even though it's required.

After about a week, return to the registry and perform the above procedure for getting a duplicate license. You can go back the next day if the DMV is a busy one. Just go to a different window.

After you get your license, return to the DMV and change your address back to your cousin's address.

If your cousin is pulled over during this time, a police officer may note the disparity between the address on your cousin's license and the address that comes back on the officer's computer. This could cause problems, which is another reason to target goody-goody types. In most cases, however, the officer and the goody-goody will probably write off the disparity as typical DMV chaos.

Driving Without a License

We've already established that the only time you need to have a driver's license is when you are pulled over. Let's just qualify that a bit. Add the word "legally" before the word "need." That's right. Legally, you're supposed to present your valid driver's license to a police officer when you are pulled over. But have you ever forgotten your driver's license at home? As I told you earlier, I have. Isn't it always the way? The *one* day out of 365 that you forget your driver's license you get pulled over?

Once when I was pulled over I was genuinely surprised that I'd left the house without my driver's license. This is precisely what I told the officer. I gave the officer my name, but he could not find it in the state's computer. I was driving the company van, so I couldn't even prove I owned a registered vehicle. I even cooperated and offered some common misspellings of my name. No dice. The computer just couldn't match it that day.

The most interesting thing is that the officer was never concerned or surprised that he could not find me in his computer. When I did not become flustered or nervous, he (like most people) had no trouble believing it was the computer that was in error.

Did I get a ticket? Yes, I did receive a ticket for not having my license in possession. The officer was even apologetic, stating, "Look, even I have to carry mine . . ." By all rights I should've gotten a speeding ticket, so I was given a break. But the main point is, I could very well have been unlicensed and the result would have been the same: I drove away from the scene.

Until people (police officers loosely included here) come to believe that computers are foolproof, the "I forgot my license" trick may prove to be the identity changer's best bet for many years to come.

A Variation on This Theme

I've known others who have been pulled over without their driver's license. Two of my friends told me the police officer gave them 24 hours to produce the license or suffer the consequences of a citation for failure to have it. Well, both times my friends drove home, got their licenses, and brought them immediately to the police station. So, what's to stop an identity changer from driving home, selling the car, and creating another driving identity? For this to work you must:

- Give the officer a fake address
- Sell your car to a distant buyer since the cops will be looking for it
- Buy another car under a new name
- Register that car under a new name
- Not get pulled over by the same cop

This is a major hassle, but it works. Having to do this every time you are pulled over will certainly make you a better, safer, and more conscientious driver.

Another Variation on This Theme

I'm sure there are cops out there who will impound your vehicle until you can produce a license. For this reason it may be better to purchase and register the vehicle in the name of a corporation. A cop will still have the right to impound the vehicle and make you walk home. But you can then elect a friend to a clerk position in your corporation and send him to pick up your car from the impound yard. If the cop or yard boss asks to see the original driver, your clerk-friend says, "He was hired just last week and we haven't seen him since the car was impounded. He probably figures he's been canned." If they ask for address information, your friend says, "I'll pull his records and fax the information to you. Is he in some kind of trouble? Blah, blah, blah." The point is you get your car back.

LIBRARY CARD TRICKS

Every U.S. citizen has a right to a library card. Libraries in smaller towns are usually staffed by friendly, soft-spoken people who are often volunteers. These people will bend over backward to help you, especially if you talk about becoming a volunteer or "friend of the library" yourself. Because of these facts, a library card is a fairly easy piece of identification to obtain in any name you like.

Small-town libraries will usually issue a library card if you show them two forms of identification. You can use a birth certificate (*MIC*, Chapter 3, Part Two), student ID, or employment ID as identification. If you only have one of these three, then a good second piece of identification is mail that is addressed to you, which most library volunteers will accept rather than putting you both through the embarrassment of rejection.

If you have an address such as a mail drop under your new identity and you don't mind the library knowing about it, get yourself on some junk mail lists. It's best to get yourself on official-type lists like those used by insurance carriers and credit card companies. When your junk mail arrives, simply bring a handful of it with you to the library as ID.

If you don't have an address or would prefer to apply for your library card with complete address anonymity, simply invent a plausible address and print up some mailing labels using different fonts and, if possible, different printers (i.e., type some up on and old typewriter, write some by hand, and print some out on your computer). Once you have some mailing labels, get some junk mail (it's just about everywhere) and put your label over the existing label or, better yet, neatly remove the existing label and put yours in its place. This way you don't have to worry that print from the old label will show through yours. Now you have some untraceable mail as ID.

Don't try to endear the librarian to you by saying, "I've lived here all my life." The librarian may begin to wonder why you don't already have a card! Just act like a confused newcomer.

PASSPORTS

Passports are probably the most secure forms of ID available. They are also the hardest to forge or ghost into. Even with the very best technology available, they are damn near impossible to copy.

Some of you who wrote me after reading my first book pointed out that the subject of passports was not even broached. This was intentional. If you are thinking of applying for a passport under a fake identity, you have your work cut out for you. Enforcement in this area is strict. If you are caught attempting to obtain falsified federal documents—and there's a good chance you will be—you are almost guaranteed a prison sentence. I would not want my readers to think I set them up to be caught, and that's why the subject was omitted from my last book.

Now that you've been duly warned, I will also say this: it is definitely not impossible to ghost into a U.S. passport. In 1997, the United States issued 6,295,003 passports. With that much of a caseload, there're bound to be some mistakes made, security measures relaxed, and clerks who need lunch more than they need to check on your birth certificate. If you are desperate enough and have nothing to lose, it's worth a shot. But if you value your freedom, there are other ways around the problem of getting out of this country and into another one.

First Things First

If you need to leave the country, there's always Canada. You don't need a passport and, although a birth certificate is technically required, you can easily cross the border without it. Tourist crossing points like Niagara Falls are simply too busy for border patrols to check all IDs. Avoid matching profiles (i.e., official, preconceived notions of how a troublemaker looks and acts) and they'll usually let you through after asking four questions:

1. Where are you from?
2. Where are you going?
3. What is the purpose of your visit?
4. How long are you staying?

Some safe replies:

1. Long Island, New York (only if you have the accent).
2. Niagara Falls, Canada.
3. To view the falls from the Canadian side.
4. Just a day.

Once you're in, you can do whatever the hell you want. Even if you're confronted by the authorities two months later, just tell them you've been in Canada for a few days touring. They have no way of knowing how long you've been around.

Coming back into the U.S. is a little harder. Same questions really, but the border agents can be real assholes. They're more likely to demand, "Citizenship!" or ask vague questions like, "Where are you from?" No matter what you say, it's not right. If you reply, "the United States," they'll act all condescending and say, "City and state would be more specific, don't you think?" If you give your city and state, they'll say, "You mean from the United States, then?" Don't let it get to you. Who knows who they had to piss off to get their miserable jobs. If exercising their minuscule iota of power keeps them from kicking their dog when they get home, then you've done a good deed. (For great insider information on how the U.S. border and its gatekeepers *really* operate, read the excellent book *Beat the Border* by Ned Beaumont, available from Paladin Press.)

If you don't like border cops—and I can't think of any reason why you should—then you can cross the border somewhere else. The U.S.-Canadian border is almost 5,000 miles long if you include Alaska, and most of it is wilderness. If you get caught traipsing though the wilderness into Canada by a border patrol, just say, "Oh, thanks. I didn't realize Canada was so close. I'd better get back. It's getting dark."

You can also cross any of the Great Lakes into Canada. If worse comes to worst, you can canoe or kayak around the perimeter of Lake Ontario, making frequent stops along the way at beaches and chowder houses. If one of those chowder houses happens to be in Canada and if you happen to spend the night at the hotel next door, you may just happen to forget to kayak back to the States for a few months, or seven years, or whatever the statute of limitations is for whatever offense you've committed.

There are a few other noteworthy ways to get into Canada. The CANPASS–Remote Area Border Crossing permit, a joint initiative of Citizenship and Immigration Canada (CIC) and Revenue Canada, allows the bearer to cross the border into Canada at certain remote areas without reporting to a port of entry as long as imported goods are declared. (Source: Citizenship and Immigration Canada Web site at http://cicnet.ci.gc.ca/english/visit/rabc_e.html)

You can apply for a CANPASS by mail. At the time of this writing, the fee is $30 per person or family. All you need is a completed application and a photocopy of your birth certificate. For more information, write to either of these addresses:

Canada Immigration Centre
301 Scott Street N., 2nd Floor
Fort Frances, Ontario
P9A 1H1

Canada Immigration Centre
Customs-Immigration Highway Building
Highway 29 (Emerson West)
P.O. Box 425
Emerson, Manitoba
R0A 0L0

Your family includes your spouse and dependants. Your dependents are not necessarily your children. A creative identity changer will certainly see opportunities here! CIC does reserve the right to request an in-person interview, so make your application neat and professional looking to avoid matching any of their paper profiles.

You can also get into Canada by taking a scenic boat tour of Niagara Falls, which stops in Canada. There is very little checking, if any. Or you can book a trip to Nova Scotia on the *Scotia Prince* out of Portland or Bar Harbor, Maine. It travels overnight when all the customs officers have gone beddybye. You wake up in Nova Scotia and nobody gives a hoot that you're a U.S. citizen. There are countless ways. Snowmobile into Canada from Minnesota, hike in from the Cascadian mountains, or whatever floats your boat. Happy travels.

Foreign Passports

In the following chapter you'll learn how some lucky people of Irish descent can apply for an Irish passport. You can also get a Costa Rican passport if you buy $10,000 worth of land and pay taxes to the Costa Rican government on an income of at least $500 a month. It's a nice country that has no wars, no army, and a poor but democratic society. To apply for the passport, contact a Costa Rican attorney or request an application kit from:

Lel Punto Costarricense S.A.
Post Box 90
Paseo Estudintes
Costa Rica

Other countries have similar laws that grant citizenship status in exchange for supporting the government. What good is a foreign passport? Well, if you get nabbed for something, there's a good chance you'll be sent back to your "home country," at which point you can use your passport to go anywhere in the world.

Camouflage Passports

A camouflage passport looks exactly like an officially issued passport. It contains your photo and vital statistics and has various visa entry and exit stamps already inserted. The only difference between a camouflage passport and a real passport is that the issuing country of the camouflage passport no longer exists. Since the country no longer exists, it is not illegal to use its name on official documents.

A camouflage passport can mask your true identity and might well save your life. All tourists carry passports. Carrying your camouflage passport at all times will make you a tourist in any emergency event, anywhere, any time.

You can order camouflage passports in any name and address you like. Although international terrorism seems to be on the decline at the moment, there are still many situations where it may be prudent for a traveler to keep his or her real passport well hidden and carry a camouflage passport in a pocket. This is especially true when traveling in or through countries that are less than hospitable.

Case in point: the Persian Gulf. Would you want to be identified as a U.S. or British citizen if you were traveling through the Middle East and stopped by an armed terrorist group? Better to be seen as a harmless tourist from Dutch Guiana than a wealthy businessman from New York. Your camouflage passport could be a lifesaver, as indeed many were during the Gulf War.

Camouflage passports are officially recognized by the U.S. government for use by members of its armed forces when off duty in difficult countries. Their use by businesspeople worldwide is well known. One company that sells camouflage passports is the FINOR Organization. It is an Internet-only company and can be found at http://www.finor.com. Much of the information in this section was provided courtesy of the FINOR Organization. They are quite knowledgeable, and I highly recommend their services.

Here is a list of some former country names from which the FINOR Organization can issue a passport:

British Guiana
British Honduras
British West Indies
Burma
Dutch Guiana
East Indies
Eastern Samoa
Netherlands
New Grenada
New Hebrides
Rhodesia
South Vietnam
Spanish Guinea
USSR
Zanzibar

Aside from the USSR, South Vietnam, Rhodesia, and Burma, most people wouldn't know the above countries are nonexistent, defunct, or now operating under a new name. For this reason, a passport from one of these countries may accidentally be accepted as ID when applying for a driver's license or opening a bank account, among other things. They've even been known to work on border patrols from time to time.

Mail and Address Privacy

Pay no attention to the man behind the curtain!
The Wizard of Oz

Wouldn't it be nice to control all your life's affairs from a secure location? To deal with the daily minutiae of your private kingdom from a safe, detached vantage point, like the Wizard of Oz? The trick is to go one step beyond Oz, to have everything the Wizard had minus that pesky yellow brick road that leads needy characters right to your inner sanctum. This is the privacy seeker's goal.

No matter who you are or who you're trying not to be, you need a home. That is to say, you need the appearance of a home. I covered the basics of establishing residence in my first book (see *MIC*, Chapter 4). This chapter will expand upon the topics brought up in that text and also explore some new territory on domicile, nationality, and where the hell you can go these days to find privacy and personal freedom.

DOMICILE: WHERE THE HELL ARE YOU, ANYWAY?

Virtually anytime you buy something, request information, tend to an account, or meet someone new, your domicile becomes hopelessly and forever entangled in the transaction. Every day, it seems, somebody wants to know where we live. Even when not asked directly, we unwittingly give up our location simply by writing checks, allowing access to our credit report, or handing over our phone number (which can be quickly cross-referenced on inexpensive computer CDs).

People—bureaucrats especially—want to know where you go when you're not doing business with them. *They* want to know where *they* can find you when *they* decide that *they* need to have a word with you.

Well I say, fuck *them*.

There is absolutely no reason why this madness should continue and the masses have their addresses branded on them like so many cattle. Has anybody seen the six o'clock news? Do the words "credit card fraud," "identity theft," "stalker," "fatal attraction," or "psycho-killer" mean anything to anybody? Do we, as a society, really need to give complete strangers our precise earthly location on a daily basis?

For a few dollars a month, you can rent a post office box or a mail drop that just might save your life. At the very least, it will allow you to keep your real location, or "domicile" as bureaucrats prefer, private. If you don't want to spend the money, then I suggest you either lie about your address to everybody you do business with or refuse to do business with anybody who foolishly expects you to give up the location where you are expected to sleep peacefully.

Mail Drops vs. P.O. Boxes

Many of you have written asking whether I prefer mail drops or post office boxes. The answer is, it depends. P.O. boxes are cheap and great in a crunch. If you need an address fast, a P.O. box may be a solution to your problem. But if your needs require privacy or the appearance of legitimacy, then a mail drop is a better, albeit more expensive, way to go.

Without rehashing the whole issue, I thought it'd be nice to include a quick reference table detailing the major differences between P.O. boxes and mail drops.

TABLE 5.1
Mail Drops v. P.O. Boxes

Feature	Mail Drop	P.O. Box
Allows legitimate-sounding street address instead of box number?	Not any more	No
Accepts private-carrier packages (e.g., UPS, FedEx)?	Gladly	Illegal!
Offers remailing service?	Yes	No
Allows you to call and check for mail?	Yes	Absurd!
Offers mail-forwarding service?	Yes	No (will forward mail for closed box only)
Will defend your privacy?	Yes	Privacy? What's that? Will give you up in a heartbeat.
Will not give your real address to inquirers?	Their business depends on it.	A 1994 directive states address info can be given only to postal inspectors and those with subpoenas. I have a contact who'll give me a box holder's address with one day's notice. So much for the directive!
Can open with fake ID?	Easily	More difficult
Can open without ID?	Not any more	Ha! Ha ha ha ha! Very funny.
Offers secretarial services?	Sometimes	See above
Can be rented on a monthly basis?	Yes	Six months at a time
Rate of payment?	Reasonable	Very reasonable
Industry competition leading to customer satisfaction?	Yes	Monopolistic and self-interested
24-hour access?	Not usually	Large cities only

Identity, Privacy, and Personal Freedom

Junk Mail

Does anybody really care if they get junk mail? Is the actual act of throwing it away really that difficult? Is the mail itself offensive? These are questions often posed by the pro-junk-mail public.

Well, my friends, I say it goes much deeper than that. For mail privacy really means home privacy. After all, the mail does come into your home, does it not? Anybody who has ever opened a new piece of junk mail has had at the back or their minds a lurking thought: now *they* know where I am, too!

It's uncomfortable to know that, without your giving permission, your name got on a list somewhere. A list that was probably compiled by someone you trusted who then willfully sold it to someone you never heard of who eagerly paid for it.

I. Thou shalt not file a mail-forwarding card with the U.S. Postal Service.

II. Thou shalt use a mail drop or, if absolutely necessary, a P.O. box, preferably in another city, for all correspondence.

III. Thou shalt open such mail drop or P.O. box in another name or a company name.

IV. Thou shalt order all utility services in another name, the landlord's name, or a company name.

V. Thou shalt never fill out applications, forms, or surveys using thine own home address.

VI. Thou shalt always omit phone numbers from applications, forms, or surveys.

VII. Thou shalt always order magazines and information packets under an assumed name or company name.

VIII. Thou shalt register and insure all motor vehicles from a mail drop or, if allowed, a P.O. box.

IX. Thou shalt apply for a new state driver's license using a mail drop or, if allowed, a P.O. box.

X. Thou shalt always refuse correspondence addressed to thine own real name at thine own home address.

After enough of this abuse, it becomes clear to us that our name and address must also be in searchable databases offered to police, private detectives, and anybody with prying eyes. Isn't that what really unnerves us about junk mail?

Junk mail is the envoy of disintegrating privacy. It is the reminder that, at any time, someone can easily find us, come into our home, and do us harm—just because they paid for a list. In case you forgot them, or never knew them, above are the Ten Commandments of moving to a new address.

What happens if you move and slip up by giving your real address to the motor vehicles bureau or otherwise break a commandment? Must you move again? Below you will learn some very valuable strategies for dealing with slip-ups.

Regaining Address Privacy

So, you move to a new place and find it refreshing that your mailbox is not filling up with junk mail, and those pesky bill collectors have stopped sending you nasty letters. Isn't it nice that, for a change, nobody knows where you are unless you want them to? You've read some privacy and ID books and know better than to fill out a mail-forwarding card, so you figure you can structure your new life in a completely private fashion.

Then you make the mistake of registering your new car with the Department of Motor Vehicles. Pretty soon you start receiving advertisements from automobile dealerships. A little while after that, an offer for a Visa or MasterCard. What's going on? Banks know where I am? Wait a minute—bill collectors share mailing lists with banks. Is my new-found privacy over?

Maybe. If you don't take action, your mailbox will soon be drooping like a sunflower from the oppressive weight of junk mail, and yes, the U.O. Collection Agency's letters will be at the top of the heap.

It's easy to look back and say, "I shoulda never've gave the DMV my home address." That's true.

When you move to a new address, you should not use it for any correspondence whatsoever. Fortunately, there are steps you can take to regain your private status if you ever slip up.

Continuing with the above example, you should immediately apply for a mail drop and report your "new address" to the DMV. Next, immediately send a copy of the following letter to anybody who has gotten your home address from the DMV's cancerous mailing list:

> *Your Name*
> *Your Mail Drop Address* ★
> *Anytown, Anywhere 00000*

January 1, 2010

Nosy Pants Business
Their Address
Goes here 00000

ATTN: Legal Department
RE: Unauthorized use of name and address

Dear Madam or Sir:

Please remove forthwith my name and address from your mailing list. All persons with whom I do business are told specifically that I do not wish my name, address, or telephone number to be sold as part of a mailing list. I am registered with the mail and telephone preference services listed below. ★★ *I suggest that you consult these services before compiling mailing lists. Privacy is a serious issue with American consumers.*

Telephone Preference Service
Direct Marketing Association
P.O. Box 9014
Farmingdale, NY 11735

Mail Preference Service
Direct Marketing Association
P.O. Box 9008
Farmingdale, NY 11735

You are not authorized to maintain my name, address, or telephone number in your database, **and you are specifically not authorized to resell the same.**
Please let me know where you bought my name and address so I may contact that business entity and inform them of their error. I have enclosed a SASE for this purpose.

Respectfully,

Private Citizen

Private Citizen

★ Always use your mail drop address as your letterhead and return address. If a bill collector or attorney is trying to prove that you live at your home address, the last thing you want to do is send a signed letterhead indicating you do.
★★ Whether or not you actually sign up for these services is optional. They do exist, and more and more companies are beginning to use them. Some people don't like them because it involves actually sending them a name, address, and telephone number.

Mail Phone Preference Services

The Mail Preference Service (MPS) is a free consumer service sponsored by the Direct Marketing Association (DMA). Established in 1971, the DMA is the oldest and largest national trade association serving the direct marketing field. Members of the DMA market goods and services directly to consumers using such media as direct mail and catalogs, telephone, magazine and newspaper ads, and broadcast advertising.

If you register with MPS, DMA associates subscribing to the plan will delete your name and address from their mailing list. Be sure to include as many versions of your name as it appears on mailings that you receive. If your family is as privacy minded as yourself, encourage them to register with MPS as well.

Mail of a business-to-business nature received at your business address will not be affected by registration with MPS. Business names and addresses are not placed in the file, and business-to-business mailers do not use the consumer file.

Sign up at:

Mail Preference Service
Direct Marketing Association
P.O. Box 9008
Farmingdale, NY 11735

To request a similar service to weed out unwanted phone calls, put "Telephone Preference Service" on address line one and use P.O. Box 9014.

You can visit DMA's Web site (http://www.the-dma.org) for more information, but you cannot sign up on line because they require your signature on all requests, which must be sent by U.S. mail.

Similar services are also available for e-mail. In order for any of them to work, you must send them your real information. This is the only downside. I've never had a problem with them, but once your name goes on a list, it can possibly wind up in the wrong hands.

On Notice

Anytime you place an order, request information, or make a donation by mail, phone, or e-mail, include the following notice in red ink. You may wish to print up some stickers from your computer and keep them next to your envelopes and stamps.

NOTICE

You may not rent, sell, trade, or give away my name, address, telephone number, e-mail address, personal information, or other information to any person, company, or other entity for any purpose. Upon violation of this demand, I will terminate my business relationship with you and seek all remedies afforded by applicable statutes and common law. A copy of this notice has been sent to your company's home office and legal department.

You should do this even if you've already protected yourself with a P.O. box, mail drop, or answering service. You don't want to pay for unnecessary mail forwarding or telephone answering. Besides, it sends a strong message to Corporate America that their customers are taking privacy very seriously. This is perhaps the most important reason of all.

Subtlety Will Get You Everywhere

A subtle trick for keeping yourself off a company's mailing list is to appeal to their sense of efficiency. Tell them you already receive all their happy junk mail at your "other" address. Companies are always trying to eliminate redundancies in their files. If they don't get the message, write to them as a concerned tree lover and ask them to stop wasting paper.

Do the Two-Step

This approach requires more work, but it's slick. When you receive junk mail from a new solicitor, write the company informing them of your new address, which can be a P.O. box, mail drop, abandoned house, bar, or gas station. More often than not, the clerk who receives the letter below will mindlessly key in the new information.

> *Your Name*
> *Your Fake Address*
> *City, State, Zip*
>
> *Their Name*
> *Address*
> *City, State, Zip*
>
> *ATTN: Mail room/account retention*
> *RE: Address Correction*
>
> *Dear Madam or Sir:*
>
> *Enclosed is a copy of your most recent correspondence showing the address you have on file for me. Please note that this is not my correct address.*
>
> *So that I may continue to receive your lovely [publication/credit card offers/charitable solicitation], please update my address in your files. My new address is at the top of this letterhead. My mail forwarding expires next week, so please take the time to do this now.*
>
> *Also, could you please be so kind as to tell me where you got the erroneous address information so that I may update that source as well? I've enclosed an SASE, and your reply would be very much appreciated.*
>
> *Very surly yours,*
>
>
> *Your Name*

Now you've diverted the bastards from the address you wish to protect. After a month or so you can ask them to remove your address from their files altogether. If they ignore your request, they will still be diverted. If they piss you off, you can divert them again. Divert them to 1600 Pennsylvania Avenue, Washington, DC, if you want.

PRIVATE PARTS

Aside from having the appearance of a legitimate residence for deflecting creditors, bureaucrats, and the generally nosy, there are times when you need an actual place of privacy where you can lay low for awhile. Maybe you're a heavy cat in need of a police-free zone where you can decide whether to turn yourself in or remain on the lam. Maybe you just need to collect your thoughts.

Although they're dwindling in number, you can still find pockets of privacy in this country. When a citizen becomes overwhelmed, these places offer a temporary respite from the Bureaucratic Machine.

Hiking Trails

The best hiking trails are the remotest ones where park rangers and ticket takers are nowhere to be found. With a tent you can live on the trail for days—or even months in temperate climes—provided you stay near water and know how to live off the land. Fortunately, Paladin Press, Loompanics Unlimited, and other freedom-oriented publishers offer books and guides on doing just that.

If you do run into other people, or if they run into you, you need not be overly concerned. Camping in the wilderness is not uncommon, and most hikers won't think twice about seeing a fellow camper deep in the woods. Even a ranger who spots you cannot do anything unless you are breaking the law. Just be sure to check applicable statutes pertaining to campfires, hunting and fishing, and public use of lands. If your particular trail is in a state park or national forest, be sure you know all the park rules (some, for example, require a permit during the high season). In any case, if you do encounter a ranger or group of hikers who ask too many questions, you can just pick up and move on.

Student IDs, even ones from clear across the country, are readily accepted by park officials. Why? Because you have been stereotyped, my friend. You're just some college chump still trying to find your way, taking the semester off to enjoy the great outdoors and introspect on life and your future. (For information on constructing foolproof student ID cards, see Chapter 3, "How To Manufacture Professional Quality Identity Documents.")

If a nosy ranger wants backup ID such as your birth certificate or Social Security card, tell him he can find both at your school's financial aid office, where you left them along with your financial assistance application for the upcoming school year. Or even better, "I left them in my dorm. I figure if I lost my wallet in a stream, it's two less things I'd have to replace. Is ID required to enter the park?" You already know it isn't because you've done your homework.

The ranger, fearing liability for violating the civil rights of an educated person, will usually save face by saying something like, "You really should have it, but I'll let it go this time," and move on down the trail to harass other, less politically alert campers.

Rotaries

Perhaps you're in a big hurry for some perfectly legal reason and you don't have time to travel 500 miles to the wilderness. And just maybe, for the same perfectly legal reason, you can't show your face in public for the next 24 to 48 hours. The island of a highway rotary is a perfect temporary hideout. Find a nice wide one with thick vegetation and make a little clearing for yourself right in the center of it. Wear green or brown to match the vegetation, and make sure you are invisible to the passing traffic. Almost nobody looks at rotary islands because they're too busy driving. Police don't patrol them either, and as long as they don't see you, they won't suspect you're there. Approach it at night, of course, or during times of little traffic.

If you're planning an extended stay, you may wish to bring food, water, personal supplies (such as toilet paper, toothpaste, and brush) and a camouflage tent or tarp. Also bring a dim flashlight for inside the tent, and always point it downward so passing motorists won't see it.

Sometimes girders and pipes are temporarily stored on rotary islands when construction is going on. Avoid islands that are within a few miles of highway construction areas; police are more likely to have an eye out, and contractors may show up anytime to pick up materials or park vehicles.

Burger Joints

McDonald's, Burger King, and other fast-food restaurants make for good temporary cover. Police will pass through to pick up lunch and dinner, but as long as they're not looking for your car, they won't think twice about seeing someone parked in the lot stuffing burgers in his face (as long as they don't recognize the face, that is).

There is a limitation to how long one can sit in a fast-food parking lot, though. The kid taking out the trash every hour is likely to notice you after a while. In this case, a newspaper as a prop will help you extend your stay. But three to four hours is probably the limit.

College Campuses/Universities

College campuses are like separate towns. As long as nobody calls the police, they won't show up. Once you're safely on campus, it's a virtual sanctuary; just sit in the corner somewhere and stuff your face in a book. Nobody will suspect you are anything but a busy student.

Most colleges have libraries you can get into simply by flashing a student ID. In most cases the ID need not be the college's own, and some colleges allow you to walk in and out of their libraries without any ID at all. Once inside you can lay low for hours without arousing suspicion.

The main student building, sometimes called the "student center" or "student union," is also a good place to lay low for a while. In this case, bring a textbook from the campus bookstore and pretend to be working through it. To pass the time, do a crossword puzzle on top of the workbook, being sure to flash the workbook's cover now and then. You'll appear to be studying, and no one will become suspicious of your presence.

Labs and lecture halls are often not patrolled. Hell, you might even learn something while you're waiting for things to cool off.

Specialty colleges like music and art schools often have practice rooms and drawing areas set aside where students can polish their skills. Even if a campus ID is required, most such IDs are easily manufactured. Just make sure your ID number matches the college's format.

Beware: many colleges (and other once innocuous institutions, like gyms and YMCAs) are beginning to incorporate bar codes onto their student IDs. The proctor covering the lab or practice room need only read your card with a laser and your "time in" and "time out" are automatically registered. But if your ID has gone through the wash a couple of times, the proctor (usually just a student in a work-study program) will have to log you by hand. Just make sure your ID has something resembling a bar code, and make sure it is unreadable.

Public Libraries and Museums

Quiet, peaceful, not patrolled. Need I say more?

Make it a daily habit to look for these minisanctuaries of privacy during your travels. I'm sure you'll find many places where you can escape if the time ever comes. By preparing yourself beforehand, you do not have to scramble to find a hideout if the occasion should ever present itself. Write down some of your favorites and keep the list with your stash of running money. An ounce of prevention is worth a pound of cure!

OBTAINING DUAL IRISH CITIZENSHIP

Did you know that if you have an Irish-born parent, you are considered a citizen of Ireland? Or if you have an Irish-born grandparent, you are eligible to apply for Irish citizenship through registration? If you were born in Ireland after your parent was naturalized as an Irish citizen, you are also eligible to become an Irish citizen.

Why Apply?

The United States has become the world's police, and most of the world resents this. As a result, there has been a renewed interest in Irish passports as the world's safest international documentation. Ireland is known around the globe as a neutral nation that donates the most per capita to international causes, and its citizens staff hospitals and schools in developing nations. In much of the Muslim world, Celtic Christianity is seen as distinctively different from Roman Catholicism or the other basic Western religions (source: Dr. Frank Faulkner, author of *The Irish Citizenship Handbook*). In short, traveling abroad under your Irish passport will subject you to considerably less prejudice than traveling under a U.S. passport.

Identity, Privacy, and Personal Freedom

How Is This Possible?

In an apparent effort to stem emigration from Ireland, the Irish Parliament enacted the Irish Nationality and Citizenship Act of 1956. Under Section 27 of this act, certain persons of Irish descent are eligible for Irish citizenship through registration.

Originally the act granted citizenship from birth to eligible registrants. This means if persons were born outside Ireland in 1920 and registered for citizenship in 1960, they were considered to have been Irish citizens all their life.

The 1956 act was amended in 1986, and now registrants are considered citizens only from their registration date. Either way, you may be eligible for an Irish passport, which has advantages for the ordinary citizen and identity changer alike.

Will I Lose My Current Citizenship?

Well, that may depend on what your current citizenship is. There are many countries and at least as many rules. I will say this, however: if you happen to be a U.S. citizen, following most of the procedures below will make you a "dual national" in the eyes of the United States and Ireland. As a dual national, you will be required to use your U.S. passport when leaving or entering the U.S. However, pay attention to special notes under the heading "Applying as the Spouse of an Irish Citizen" below.

My parent was born in Ireland: what do I have to do?

Nothing. Congratulations, you're an Irish citizen. Throw yourself a citizenship party. If you'd like, apply for your passport (see below).

My parent wasn't born in Ireland but later became a citizen. Is there any hope for me?

It depends. Were you born after your parent became a naturalized Irish citizen? If so, you are eligible for citizenship through registration. If not, talk to your grandparents—now!

Okay, I'm none of the above, but my grandparent was born in ireland. Am I in?

If you have an Irish-born grandparent, you may apply for Irish citizenship through registration. And, yes, you only need to have *one* Irish-born grandparent. This multiplies your chances by four!

My grandparent can't help me. What about my great-grandparents?

Thanks to the amended Act of 1986, probably not. There are some very special exceptions, though. To find out if any of these exceptions apply, answer the following questions:

1. Do you have an Irish-born great-grandparent?
2. If yes, continue. If no, you are not eligible via this method.
3. Were you born after July 17, 1956?
4. If yes, continue. If no, you are not eligible via this method.
5. Did your parent register for Irish citizenship before July 1, 1986?
6. If yes, you are eligible via registration. If no, continue.
7. Did your parent register as an Irish citizen after January 1, 1987?
8. If yes, continue. If no, you are not eligible via this method. ★
9. Were you born *after* your parent registered as an Irish citizen?
10. If yes, you are eligible via registration. If no, you are not eligible via this method.
    ★ If your parent registered between July 1, 1986, and December 31, 1986, and you were born before they registered, you were only eligible for registration during that six-month period.

If You Are Eligible via Registration

If you've read through the above and have determined that you are eligible for Irish citizenship via registration, you will need to contact one of the following agencies to apply for your citizenship.

In the United States, you must apply to the Foreign Birth Registration Department of the appropriate Irish diplomatic mission or consulate. These are:

Consulate General of Ireland
655 Montgomery Street
San Francisco, CA 94111

Consulate General of Ireland
400 N. Michigan Street, #911
Chicago, IL 60611

Consulate General of Ireland
515 Madison Avenue
New York, NY 10022

Consulate General of Ireland
535 Boylston Street
Boston, MA 02116

If you do not live near any of these cities, application must be made through the Embassy of Ireland. Their address is:

Embassy of Ireland
2234 Massachusetts Avenue NW
Washington, DC 20008

You must also use the above agencies if applying for an Irish passport. If you live in Ireland, you must apply through the Department of Foreign Affairs.

What Will They Want from Me?

Depending on how you are eligible for Irish citizenship, these agencies will require a different set of documents. Where it is noted below that an "original" document is required, you *must* submit the original. Upon acceptance or denial of your application, all original documents will be returned to you.

My Parent Was a Naturalized Irish Citizen

If your parent became a naturalized Irish citizen before you were born, you must submit the following:

- Your parent's original naturalization certificate.
- Your parent's birth certificate (civil long form).
- Your parent's marriage certificate.
- Your parent's death certificate (if applicable—don't kill your parent!).
- Your birth certificate (civil long form).
- Your marriage certificate (if applicable—don't run off and elope!).

My Grandparent Was an Irish-Born Citizen

- Your grandparent's Irish birth certificate (civil long form). If the grandparent was born before 1864, an original baptismal certificate will suffice. For help in finding and applying for these documents, obtain either of the publications listed below under "Additional Notes and Credits."

- Your grandparent's marriage certificate.
- Your grandparent's death certificate, or, if the grandparent is still alive, alternative documentary proof that supports the grandparent's birth in Ireland. This could include U.S. naturalization papers, passport, or an appropriate extract from the U.S. Census Returns.
- If maternal grandparent, your mother's birth certificate (civil long form). If paternal grandparent, your father's.
- The appropriate parent's death certificate (again, only if applicable, please!).
- Your birth certificate (civil long form).
- Your marriage certificate (if applicable).
- Your current passport, driver's license, or state ID and two additional proofs of identification (bank statement; pay slip; credit card; utility, cable, or phone bill).
- Two recent passport photographs. These must be signed and dated by the witness who completes section "E" of the application.
- The completed Application for Irish Citizenship.

My Great-grandparent Was an Irish-Born Citizen
The requirements are the same as if claiming citizenship via your grandparent, except you will also need:

- Your great-grandparent's birth certificate (civil long form). If your great-grandparent was born before 1864, a baptismal certificate will suffice. For help in finding and applying for these documents, see the *Dual Irish Citizenship Guide* (details below).
- The original copy of the Foreign Births Register entry registering the appropriate parent's birth (mother if maternal great-grandparent; father if paternal). This entry may also be found in the Foreign Births Entry Book.

Minors
If the applicant is under 21 years of age, a parent or legal guardian must apply on their behalf. Application is made on a special form, so be sure to ask for it if this is the case. The proofs of identification mentioned above should be those of the person submitting the application, not the child. However, if the minor applicant is of age to have any form of photo identification, that should also be submitted.

Applying as the Spouse of an Irish Citizen
As the spouse of an Irish citizen, you may be eligible to acquire Irish citizenship via postnuptial declaration. The requirements are:

- You must have been legally married for at least three years.
- Your spouse must complete an affidavit that states you have indeed been living together as husband and wife and the marriage is not a sham. The affidavit must be witnessed.
- You must submit at least three but not more than five proofs of identity that reflect the fact you and your spouse have been domiciled at the same address. Valid documents include driver's license, passport, picture ID, bank statements, pay stubs, and phone, electric, or gas bill.
- Your civil long-form marriage certificate.
- Your civil long-form birth certificate.
- Your spouse's civil long-form birth certificate.
- If your spouse was born outside of Ireland, you must submit proof of his or her Irish citizenship. You must have all of the documents used by your spouse in obtaining his or her Irish citizenship as well as a copy of your spouse's Foreign Births Registration Certificate.
- If either spouse was previously married, a copy of the divorce decree.
- Two passport photographs of yourself.
- Two passport photographs of your spouse.

If you are already married to a person eligible for citizenship via registration, your spouse must register for citizenship first. The three-year waiting period begins after registration is complete.

CAUTION: When acquiring Irish citizenship via postnuptial declaration, you will be making an actual declaration accepting Irish citizenship. You may wish to contact the U.S. Department of State's Dual Citizenship office to determine its current views of making such a declaration. It is possible that at some point in the future, such a declaration may be considered a renunciation of your U.S. citizenship.

Fees

At the time of this writing, the registration fee for adults is $169, which includes a short-form certificate of registration. Add $17 if you'd like the long form.

The registration fee for minors is $57 for the short form and an additional $17 for the long form.

Applying for Your Passport

Before filing, the applicant should call the appropriate consulate and arrange an appointment for preliminary checking and submission of the application.

The documentary requirements for an Irish passport vary depending on how you are claiming citizenship. Listed below are only those requirements specific to the dual Irish citizen. In addition, you will need to fill out a passport application and supply photos, etc.

Application must be made through the diplomatic missions and consulates previously listed under the "Eligible via Registration" subheading.

All Applicants

- Must have their application witnessed.
- Must submit two passport photos, signed on the reverse side by your witness.

If Your Parent Was Irish-Born

As mentioned above, if your parent was born in Ireland you are already considered an Irish citizen. As such, you will need less documentation than those claiming citizenship through registration. You will need:

- Your civil long-form birth certificate.
- Your Irish-born parent's civil long-form birth certificate.
- Your parents' marriage certificate.

Additional Notes and Credits

All applicants will be registered in their given names. All documents must be originals. Those that are in a language other than Irish or English must be accompanied by a certified translation.

All of the above information was compiled from material sent to me by the Consulate General of Ireland and from the *Dual Irish Citizenship Guide*. The latter is available from:

Sidhe Information Services
9104 Willow Pond Lane
Potomac, MD 20854

The cost is $30, which includes shipping. *The Dual Irish Citizenship Guide* is a must for anybody seriously considering dual Irish citizenship. It contains the complete history of the Irish Nationality and Citizenship Act, detailed instructions, citizenship application forms, Irish birth record application forms and addresses, and phone numbers of Irish county registrar's offices where application for birth records can be made. The guide also contains a nice section explaining the European Union and social benefits available to the dual Irish citizen. Sidhe Information Services will soon have other publications available that will be of interest to dual Irish citizens or those intrigued by the subject. Ask to be placed on their mailing list.

I also consulted the *Irish Citizenship Handbook* while compiling the above section. The book offers a different take on the subject and includes sections on Irish history, Gaelic surnames, and tracing your Irish lineage. There's also a nice section on the legal framework of dual citizenship in the United States and your rights regarding the same. Ordering info:

Hungry Hill Press
192 Springfield Street
Springfield MA 01107
Web: irish@map.com

At this writing, Dr. Frank Faulkner's book retails for $16.95. You can also order it from Amazon.com on the Web. Shipping and handling is $1.50 from Hungry Hill Press, and credit cards are accepted.

You may also wish to write to the Embassy of Ireland in Washington (address given above) for some of this information. When doing so, ask for the Dual Irish Citizenship package.

After compiling this section, I came across a good article on Irish Citizenship in the *Freedom, Wealth and Privacy Report*, Issue 23, page 15. The article approaches the subject from a fresh angle and is worth checking out. Their address and subscription information is listed in Chapter 2 under the subheading, "The New Resistance."

JOIN A FLEDGLING COUNTRY

If all that paperwork and records searching seems like a hassle just to get an address, bank account, and passport from another country, why not "join" a country that is just starting out? No, I don't mean you have to throw yourself in the middle of a third-world nation whose government has just undergone a coup d'état. With advances in material fabrication and building construction technology, the human race no longer needs to rely on landmass to start a new country. We can build on oceans.

And one man is already doing just that.

His name is Prince Lazarus, and he's already begun construction of a country in the Caribbean called the Principality of New Utopia. It will be located 115 miles west of the Cayman Islands (its nearest neighboring country), and its 284 square miles of surface area will be subject to no authority except its own.

Once completed, New Utopia will be an oasis in the middle of the ocean. It will have office buildings, hotels, theaters, hospitals, and shopping centers sitting 10 feet above the ocean's surface in neat rows, surrounded by greenery and flowers, with canals of clear blue water, water taxis, and gondolas providing transportation for its citizens. Marinas, waterfront restaurants, and oceanfront villas and condos, and a magnificent casino are also planned.

New Utopia is a new nation operated as a principality, much like Monaco, and managed by a board of governors, blending the philosophies of both Ayn Rand and Robert Heinlein. The principality is a constitutional sovereignty based on the principles of free enterprise and capitalism, embracing a tax-free economy, with the assurance of freedom and privacy in connection with any commercial enterprise. The founders of New Utopia believe that he who governs least, governs best. There will be unobtrusive laws to protect the citizens, making it a safe haven for citizens and visitors alike.

Specific legislation has been drawn and enacted by the board of governors for the purpose of regulating commercial enterprise and ensuring the rights of the citizens of the principality. The legislation is designed to promote the development of banking, financial services, insurance, trust and securities brokerage services, and many other businesses.

Dual citizenship is recognized by the principality, and it offers citizenship to those of good character and the financial means to support themselves and their dependents. Privacy and freedom are ensured by statute, with emphasis placed on confidential banking and business laws. Businesses owners of all types are encouraged to examine the potential of New Utopia.

It appears that New Utopia will be recognized as a new nation by at least one country, Honduras, by the time you read this. What sold me on New Utopia is the fact that the U.S. Securities and Exchange Commission (SEC) has already dealt Prince Lazarus a serious ration of shit. It seems the SEC sees that Prince Lazarus has a legal and workable plan or else they wouldn't so much as wink in his direction.

If you are interested in becoming a charter citizen, an application has been provided in Appendix B. For more information contact this source:

Freedom Development Corp.
125 S. Merdian St. Suite G
Lebanon, IN 46052
USA
E-Mail: info@freedom-corp.com
Web: www.new-utopia.com

Telephone Privacy

"Watson, come quick. I need you!"
Alexander Graham Bell

Thomas Watson, Alexander Graham Bell's assistant, was the first person to ever hear a telephone transmission—except he didn't actually hear it. Rather, he *overheard* it. That's right. The very first telephone transmission was an accidental eavesdrop.

On March 10, 1876, Bell and Watson set out to test their newly patented voice transmission apparatus. Bell was stationed in the transmitting room going about his business and Watson was tidying up the receiving room. Before actual testing began, Bell accidentally knocked over a beaker of battery acid. Reacting to the spill, Mr. Bell shouted, "Watson, come quick. I need you!"

Watson indeed heard Bell over the wire and rushed to his aid. Perhaps this should have been a sign of things to come. It didn't take long before the telephone became man's most popular eavesdropping device, a classification it still holds today.

After Watson came rushing to Bell's aid, both men were beset by a loud, droning sound. At first they thought it was coming from the telephone, but as it got louder they realized it was coming from outside. The sound soon grew to shake the entire house vigorously to the point where the men could barely keep their balance. When they stumbled outside to see what was going on, they saw a colossal, metallic disk hovering overhead. Before they could bring themselves to react, the saucer landed and the men were greeted by visitors from another galaxy who wore hot-pink sandals and drank lemon Slurpies . . .

Okay, okay. So everybody knows the Watson and Bell story has about as much merit as the George Washington cherry tree story. But the point should be clear: telephones demonstrated their capacity for privacy abuse from the git-go.

KEEPING YOUR CONVERSATIONS PRIVATE

Just how should a privacy seeker keep telephone conversations private? Fair question. Tough answer. These days there are many different modes of telephone communication. Standard landline, pay phones, cordless (including analog, digital, and spread spectrum), cellular (including analog, voice-inverted analog, and digital), satellite, mobile, and ship to shore. Any of these methods can be violated. (For proof, see *Electronic Circuits and Secrets of an Old-Fashioned Spy* by Sheldon Charrett, available from Paladin Press.)

Among these, the pay phone is still the best bet as far as maintaining your privacy is concerned. Unfortunately, it's extremely inconvenient to run out to a pay phone every time you need to place a private call. Moreover, for pay phones to effectively protect your privacy, you need to use a different one every week. It won't take long before pay phone runs are bringing you across town and over the county line.

For the Ordinary Consumer

Even, if you're not on the FBI's most wanted list, there are still some precautions you should take to keep your phone life in the same realm as your private life. First, you must understand that if you use a cordless phone, there is a very good chance that someone is listening in on your conversations. You don't have to be under investigation for this to be the case. There are literally thousand of crooks out there with scanners, just waiting for you to order something by credit card or use your bank's automated account inquiry system. As soon as you start punching numbers into your telephone keypad, some wise guy three miles away with a scanner, long-wire 49 MHz antenna, and DTMF decoder is jotting those numbers down. After that, it's a simple matter to get your mother's maiden name from the state's vital statistics registry and a-spendin' they will go—with your credit!

"But I got me one of those voice-scrambling cordless phones," some of you may say. Well, let me tell you something. If you spent less than $100 for it, it's probably not a voice scrambler. Rather, it's a voice-inversion circuit, which can be decoded with about $15 worth of components and a fundamental knowledge of electronics.

The best thing for the ordinary consumer is to use a standard, corded telephone. Further reinforce this precaution by familiarizing yourself with the phone wiring coming into your home or apartment. Specifically, be able to identify and locate the incoming service line. In an apartment building there will be more than one, so know which one is yours. There is a terminal where the line comes through the outside wall. It is usually covered by a rubber or plastic boot to keep the rain out. Find this terminal and look behind the boot.

If you've had your service for any length of time, you should find some insect pupae, dead spiders, and cobwebs in there. Regardless of how long you've had your service, you shouldn't find anything but a two-wire terminal. A large center bolt keeps the terminal attached to your house. The outside line is tied on either side of the center bolt to two smaller bolts. The red and green wires of a standard four-conductor phone line should be held on the smaller bolts with brass nuts. You should be able to follow the four-conductor wire through a small drill hole where it enters the house.

You should check the terminal often and make sure there is no printed circuit board attached to it. A circuit board of any type indicates a phone tap.

Now, go inside the house and trace where the wire comes though the wall. Trace it to any junction terminal that may be used to wire multiple extension phones. Trace each line to its corresponding extension. Make sure there are no mysterious lines leading off in any direction. If there are, follow them and see where they terminate. Hopefully, it will not be to a tape recorder in the landlord's basement!

Once you have completely familiarized yourself with the telephone system as it applies to your residence and have committed yourself to inspecting it periodically, you can be reasonably that assured your ordinary corded phone conversations are private. As an added measure of privacy, use pulse dialing instead of tone dialing to defeat any DTMF decoders that might be lurking up-line. Please be aware, however, that this advice applies to ordinary citizens who are not wanted by the FBI. Court-ordered phone taps are often set up right at your local phone company. These taps are not traceable, and you'll never have any way of knowing if one is present. So if you're a heavy cat, don't blab on the phone.

If you're going to use a cordless phone despite my warnings against doing so, invest in a digital spread-spectrum version. It'll cost you about a $100 more, but your privacy is worth it. Keep the "pulse/tone" switch set to pulse. Again, this defeats most DTMF decoders and, if you tell the phone company you don't wish to carry tone dialing, you save a dollar a month on your phone bill—at the end of the year you'll have saved enough to see a movie and buy a sandwich!

Cordless Channels

The scan button on cordless phones, sometimes labeled as "channel," is severely underused by most home consumers. Most people who set up their cordless phone never give channels a second thought. This is very convenient for private detectives and nosy neighbors. Once they figure out which channel your cordless is operating on, they can pretty much set up a scanner and tape recorder to do their work for them. This is referred to as an unattended listening post.

There are only two ways your cordless phone will change channels. It will do so automatically if it picks up any interference from another cordless phone or anything else operating on or near the same frequency. After a cordless phone's initial setup, it may scan for the best frequency. However, it will stay on that frequency for months, even years, until something interferes with it. This is where you come in.

Pressing the "scan" or "channel" button is the second way to change frequencies. Pressing these buttons often during conversations will help deter casual listeners and defeat unattended listening posts. Don't mention to the person you're speaking with that you're "going to scan now." Just do it. If they ask what the buzzing sound was, just say, "I'm on a cordless phone," and continue with your conversation.

The above methods do not apply if you are a high roller, extraordinarily rich, or on the FBI's inquiry list. This subheading applies to ordinary consumers only.

Cellular for the Ordinary Consumer

If you make cell calls from your home because you don't trust landlines, you may be making the nosy neighbor's job easier. This is especially true if the cellular system to which you subscribe is an analog system as opposed to a digital one.

When you make cell calls from your moving vehicle, the radio frequencies used to establish the connection will change as you make turns and drive from one cell to another. Spies, of course, have ways of tracking these signal changes, but for those of us who've led a good, clean life, mobile cell calls are fairly safe—just be aware that people *will* hear snippets of your conversation.

Conversely, if you're sitting in your living room chatting on a cell phone, the radio frequencies used to set up the connection will remain constant. Since you're not moving, the cell company's computer has no reason to hand off your conversation to another antenna. This means that any of your neighbors within a one-mile radius can monitor your handset, which will provide them with half of the conversation (your half). More disturbing, anybody within a six- to 20-mile radius of the cell tower need only turn on a police scanner and listen in on both halves.

Digital cellular is the ordinary consumer's safest bet cell-wise. It is by no means foolproof, however.

HOW TO MAKE FREE PRIVATE PHONE CALLS

Maybe you have a little business that operates in a legal gray area? Perhaps you have several spouses or just one persistent ex? Or is it just that you and your buddy like to talk about new ID over the phone? Whatever your bag, it will inevitably happen . . .

It starts with a funny background click right after you tell your buddy how to make a kick-ass hologram for a New Jersey driver's license. Abruptly, you change the topic. Then it's the one-ring hang-ups that come at odd hours. An infinity transmitter? Before you know it, you're talking in a stilted code every time you answer the phone. You've simply lost all faith in those telltale wires leading from your house out to the pole and onto God knows where.

So, you "red box" calls from pay phones for a while (see *Electronic Circuits and Secrets of an Old-Fashioned Spy*, Chapter 4). Inevitably, winter arrives and your knuckles turn white as you spit out shivers of conversation during 20° cold snaps. Wouldn't it be nice if you could sit in the comfort of your heated automobile and make your important phone calls? So you sit in your car, cell phone in hand, and begin to dial. Who's in that black LTD parked up the street? Do I see an antenna? Is he holding a scanner? There's got to be a better way!

There is.

In the old days, you could take your cordless phone handset for a Sunday drive, park in front of a house that had the same model phone system, and dial away. The taps the feds placed on your home line would be of no consequence because all your calls would be made from somebody else's line. If you had the same model garage door opener, you could go inside and make yourself a sandwich, but that's another topic altogether.

Anyway, it wasn't long before people started complaining and the cordless phone companies came up with a few security measures that pretty much put an end to the old days.

Today there is a variation on this theme. You personally attach your own base to a working phone line that you don't own and that your trackers will not suspect you of using. You keep the handset in your car, and when you need to make a private call, you drive to the base's location and dial away.

To use this method, you must work in or have access to a business office with a dedicated fax or modem line that is *not* part of a multiline system. If you don't like the idea of stealing, I'll tell you up front that this method will not cost the target office more than a few pennies unless you make long-distance phone calls. Even if you do "accidentally" make a few long-distance calls, the overworked administrative assistant will never notice the negligible cost of three calls out of 300 on the company's phone bill.

My office of choice is a real estate office. I hold a real estate broker's license, which is easily obtained under a new identity (see Chapter 8, "Freedom of Employment and Income" under the real estate subheading). It is also extremely easy to obtain "work" as a real estate salesperson. Walk into any nonfranchised real estate office and tell the office manager you have the following:

- A real estate license (salesperson or broker, but make sure you can produce one)
- At least one "listing" (i.e., house you want to sell, which can be your own provided you disclose this fact to prospective buyers)
- Two hours a week where you can "cover the floor"

Office managers are always in need of new listings and an extra body to cover the floor, if only for a couple of hours per week. If the manager doesn't have enough brokers willing to take floor time, or "duty time" as it is sometimes called, the broker will be the one covering the floor on Friday nights when nobody else is willing.

If all goes well, you'll be given a closing shift, which will probably be Friday since you're the "new guy." After a few Friday nights of casual office banter, the office manager will feel comfortable giving you an office key and leave you alone to play with the phone system. If you don't want to go through all that trouble, or if you don't like real estate, you could set up a night cleaning business and get yourself in the door that way.

These are just two ideas; it really doesn't matter how you get access to the office. But once you're in, it's time to make some slight modifications to the company's phone system. You will need to bring a 900 MHz cordless phone system to work with you. If you can afford it, get a model with digital spread spectrum or at least voice inversion for an added measure of privacy. Other items you might need include:

- Standard modular telephone line cord (not handset cord)
- A roll of four-conductor phone wire
- A wall-mount modular phone jack
- Wire strippers
- Phillips screwdriver
- Slotted screwdriver

- Electrical tape
- Rubber gloves
- A stovepipe hat and tobacco pipe for ambiance

All needed items, with the exception of the hat and pipe, are available from your local surveillance supplier, aka Radio Shack.

On Friday, when everybody calls you a chump and goes off to party, lock yourself in the office and get to work. By now you should have already located a hiding place for the phone's transponder (the part you plug into the wall). This can be almost anywhere, even in your desk, provided you have access to the twisted pair (phone line) leading to the dedicated fax or modem line. Most offices make this easy by having a telephone company junction box in the wall or floor conveniently hidden behind each desk. It may not matter if the fax machine is across the room or even down the hall. There's a good chance you can splice into the line at your desk.

This procedure requires a bit of telephone experience. If you don't have such experience, I suggest you do some reading and research before assuming your role as a TelCo repairperson. Experiment on your home phone for a while until you learn the proper way to splice into a twisted pair and hook up extension phones, taps, DTMF decoders, etc. You may wish to consult my aforementioned *Circuits and Secrets* book, which will get you started on the subject.

Quick and Dirty Procedure

1. The rubber gloves are important. If someone tries to send a fax while you're working on the wires, you could get a nasty shock from the ring signal. People have died this way. Wear the gloves!
2. Go to the fax machine (or modem) and trace the line back to the wall or floor.
3. Unscrew the junction box or jack cover and pull it away from the wall.
4. Note the color of the wires that pull out with it. Specifically, we're interested in the two wires *connected to the jack*. There will only be two, and they will be colored in any of the following ways: red and green, yellow and black, white/black stripe and black/white stripe, white/orange stripe and orange/white stripe, white/green stripe and green/white stripe. Larger offices may have more color patterns. Just make sure it's a matching pair and write down the colors.
5. Screw the jack back into the wall so the office manager doesn't get upset.
6. Go back to your desk and trace the phone line back to its jack.
7. Pop that jack and find the same pair of wires.
8. Cut both wires and strip the insulation back about 3/4″ from each end, revealing the bare copper. You should now have four stripped ends.
9. Reconnect both wires by twisting their respective copper ends together. Don't cross the wires. These will be your "splice points."
10. Cut a 4″ length of four-conductor phone line and remove the red and green wires.
11. Strip the red and green wires at both ends.
12. Twist one end of the green wire onto one splice point.
13. Do the same with the red wire to the other splice point.
14. Tape each splice point with electrical tape to prevent shorting. Do not tape the splice points to each other! You may also use small wire nuts.
15. Screw the other end of the green wire to the green terminal of the new wall jack you bought at Radio Shack.
16. Screw the other end of the red wire to the red terminal.
17. Screw the office's jack back in place, being careful not to crush the red and green wires that run out from under it.
18. Screw the new wall jack right next to the existing one.

19. Connect the cordless phone base to the new jack via the line cord.
20. Plug the base into an electrical outlet behind your desk.
21. Place the handset on the base and let it charge according to the owner's manual. *
22. Hide the base behind, under, or in your desk. **

* Most new models establish an internal handset identification number each time the handset is placed on the base. This means you may not charge your handset at home on another base. Doing so will cause the handset to establish an identification number with the wrong base. The handset will then not work at your office. The quickest way to avoid this problem is to buy an older model that doesn't have this security feature. If you're electronically literate, note the voltage and current rating of the AC adapter and get a comparable replacement at Radio Shack. Use it to build your own charge stand for the handset. I built a charge stand in my truck so the handset is always ready. In this case, an AC adapter is necessary. A car battery supplies plenty of current, and a 9-volt regulator gives the required voltage.
** Hiding the base in a metal desk will severely limit the handset's range, unless you supply a port for the antenna.

You may wish to implement this over several office visits, particularly if your office's layout requires significant modifications to the procedure.

You now have a phone line that doesn't belong to you. Nobody will ever suspect you of using it. Therefore, you no longer have to worry about phone taps! Even if your target office comes under investigation, the investigators probably won't be monitoring the fax line. Even if they do, they won't know or care who you are or how you're doing what you're doing. The investigators, for a change, will be after somebody else.

How to Use It

Simple really. Keep your handset in your car, preferably on a charge stand. When you need to make an anonymous or private call, drive to your office. You can place the call right from the parking lot or even down the street a bit. It's probably best to do this at night, especially if the office crew knows you.

You don't have to worry too much about someone picking up the line and listening in because it's a fax line. However, if someone tries to send a fax, the fax machine will tell them the line is off hook. This may spark an investigation. So, to be perfectly safe, use your newfound private phone line only when the office is closed.

Actually, this is another reason why I like real estate offices. Salespeople pop in all the time to make copies and send faxes. So when the administrative assistant notices Sunday phone activity on the fax's phone bill, it's no big deal. If your chosen office is strictly 9 to 5, however, numerous off-hours calls on the bill may spark inquiry. The calls do not have to be long distance, either. Many phone companies charge businesses a small per-call fee ($.01/minute) even on local calls. Every situation is different, so use common sense.

SETTING UP A PRIVATE MESSAGING SYSTEM

There are a couple different ways to do this. The first one is in keeping with the above scenario. My real estate office, like most, also has a dedicated modem line where salespeople can dial up a master list of real estate listings in the area. The modem line is actually part of a multiline system, but in this case it doesn't matter. A quick investigation showed that the line was fifth in the trunk and, of course, did not roll over to or from the other lines, hence "dedicated." For example, let's say the office's main number is 611-4000 (not a real number). The advertised number is 611-4000, which rings quietly at the secretary's desk when customers call, and the secretary in turn transfers the call to the desk of the called party, usually a salesperson. Now, 611-4000 is in use until the salesperson hangs up.

When another customer calls, the secretary's phone will automatically ring on 611-4001, the next rollover line. If all subordinate lines are busy, calls will roll over up to 611-4003, at which point the office's messaging system kicks in. I knew the office had four lines (4000–4003). I knew that the fax line, for whatever reason, was dedicated on a separate bill altogether. It was common knowledge in the office that salespeople (and anybody) could direct dial any of the lines. In fact, in an emergency, a salesperson on the road would dial 611-4003 to defeat the rollover protocol. The other salespeople would see the premature rollover by the telltale desk-phone LEDs (light-emitting diodes) and immediately pick up the line to get their frantic message.

So for the hell of it, I picked up line 1 and dialed 611-4004, which rang and rang and rang. The next time I was left alone in the office, I started a communications program on the computer (Windows Terminal for IBM users) and called the line again. The program spit out RING RING RING. That's how I figured out which line it was. Sure, you could always ask, but this may arouse suspicions.

Now it was time to set up my private fax and voice mailbox.

I installed Faxworks voice messaging software on the office's computer because it runs in the background with no icon. Other voice messaging software will also work. Unless your office's PC is very new, you'll need to open it up and swap out its modem card with the voice/fax/modem card that comes with the software. Again, a little training is required to do this. Practice on your PC first.

Once done, I set up the messaging software with several mailboxes, which could now be programmed simply by calling the office. Today, I receive, retrieve, delete, and save voice messages and faxes from any of the mailboxes I set up. I haven't been to the office in months.

Low-Tech Method

You can only use the following method in areas where the telephone company offers a call answering service. If your area doesn't have this, it probably will soon. This procedure can be adapted to suit your needs:

1. Find a three-family apartment building that you know for sure has no "in-law" apartment in the basement.
2. Call the telephone company and order residential phone service to the "new basement apartment." Give your hookup address as 123 Nowhere Street, Unit B1. Specifically tell them you want service brought to the outside of the house only and your electrician will do the rest.
3. Give your mail drop as the billing address.
4. At this point the nice TelCo salesperson will try to sell you every service you've ever heard of and a few you didn't. Order the most basic service possible and tell them you do not wish to designate a long-distance carrier at this time. Then order your call answering service, get your phone number, and tell the nice TelCo salesperson to have a lucky day.

To make the hookup you requested, the installer does not need to enter the house or talk to anybody. Next time you drive by the three-family apartment building it will look exactly the same. If you're particularly observant, you may notice an extra wire running from the telephone pole to the side of the building.

So now what do you do? How do you get in to set up your phone? Why did you just blow $35 to hook up a line to some stranger's house? The answers are nothing, you don't, and you didn't.

In a couple of days, go to your mail drop and get the package the phone company will send you. It will give you instructions for setting up your mailbox as well as access numbers and instructions for checking your messages. Follow the instructions to set up your voicemail system.

When you're done, call yourself and leave a message. It will work. You don't need to have an actual phone connected at the residence. If necessary, you can even rip the phone wire right off the apartment building and never worry about it again.

Now you have a phone number to give to bill collectors, business partners, dates, banks, credit card companies, employers, and others. With the minimal service you ordered, it shouldn't cost more than $20 to $25 per month.

MAKING THE MOST OF CALLER ID

Caller ID, or CLID for Calling Line Identification in TelCo-speak, allows you to see exactly who's making your phone ring. Well, you don't actually see the person, but his phone number will pop up on a little LCD (liquid-crystal display) screen connected between your phone and the wall jack. By the time you read this, most CLID systems will also identify the calling party's name and address. In this way you can choose whether and, more important, *how* to answer the phone. If the call is from your new lover, you may wish to answer it differently than if it's from a potential employer, bill collector, or FBI agent.

Great privacy tool, right? Well . . .

The flip side is that anybody you call might also have Caller ID. If so, your name, address, and phone number will pop up on *their* screen.

Caller ID can be your best friend or your worst enemy. I believe Caller ID is worth having if you can maximize its advantages and minimize its disadvantages. The fact of the matter is it's out there. And if it's out there, you are obligated as an embattled privateer to make the most of it. Here's how.

Line Blocking

Line blocking is a way to prevent your name, address, and phone number from showing up on Caller ID screens. You request this service directly from your local phone company, and it remains activated until you drop the service. When you call someone who has Caller ID, his display will indicate PRIVATE or BLOCKED. The only problem with having permanently installed line blocking is that you will be unable to connect with any phone number equipped with Anonymous Call Rejection (see ACR below), unless you subscribe to per-call unblocking (*82), which you must pay for in many states.

Per-Call Blocking

Dialing *67 will block outbound Caller ID on a per-call basis. You do not have to sign up in advance to use this service. Any area that has Caller ID allows free per-call blocking. The obvious disadvantage is you have to remember to do it. If you are handy with electronics, you can build a circuit that automatically dials *67 for you whenever you pick up your phone.

Neither line blocking nor per-call blocking will prevent your number from being displayed at toll-free (800/888/877) or pay-per-call (900/976) numbers, which use Automatic Number Identification. Also, emergency numbers (e.g., 911) are unaffected by CLID blocking.

Automatic Number Identification and How To Avoid It

The privacy seeker must be aware that CLID differs from Automatic Number Identification (ANI). CLID is a service offered to consumers, whereas ANI is a feature inherent in existing telephone company business services. For example, if you establish a toll-free or pay-per-call number, you pay for all incoming calls. To account for these calls, the phone company supplies the calling numbers in a monthly statement. This is exactly how credit card companies catch unwitting fraudsters.

The only way to completely avoid ANI is to call from a number you don't mind having identified, such as a pay phone or office phone. Large PBX (Private Branch Exchange) systems that have all their calls billed to a single line will offer some ANI anonymity because the billing number will be the number identified. This means extensions in large office buildings and off-premises extensions will not be pinpointed by ANI.

Miscellaneous CLID Avoidance

Even though many Caller ID systems will identify out-of-state numbers as "out of state," the system is constantly being upgraded and soon all numbers will by identified by CLID. In fact, some CLID systems are already pretty good at identifying out-of-state callers. You can avoid CLID by using an operator to dial your call for you. Just dial 0 and tell the operator what number you're trying to call.

The called party's Caller ID box will have no way of knowing what number has called it because the connection was "broken" at the phone company.

You can also place local calls through an operator to avoid CLID. Some operators may be curious if you ask them to dial a number that is local to you. Just tell them you've tried it several times and you keep getting a weird noise.

Some other ideas:

- Use a *prepaid* calling card. Such calls are rerouted through the card's long-distance service. *Credit-based* calling card services leave a paper trail for investigators to follow.
- Use a call rerouting service, usually a 900 number, and be prepared to pay the bill.
- Call from a cell phone. This is chancy at best because many areas are testing cellular CLID services, and cellular calls open other avenues of privacy invasion.
- Use a loop line. A loop line is two consecutive numbers established by the phone company for testing local phone circuits. The TelCo repairperson dials one number, which plays a high-pitched tone, feeds that tone into a loop, dials the other number, and tests to see if the tone is present. You can also dial one number, have your friend dial the other number, and talk to each other for free.

Due to abuse, most loop lines no longer allow voice frequencies to pass, so voice-pass loop lines are all but defunct. If you're lucky enough to live near one, dial the number that produces the tone and wait for the operator to pick up, which may or may not happen. If you're lucky and the operator picks up, say, "Hello? Hell-o-o?" and the operator will think they've answered an operator-assisted call. Say what number you are calling and the operator will connect you and bill the call to the loop line. You can find loop line numbers listed on the Internet. I don't consider these practical methods of communication, but people do use them so you should be aware of it.

Using Inbound Caller ID

Simply put, don't answer any call unless you know who's calling

Anonymous Call Rejection

Anonymous Call Rejection (ACR) will peremptorily reject any caller who has blocked Caller ID. Your phone will not even ring. Instead the caller will receive a message to the effect that you don't accept calls from blocked lines.

I don't recommend this service for several reasons:

- You have to subscribe to it, and it costs money.
- You will not know you were called.
- It gives bill collectors, private detectives, and others a reason to find some other way of contacting you.
- It advertises to your friends, associates, family, and enemies that you have Caller ID.
- It's hypocritical: you're professing to be pro privacy while at the same time not allowing others to exercise their right to privacy.
- You will lose a lot of dates, especially if you're male.
- It's just as easy to ignore the call.

The only upside to having ACR installed on your line is that you can turn it off (see Table 6.1).

Free Caller ID

When your phone rings, answer it but don't say anything. The other person will become confused and say, "Hello?" If you don't recognize the voice, say, "Who's this?"

This seems obvious, but it's a very powerful tool. You have reversed the flow of conversation.

Typically, you say hello first and the caller says, "Is this Bozo T. Clown?" At which point you are on the defensive. Even saying, "Who wants to know?" is like saying, "Yes, and I'm in a bit of trouble so I don't want to admit anything until I know who you are." The conversation turns into a power struggle.

By using the above trick, you are immediately in control and the other person is forced to identify themselves first. If you don't like who they are, simply hang up and put the receiver in the fridge for a half hour.

After you use this method for a while, your friends and family will get used to your little "quirk" and identify themselves immediately when they call. If you'd rather not have a quirk, you could always say your cordless phone cuts off the first few seconds of conversation, which is true of many models.

This method really works, and it's much more civil than asking your close friends to go through a special ringing ritual in order to reach you. And—oh yeah—it's free.

General Caller ID Tips
Here are a couple general tips before we move on.

- Whenever an unrecognized caller asks, "Is this Mr. So N. Sew?" you can respond by saying, "Who's calling?" If they repeat their question, simply repeat yours. After three times, gently place the receiver in your refrigerator.
- Don't tell people you use Caller ID. That's your business. Also, don't "telegraph" to them that you're using it by calling them back when their number appears on your Caller ID screen. This is a common mistake. A friend or business associate calls you but does not leave a message. You see his number on your Caller ID screen and mechanically return the call. "How'd you know I called?" they ask. Bingo. You're bagged.

For your convenience, I've provided a quick-reference chart of common TelCo service codes in Table 6.1. Those service codes that are not self-explanatory will be elaborated upon below.

TABLE 6.1
Telephone Service Codes

TelCo Service	DTMF (tone) Code	Pulse Dialer's Code
Call trace	*57	1157
Call cue	*66	1166
Per-call blocking	*67	1167
Activate ACR	*77	1177
Per-call unblocking	*82	1182
Deactivate ACR	*87	1187
Dial last caller	*69	1169
Activate call forwarding	*72	1172
Deactivate call forwarding	*73	1173
Deactivate call waiting on a per-call basis	*70	1170

Call Trace
Call Trace allows you to do something about threatening and offensive calls. If you or a family member receive one of these calls, you can press *57 and Call Trace will automatically trace the last call you received. The caller's phone number will be recorded at the local telephone company along with the time and date, if possible. You will be charged each time you activate a successful trace.

If you wish to initiate an investigation, contact your local TelCo office and law enforcement agency. The TelCo will then supply law enforcement with the recorded information.

This service is limited to certain areas.

Call Cue

If you dial a number and it's busy, you can have the phone company retry the number for you by dialing *66, then hanging up. The TelCo will keep trying the party until the line is no longer busy. At this point your phone will ring and you will be connected with the party you so desperately need to talk to (or their answering machine).

FREEDOM FROM LONG-DISTANCE CHARGES

Though Ma Bell has been broken up for many years, the phone company still seems a recalcitrant monopoly. Most people in fact still refer to it as "the Phone Company." Indeed we have all felt the aggravation when the pay phone operator asks, "Which long-distance company would you like?"

"Which company?" we ask. "I want the f***ing Phone Company! What do you mean *which* company?"

Despite the aggravation that ensued after Ma Bell's federally forced breakup, it has all been for the best. Had the feds allowed her to continue wielding her monopoly, the advances we've seen in cellular networking technology would never have transpired. Long-distance price wars would not be driving down rates, and I wouldn't be able to teach you the following goodies. Once enough people learn what I'm about to teach you, you'll see long-distance rates decline even further as competition becomes more fierce.

How Long-Distance Service Works

When you sign up for phone service, the sales rep asks which you want as your primary long-distance carrier, also known as an Inter-Exchange Carrier, or IXC. If you ask which ones are available, the rep will probably name two or three of the biggest companies such as Sprint, MCI, or AT&T. Most people don't know they can choose from any of dozens or even hundreds of companies that also serve their calling area. More important, you don't have to choose a carrier at all! You can simply elect not to do so at that time and avoid the setup fee.

Assuming you're like most people and you choose a long-distance carrier, your phone company ties the carrier's four-digit code to your number. Each time you dial a 1+ or 0+ number, that long-distance company automatically carries your call.

PICCy PICCy

Because you declared them as your primary carrier, the IXC is subject to a Primary Inter-Exchange Carrier Charge (PICC). This is a mandatory per-line charge levied by the LEC (Local Exchange Carrier) upon the IXC for using its local loop. The IXC used to pay the LEC a per-minute charge, but this was eliminated by Federal Communications Commission reforms. The charge only applies if the IXC is predesignated by the subscriber (another reason to not declare an IXC during the signup process).

Dialing Around Your Primary IXC

Notice all those new TV commercials offering special long-distance rates if you dial 10-10 this and 10-10 that? Perhaps you even tried it once or twice wondering what it's really all about and if you can really save money. If you did, you also found that it really doesn't make too much of a difference price-wise, as, more often than not, there is some hidden charge you don't know about.

So can these services save you money? If you use the ones advertised on TV, probably not. If you do some hunting around, however, you can save a lot of money.

First, you must understand how "dial around" services work.

Understanding "Dial Around" Services

Remember how your local phone company input the code of your primary long-distance carrier when you signed up for service? Now, whenever you dial a 1+ number, you're stuck with that carrier. Or so they'd like you to believe. The IXC code input by your local phone company is simply a default code used if you don't dial your own. In other words, when you place a call, you can choose from *any* of the long-distance carriers servicing your area—and there may be dozens. You do this by dialing 101 + IXC Code + 1 + Area Code + Number. Even if AT&T is your primary IXC, you can dial 101 + 0222 + 1 + Area Code + Number and MCI (whose code is 0222) will carry the call. That is exactly what you are doing when you respond to TV ads requesting that you try their service.

For a long time, IXC codes were only three digits long and were accessed by dialing 10. But since the breakup of Ma Bell, so many IXCs have come into existence that a new numbering scheme became necessary. This scheme went into effect July 1, 1998. You may have seen TV commercials at that time saying 10xxx is now 1010xxx or 10xxx is now 101xxxx.

That's All Very Interesting, But How Do I Save Money?

There are literally hundreds and soon to be thousands of long-distance carriers. Your job is to find a few that offer low "dial around" service rates in your area. As more companies spring into existence, competition will drive dial-around rates even lower. Each month, use the IXC offering the lowest rate. You can even sign them on as your primary carrier if and when they offer to guarantee the rate for a specific period of time. You can and should hold out for a one- to two-year guarantee.

Currently the best source for this information is the Internet. Use the keywords "dial around." If you don't have Internet access, find a library that does. There are a lot of new companies out there, so you must be certain to ask the right questions and be vigilant in avoiding hidden charges.

Caveats

When dialing around, many IXCs will not give you their advertised rate unless you register your phone number with them. As long as there is no registration or "sign up" fee, go ahead and do it.

When predesignating an IXC, most carriers will waive their monthly fee if you meet their minimum use requirement. This is only fair. Why should they spend the administrative expense to send you a bill every month if you only make 30 cents worth of calls? Look for a company that offers a low minimum and a low fee for the months you fail to meet it. I would suggest a minimum use of $25 and a billing fee of $2 if you fail to meet it. You may even find better deals as competition grows. Be sure there is no minimum billing during months you place no long distance calls at all.

Make sure the advertised dial-around rate is the same for the first minute as it is for the last. Make sure there is no per-call fee and no penalty for calls under a certain time limit.

Ask how long the rate and terms will be valid. If they say they are subject to change at any time, then tell them you cannot use their service. Tell them you'd rather not have to verify their rate before each call, then go elsewhere. Make them compete harder for your patronage.

Final Note

If you have Internet access, several software packages allow you to talk via your modem connection. If your Internet connection is a local call, you will only be charged for a local call—even if the person your chatting with is halfway around the globe.

There is already a movement by the telephone companies to charge extra for this sort of connection. At the time of this writing, however, thousands of people worldwide were communicating long distance and saving hundreds and sometimes thousands of dollars a year using this method.

Internet Privacy

How can we expect another to keep our secret if we have been unable to keep it ourselves?
François Duc de La Rochefoucauld

Every day, the Internet receives thousands of new subscribers through hundreds of Internet Service Providers, or ISPs. An entire cybersociety has been created and continues to grow rapidly. Just as with ordinary society, there are friendly people, people just trying to make a buck, and people trying to molest your children and kill you. Just as you take safety precautions in your everyday life, so should you in your Internet life.

This chapter will show you some simple methods of remaining anonymous while you're surfing the Net. Since Netscape Navigator and Microsoft Internet Explorer are the most popular products for accessing the Internet at this time, they will be used to demonstrate techniques described in this chapter. The techniques, however, may be easily adapted to other Web browsers.

UNDOING SETUP'S "FAVORS"

The first thing I did after installing Netscape was to remove my name from the data file created during setup. If you fail to do this, every site you visit will be handed your real name, often without you knowing it. If you use Netscape, you can do this right now. Click on Options, then Mail and News Preferences, highlight your name, and delete it! You may replace it with an on-line name, or "handle," or you might simply choose to use only your first name.

WHAT'S A COOKIE?

Real cookies are sweet, but this one leaves a bad taste in the mouths of some people. The "cookie" was quietly, suddenly, and unexpectedly introduced by Netscape and, at the time of this writing, was still considered experimental. But I can state with confidence: the cookie is here to stay.

A cookie is a small file placed by the remote server on the client side of the network interface (your computer). Ever wonder why some discussion boards seem to remember you? You log on and get the message, "Hello Barbie! You've been here 1,234 times!" Did you always assume that the remote server compared your e-mail address to an internal database? Most people think this is how it works. It isn't.

While it's true that most decent Web sites will not hassle you for your name, a name script is the best example I can think of to help me explain cookies. The first time you visit such a site, you get a JavaScript (or CGI script) message asking you for your name. The JavaScript message box results from unseen programming code embedded in the HTML (hypertext markup language) of the Web page. Once you enter your name, another unseen code snippet writes that info to a file on *your computer*.

Thenceforth, when you log on to that Web site, another JavaScript routine looks for the cookie and retrieves your name and any other information stored in the cookie, such as how many visits you've made. If your browser doesn't allow cookies or you've disabled them, you will be prompted for your name on every visit, which is a minor annoyance.

This is the same way an electronic mall remembers which items are in your "shopping cart" even if you shut your computer off and decide to finish shopping the next day.

Cookies: Are They Good for You?

Just like real cookies, they're not as bad as some people would have you believe, but I wouldn't go so far as to say they're good for you. Despite widespread skepticism, cookies are not the tools of evil. In order to keep them this way, however, one must understand what they are, how they work, and what they know about you.

Cookie files are very small, usually a few kilobytes at the absolute most, and they won't use up all your disk space. While cookies are a very powerful programming and marketing tool, they are not executable files, which means they cannot harm your computer's integrity or spawn so-called viruses. Nor can a cookie ever send private information stored in other files on your computer to the remote computer.

But there are privacy implications you should know about so you can watch for them. Cookies *can* track information, such as your buying and spending habits and the amount of time you take looking at each screen. This is done for marketing purposes.

If you ever feel that a Web site has used a cookie to invade your privacy, you can disable the cookie on your next visit or take your business elsewhere.

Show Me the Cookie!

Unlike when you were a wee toddler in search of a secret snack, cookies are not hard to find . . . on your hard disk, that is. Sixty-five percent of computer users will find cookies in one of the following two places.

If you have Microsoft Internet Explorer, your cookies will most likely be in a Windows subdirectory called . . . (drum roll, please) . . . "cookies." See? They're not the sneaky little devils you thought they were after all. Open up Windows Explorer (or File Manager if you have not upgraded to Win95/98) and expand the Windows directory. Not too far down the directory tree you will see a subdirectory called "cookies." Double-click it to make it the active directory.

Any cookies that have been set will now appear in the right-hand window. Here's what my cookie directory looked like the day I typed this:

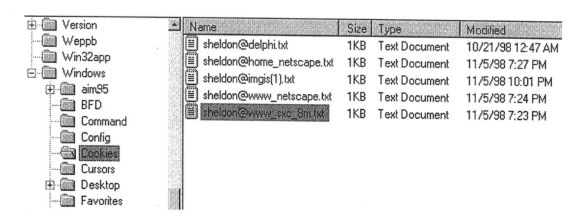

Clicking on any of the files will reveal a string of computer gibberish.

Netscape Navigator users will find a cookies.txt file in their Netscape Navigator subdirectory, usually located in the Program Files directory for Win95/98 users. Double-click the file for a complete multiflavored list of cookies. The Netscape file is neater and more readable than Microsoft Internet Explorer, though not much more useful.

Still Can't Find Your Cookies?

Win95/98 users can click Start/Find/Files or Folders. Type in cookie*.* and click Find Now. Other Windows users can do a File Manager search. If you have cookies on your system, this will turn them up. If you don't find any cookies, either your browser is not set up to receive them or you have them disabled. Speaking of which . . .

Cookie Control: A Web Browser Diet

To have your browser warn you before setting cookies, thus giving you the opportunity to refuse them, set the proper switch in your Options menu. For Navigator, click Options/Network/Protocols, then check "Accepting a Cookie" in the Show an Alert Before box. While you're at it, click Options/Mail and News Preferences/Identity. Go to the Your Name box and type in a made-up online name. You can also choose to enter "anonymous" or no name at all. Below that in the Your Email and Reply-to Address boxes, enter an alias e-mail address (see next section).

Microsoft IE users should click View/Options/Advanced, then check "Warn before accepting cookies."

I recommend using the cookie diet solely for demonstration purposes until you get an idea of just who's sending you cookies and when. From this information you can usually figure out why the cookie is being set and, you should see, it is not for malicious purposes. Leaving your browser in cookie diet mode will soon become very annoying, and you have to click "I accept" two to three times for most new sites you visit. Alternatively, you can find freeware or shareware cookie control software on the Internet, which lets you dynamically or permanently accept or reject cookies from specific sites. I use one called Cookie Pal.

E-MAIL PRIVACY

To best maintain your Internet privacy, avoid using the e-mail account provided by your ISP. In many cases, using your ISP's e-mail allows marketers, private detectives, bill collectors, and other nasty-nosies to home in on your actual location. This is especially true if your ISP happens to be a company or university. Their user base is relatively small, making you easier to find.

Today, there's absolutely no reason to use your ISP's e-mail account. There are hundreds of companies that allow you to maintain free e-mail accounts on their servers. They do this hoping you'll read the ads on their servers and patronize their sponsors, but you're under no obligation to do so. Although many of these companies request your name, address, and phone number during the initial sign-up process, I suggest you use an alias and invent any information they request. This will provide you with a totally anonymous e-mail address. Here are a few companies offering free e-mail at the time of this writing:

yahoo.com
geocities.com
hotmail.com

By taking advantage of these companies, you can create a personal e-mail account (or several) even if you don't have an Internet service provider. Using a library, company, or university computer, you can log on from anywhere in the world to check your e-mail and never pay a cent for the service.

Anonymous Remailers

When you route your e-mail through an anonymous remailer, the server replaces your e-mail address with one it makes up. It then forwards your message to its original destination. Any replies from that destination automatically pass back through the remailer, which then recalls your e-mail address and forwards the message back to you.

Andre Bacard, author of *The Computer Privacy Handbook* (Berkeley, CA: Peachpit Press, 1995), rightly makes a distinction between anonymous and pseudo-anonymous remailers. His book is an excellent one for anybody interested in privacy on the Net or the intricacies of using Philip Zimmerman's Pretty Good Privacy (PGP) encryption software. The book can be ordered from:

Peachpit Press
2414 Sixth Street
Berkeley, CA 94710

For the purpose of this discussion, I won't delve into the distinctions between anonymous and pseudo-anonymous remailers. This is because I don't recommend either for the following reasons:

- A pseudonymous remailer costs money and is less anonymous than opening a free anonymous e-mail account as described above.
- True anonymous remailing involves an inordinate amount of work for what should be a simple task.
- Recipients of anonymous e-mail can usually tell that the mail is anonymous. For this reason, many potential business contacts may not take your mail seriously. Some will even delete it unread.
- Both methods cause your mail to, at best, be delayed and, at worst, become lost.
- Neither method is convenient.
- Most modern browsers allow you to omit or change your "reply to" e-mail address anyway.

If you are in *very* serious trouble with the law or you are an international spy, then anonymous remailers *may* provide more security than free, anonymous e-mail accounts. If this is the case, then you may wish to visit Mr. Bacard's Web site (www.well.com/user/abacard) for more information.

Most average Joes and Josephines, however, can relax with their anonymous e-mail accounts nestled inside the staggering multitudes on servers such as Yahoo and Geocities. These companies are colossal money-making turbines that simply haven't the time nor desire to slow down and spy on you. Frankly, they don't give a rat's ass about you. They just want you to come to their server, read ads, and hopefully send a few dollars their way by patronizing their advertisers. Privacy-wise, at least, I find it very reassuring.

Encryption

Now consider this: the Internet was set up by the government, and now that very same government is up in arms over private citizens' use of encryption software to secure their e-mail transmissions. In fact, the government is trying to have the practice outlawed. Why? Could it be that our trusted government uses supercomputers to randomly scan e-mail for certain key phrases that *may* indicate illegal activity? Could it be that encryption will bog down these supercomputers? Could it be that Big Brother fears anything it can't control? Could it be that government's worst nightmare is the free thought and movement of the very people who established it?

I think so. I think it could be all these things. I think if government has its way, you may someday e-mail a friend that you "just had some Coke" and 44 DEA agents will be banging at your door 15 minutes later. Guess you should've had a Pepsi instead.

Personally, I don't use encryption. Again, I think it complicates what should be a very simple task. If I don't want my "secret" left for a minimum of six months on dozens of servers—encrypted or otherwise—I use a pay phone. However, if you think your boss or some other nosy bastard is perusing your e-mail, encryption software will probably preclude them from doing so. There are several available on the market, but the best known is PGP as mentioned under the previous subheading.

FORMS PRIVACY

There will be times when you're on the Internet and you wish to request a simple bit of information. Next thing you know, you're faced with the task of completing a privacy-invading form. You try your best to skip the boxes you don't think you should have to answer, but then the form doesn't go through! (An excellent—and ironic—example of this is when you try to call up an on-line article from the *New York Times*.)

Here're some quick tips for managing these hassles:

1. If a form asks you for something you don't care to give, simply make it up. Better yet, confuse the clerk who processes the form by typing something like this: (*&#UIKJencrypted~} {)%J_)(sxcencoded&^&#$IU(". Be careful to throw in the word "encrypted" or "encoded" so they think the problem is on their end and will send you the information you requested.
2. When forms ask for your phone number, "accidentally" type in your e-mail address. Sometimes, if I'm not overly anxious for a reply, I'll type, "Why do you need this?"
3. Some forms are smarter and will not accept alphabet characters where numbers are expected. For phone numbers and Social Security numbers (the nerve!), type all zeroes or all nines. This usually works.
4. Highly intelligent forms compare phone numbers with a database and return an error message such as, "Exchange does not exist in the given area code." In these cases, type the area code and most popular exchange of a major city and then 0000. This will be accepted even by the smartest forms (at least for now).
5. Other intelligent forms compare your city with your zip code. Just pick a city and zip code that are not yours. Most people know the zip codes of friends, relatives, or business associates they often mail letters to. Just pick one from memory. Here's one I've memorized from dealing with credit card companies: Sioux Falls, SD 57101. Or how about Beverly Hills 90210?
6. For any form field marked "required," type: "Why is this required?" The form will usually go through, but don't be surprised if your request or order is not granted.

THAT'S THE FACT, JACK

The Internet is a continuously evolving species. If you "get connected," I highly recommend bookmarking a few privacy Web sites such as EPIC, ACLU, or Mr. Bacard's privacy page, all of which were mentioned earlier. Visit the sites often to keep up with the latest Net privacy concerns. If you see Big Brother trying to step in, smash his toes with a sledgehammer. Write your congressional representative long before you see the whites of Big Brother's eyes. If others do the same, just maybe we can keep the Net a private and safe place, controlled by the "netizens" who use it and not by the Bureaucratic Machine.

8

Freedom of Employment and Income

Workin' for the man every night and day.
Ike and Tina Turner

Plenty of good tricks and techniques for squeezing your way into somebody's operation were given in *The Modern Identity Changer* and its predecessors. In strict observance of the no-rehash rule, this chapter will deal mostly with the joy and privacy of depending on yourself to provide for yourself. That's what freedom is all about, right?

Well, I've always thought that, but these days there's more freedom riding on self-employment than ever before. Thanks to Public Law 104-193, all employers must submit employee data to the federally mandated "new hires" database. The law, ostensibly related to welfare reform, authorized the database, which is now used to track illegal aliens and so-called deadbeat dads. Okay, fair enough. So only illegal aliens and deadbeat dads with court judgments against them are entered into the deadbeat dad-abase, right? Of course!

Oops, wait a minute here. What's this? No? *All* new hires are entered into the database? Believe it or not, it's true.

How is this possible in the good ol' U.S. of America? Because the land of the free is really the land of bullshit, my friends.

What can you do about it? Work for yourself and avoid the whole bloody debacle. That would seem to be the easiest solution.

But with Big Brother squeezing his restrictions and regulations into an increasing number of trades, where can privacy seekers and identity changers ply their wares? Well, there are many things to do in this world, and fortunately, Big Brother is a sluggish adversary. There are still trades and pastimes where identity changers and privacy seekers can support their freedom habit.

In a few moments, I will present an extensive list of income-generating possibilities. In my meandering life of keeping a step ahead of the system, I've stumbled into firsthand experience with many of the opportunities listed. Areas in which I've had no firsthand experience were adequately researched by talking to others who have.

Where appropriate, specific reasons will be given as to why and how a particular occupation is considered private, anonymous, or a safer bet for the identity changer. Where it is not readily evident, I've done my best to lend insight to why a particular occupation might be more suited for a privacy seeker and less suited for an identity changer and vice versa.

Big Brother's life-design (*MIC*, Chapter 1) offers the average citizen a handful of closely related opportunities based on our education and experience, which are also meted out by Big Brother. Often the opportunities are so closely linked (orderly, nurse, or dental assistant if you went to one school; secretary or paralegal if you went elsewhere) that in reality we have but one "opportunity" and one preordained course in life to follow.

In an effort to ensure that all my readers have diverse avenues from which to choose, the list of employment possibilities is rather large and detailed. Obviously, not all of the occupations or income techniques will appeal to you. Thus, it may be best to skim through the headings and read only those that most interest you. If you've diverse interests, you might enjoy reading the entire section and also learn a great deal from it. We'll begin with an uplifting pep talk on self-employment.

MAKING YOUR OWN JOB

Thinking about it for any length of time, one begins to realize that the words "employment" and "personal freedom" are not exactly willing bedfellows. Nor is the word "privacy" oft courted by the nefarious "employment."

This is perhaps because most of society sees employment only one way: you need a job, so you go to someone else to get one. After all, that is what most of us were taught from the time we were innocent little toddlers looking to our parents, teachers, and elders for sound advice. Did we get it? Most of us didn't.

More often than not, the gods we looked upon told us we must go to school and learn enough to be accepted into the employment market. The employment market, we were told, was controlled by "bosses" and "supervisors," and these were the people we must strive to impress.

But where did all the bosses come from? If we were bold enough little tykes to ask such a silly question, we were told that the bosses, themselves, had bosses; that's the way it works, now eat your dinner.

Pondering on it later, the curious kid knew the buck must stop somewhere. Who's the boss's boss's boss? Well, the boss's boss's boss is a kid—a kid who figured it all out, grew up, and said, "Hey, why can't *I* be the boss? I can start my own business." Sure. In retrospect this seems obvious. But this big kid admits it took many years to undo society's pervasive conditioning.

Before moving on, you may also wish to keep in mind that working for yourself is the only legal way around having to apply for a Social Security number and use it on tax returns (more on this in Chapter 9).

SOME NICE AND (MOSTLY) LEGAL
WAYS OF PROVIDING FOR YOURSELF

Listed alphabetically below are some perfectly reasonable ways to provide for yourself in this world. In most cases, no identification is required to conduct your business. No license is required for most of these activities, or, where a license is required, it's a simple matter to ignore the requirement or use novelty identification. There are some general points about business licensure later in the chapter.

The designation "tax free" as used below does not mean a particular line of business does not require income tax filing. Rather, it is used to indicate that a particular business is typically associated with failure by its practitioners to pay income tax (e.g., member of rock band, paperboy) and a general acceptance by the IRS that enforcement in these circumstances is difficult. Consequently, the IRS relies mostly on the "honor system" in these areas. Ultimately, however, you must decide whether to violate the U.S. Tax Codes. The decision is, as it should be, yours.

There are plenty of job titles listed below. You should have no trouble finding something you are capable of, knowledgeable about, or interested in enough to take the time and learn how to do.

Actor
Since there are no licensing requirements to become an actor, the privacy seeker may pursue this career under any name without too much concern over identity documents. Actors are typically poor, and it's no surprise to an agent or casting director if an actor does not have a driver's license. A well-made student or employment ID will suffice.

In "agent-free" towns such as Boston, you can be hired as an "extra" and paid $150 per day (at the time of this writing). On Hollywood productions, you will be fed like a king while you hobnob with the other extras waiting to be used.

Even the hard-core identity changer trying to keep a low profile can safely work in this profession. Most days on the job, you are not used. When you are used, it is for background, which is usually out of focus. When it's not out of focus, your face is usually not toward the camera. When it is toward the camera, nobody's looking at you anyway. They're focused on the main characters!

Antiques Expert

Unless you already have a substantial background in history and industry, becoming a general expert in antiques will be a Herculean undertaking. But many of us are knowledgeable about specific things such as cars, records, trading cards, or Hollywood memorabilia. I've known many such people myself, and a good number of them make at least a part-time living by trading in their chosen field. One man I knew did nothing else but trade in Houdini memorabilia. I'd like to say that he was an identity changer because the Houdini thing would be ever so fitting, but, alas, he was not (sigh). Nor was he much else. He was not too bright, overly paranoid of just about everything and everybody, and basically had no life outside his antiseptically spotless apartment. However, he made a living doing the one thing he'd somehow become an expert at.

As an antique expert, you can offer your services as a consultant, open up a shop, or buy and sell antiques at a profit through advertisements and swap guides.

Less scrupulous experts offer their "services" under the guise of a cleaning company: they offer free estimates to clean out attics and basements. If they don't see anything they like during their "estimate," they give the client a ridiculously high price, hoping the client will refuse their services. Sometimes the client accepts despite the high price and the antique expert makes $1,500 for an afternoon's work and a couple of trips to the dump. The particularly discerning antique expert will simply call back and decline the work, claiming illness or "too much business" at the moment.

Alternatively, if the antique expert sees a valuable painting from an obscure historical artist, a Stradivarius violin, or a Ming vase, the "cleanup" estimate will likely be more than reasonable. The expert might also offer to do the job right away. The valuable object eventually gets taken to an antique shop or auction.

Apartment Rentals

An apartment rental agency usually operates in a good-sized city and runs two ads in separate local papers or separate sections of the same paper. The first ad reads something like this:

Clean apartments, reasonable rents, landlord pays rental fee. Call 555-RENT today!

The second ad reads like this:

Landlords! Trouble with vacancies? Get that apartment filled today!
Good tenants, credit check, references. Call now! 555-RENT.

As calls come in, you accumulate a database of prospective tenants and their desires (e.g., how many bedrooms they need, do they desire a garage, how much they're willing to part with each month). When the desperate landlord calls, you explain that you charge a commission equal to one month's rent. Explain that you do all the work—you set up all appointments, show the apartment, run a credit check on the prospective tenant, negotiate the lease, and so forth. Remind him also that if the apartment is not filled soon, another month will go by where he collects no rent. So he's really not losing any money by paying you a one-month commission.

If the landlord is annoyed by your fee, offer to accept a half-month's rent, but reduce your services.

For example, you can simply set up the appointments, but it will be the landlord's responsibility to show the apartment and screen the tenant.

Another incentive many rental agents use to entice landlords is to "guarantee" the tenant for three months. If the tenant moves or skips out before three months, you refill the apartment at no charge. The same rental agencies require the tenant to pay first month's rent, last month's rent, and a security deposit equal to one month's rent in advance. What does that equal? Exactly. It equals three months' rent! So guaranteeing a tenant for three months is no skin off the agent's nose. The whole thing is wired together in advance!

Although many states require rental agents to hold a valid real estate license, I personally know unlicensed people who provide this service and who have been doing so for many years. The licensing requirement may or may not present a problem to the identity changer. If you are simply seeking privacy or personal freedom, you might wish to take steps to obtain the proper license after your business turns profitable.

If you decide to conduct your business without a license, it is only considered a misdemeanor in most states, and any fines involved are minimal. If you are ever caught, you can continue your operation under a new name and address.

Artistically Inclined

If you're the type who has always dreamed of becoming an artist or using your existing artistic skills to make a living, then why not do so now? What did you want a new life for anyway? To be trapped in the same old boring office routine? No. Most folks who pick up a book like this do so because they envision a new life—a romance. So, if you're going to make a change, why not follow that old dream. Be a romantic. Live your dream. You've heard the expression before: great artists aren't born, they're made. Who makes them? I believe they make themselves. They make the decision to bring the art outward. And many of them make some good money at it too.

Artists, Visual

If you're a painter, sculptor, or computer media wizard, there is money to be made. Many visual artisans sell their wares at art colonies, tourist strips, vacation spots, and county fairs. Less common, but considerably more profitable, is to exhibit your work at art shows and auctions in the hopes of selling a piece and obtaining recognition.

These latter situations present no problem for the identity changer because most of the business transactions can be handled by an agent. It is highly unlikely that an agent or gallery owner will request identification from you. There's simply no reason for it.

Some artists act as their own agents. They show their own work under a different name, deal with the museums and gallery owners, and take in all the feedback, criticism, and compliments, never admitting they are responsible for the work.

Even though I've never seen it done, I've often wondered what would happen if the "agent," at some point after the artist becomes well known, announces that the artist has died. It's really not commonplace for an artist's work to go up in value after death, but many people think it is. Would they then bid higher at auction? I wonder.

Crafts

Okay, so you're no Rembrandt or Michelangelo. Do you happen to have a knack for painting cute little figures on slate or making Christmas ornaments out of what most people consider trash? Is there some other craft at which you've become adept? Well, if it's novel enough, you can sell it. If it's completely stupid, you can make millions! To wit: fuzzy dice, pet rocks, pogs, beanie babies, etc. You can sell your wares at consignment shops, flea markets (see subheading below), or in mall kiosks, where it's not uncommon for cheap space to become available around holidays and special events.

If you're new to marketing crafts, try to remember that novel ideas work best. If it's new, different, and awe inspiring, you can make some good dough. If it's so cute it makes you want to throw up, your product will probably be very successful.

Musicians

There are a lot of people out there who play an instrument or sing very well but have never considered performing in front of an audience. Maybe your mother forced you to take piano lessons and you've vowed never to play again. Perchance you played the kettledrum in the high school band and you hated your instructor because he had bad breath.

I know you're out there. Ever thought about playing again?

Regardless of how you acquired your musical abilities and whether or not you still use them, there's plenty of money to be made and, more often than not, the income is tax free.

Tax free? Do you think the dude strummin' away in the subway station or city square goes home at night and does his books? Do you think the country band playing until 2 A.M. at Jumpin' Pete's Café files a quarterly return? Like I said, tax free.

I've never seen a nightclub owner issue 1099-MISC forms to band members. Occasionally the owner will have the band leader sign a receipt so that he can deduct band expenses on the club's own returns, but that's as far as it ever goes.

I've done my own stints in blues bands, and I've never received a 1099-MISC form. Ever. I've never had a club owner ask me if I was using an alias, and nobody ever asked to see my ID, not even when purchasing alcohol as a band member.

In reality, you could be anyone. Nobody cares who you are, and nobody asks. It's a largely unregulated industry and too small to attract the attention of the IRS. The IRS knows that most people in the music industry live below the poverty line anyway. Even if they were forced to file returns, the IRS would be owed little, if any, money. Certainly not enough to justify the expense of a crackdown.

The nightclub end of the music industry is wonderfully anonymous and, speaking from personal experience, you can make very good money. Minimum payment for a wedding band member is $125 for a four-hour gig. About $250 is more typical, and $500 is not uncommon.

Typical payments for members of a nightclub band are $50 a night for Tuesdays and Wednesdays, $75 for Thursdays and Sundays, and $100 for Fridays and Saturdays. Working four-hour nights Wednesday through Sunday, you can take in a minimum of $400 per week. Not bad for a part-time job.

Being "on the road" is not as hard as most sappy songs on the subject would have you believe. Many times you are playing the same club two or three nights in a row, so the torture of travel and the physical labor of setting up, breaking down, and moving the equipment is not as much of a hassle as most people think. I had nothing but fun in that business.

Automotive Repair

I picked an average town from my ProCD Select Phone database and counted the total number of listings. There were 10,000 listings. I then limited the search to automobile repair shops. There were 40 listings. This means that, on average, there is one automobile repair shop for every 250 households in the United States. At two cars per household, that's one shop for every 500 cars. Figuring the average car is in the shop three times a year, that's 1,500 visits per year per garage, or five visits per day per garage (at 300 working days per year).

Services range from a tuneup at about $60 to transmission and engine replacements running upward of $4,000 to $6,000. Conservatively figuring the average profit at $400, the *average* suburban shop is grossing $2,000 per day.

Do people say you're mechanically inclined? Have you ever been called a "grease monkey"? Perhaps you were never the type to fork over five Ben Franklins every time you visited your mechanic, so you became a do-it-yourselfer like yours truly.

Regardless of how you gained it, if you have the ability to fix automobiles and you let people know about it, they will flock to your garage as long as your prices remain competitive. People love to hear about some genius dude or dudette home mechanic who can fix cars like there's no tomorrow and will gladly do so at significant savings. Typically, these home mechanics have waiting lists much longer than the so-called professionals do.

When I was a poor teen, there was an 80-something-year-old guy whose backyard looked like a multicar pileup. There were junked cars and parts strewn all over the place, and the whole neighborhood smelled like used motor oil. When I sensed some forthcoming engine trouble that I knew I wouldn't be able to handle myself, a friend of mine told me to go to the old man for an estimate. I did. I was given an estimate of $5 per hour for about four hours worth of work. Great! When can I come back? He pointed to a calendar and said, "Write your name in the next white space." It was April, and the calendar had already been flipped to June! He advised me to "baby the car for the next couple of months. She'll make it."

He was right. Two months later he remembered me *and* the price, and about four hours later I came to pick up my car, which was running smoothly.

I never knew the guy's name, and I never thought to ask. He could've been anybody and it wouldn't have mattered.

If you have the ability to fix cars, you can do so under any identity. Many states do not have licensing requirements, and even in the ones that do, you will generally not get cracked down on if you are working by word of mouth for "friends" in your own garage. Your yard cannot look like a serious car wreck, though, or you will receive complaints. It's best to have a garage—it'll be less disturbing to your neighbors, as they will not be able to see nor hear you working, and you'll need it to store your tools and have a warm place to work once winter arrives anyway.

Used Car Dealer

If you're mechanically inclined, you can buy used cars and sell them at a profit. The backyard mechanic-dealer buys cars with semiserious problems, such as those needing a clutch, engine, or extensive body work. The mechanic-dealer then builds "sweat equity" into the vehicle by fixing the problem. Once the car is fixed, vacuumed out, washed, and waxed, it can be resold for a profit of anywhere between a $200 and $2,000, depending on what was wrong with it.

If you're a hard-core identity changer and you'd rather not deal with title transfers and registry clerks, you can use the following method, which is used by one of my clients, whom we'll call "Fred." The equity is built into the car as described above. However, title transfer is handled differently.

Fred looks through used car advertisements for hard-to-sell vehicles. Such an ad would read like, "1996 Ford F250 Pickup, seized engine, tow it away for $1,500." Fred knows that the poor bastard who ran the ad is probably desperate to move the vehicle. Who wants to buy a truck that doesn't run? Few people other than Fred, that's who. So, Fred calls the poor bastard and says, "Hey, poor bastard, I'd hate to see you take a hit on your truck. You could easily get $6,500 if you put a new engine in it."

"Yeah, but the garage wants $5,500 to put the new engine in," says the poor bastard.

Fred says, "Look, I'm a mechanic but I hate dealing with registry clerks. I'll tell you what. You buy a short block for $1,200 and I'll install it. When the vehicle sells, you keep $1,200 for the engine, plus the $1,500 you wanted in your ad, plus another $1,500 profit for working with me. I get anything over that, but I have to agree to the selling price and we have to have the whole deal in writing."

Most poor bastards say yes to Fred. In the above example, if they get the full $6,500 selling price, Fred makes $2,300. Not bad for a week's work, huh?

The sellers never ask him for ID, and Fred can use any name he wants in the contract. Since sellers are scared to violate a seemingly valid contract, they pay him what he is owed and Fred is on to the next job.

I do realize that some of you mechanically inclined folks still aren't willing to undertake engine replacements and the like, but the same principal can work on a smaller scale with ads for cars that, for instance, "need brakes," or "have a clutch slipping."

I have no experience with other twists on this idea, but I'm sure there are other items (computer systems, refrigerators, furniture) with which it could be used.

Baby-Sitting

This one's self-explanatory. It's best reserved for college-age females. If you're asked for identification, show them your student ID! (See Chapter 3, "How to Manufacture Professional-Quality Identity Documents.") Be prepared to work for minimum wage.

Bottle and Can Collecting

Although considerably less fashionable than most of the jobs we've discussed thus far, can collecting can help you bootstrap from ground zero or get you through a bad week. In order to make this occupation worthwhile, you must live in or relocate to a state that has enacted a so-called bottle bill. In New York, the law is the "Returnable Beverage Container Act" and was implemented in September 1983. Altogether, there are 10 states that have enacted such a bill:

TABLE 8.1: Container Deposit/Redemption by State

STATE	POLICY
California	Cash refund
Connecticut	Redeem 5¢ deposit
Delaware	Redeem 5¢ deposit
Iowa	Redeem 5¢ deposit
Maine	Redeem 5¢ deposit
Massachusetts	Redeem 5¢ deposit
Michigan	Redeem 10¢ deposit
New York	Redeem 5¢ deposit
Oregon	Redeem 5¢ deposit
Vermont	Redeem 5¢ deposit

The Bottle Bill

Bottle bills floundered among various northeastern legislatures throughout the 1970s. Some were enacted briefly and then repealed. The first one to stick was the one enacted by New York in 1983. The bills were designed to encourage recycling of such beverage containers as beer and soda cans. Some jurisdictions have expanded the bill to include the larger two and three-liter soda bottles, juice containers, and wine bottles.

Basically, the law states that all retail establishments selling beverages in subject containers must collect from each purchaser a sum of money—usually five cents—as a "deposit" for each container. In other words, if you buy a six pack of beer that sells for $5, you will be charged $5.30 assuming a five cent deposit and no tax.

When you are done getting shit-faced, you bring the six cans back to the store and the proprietor gets grumpy and gives you back your thirty cents so you can buy a pack of gum (or not). Most people hang on to their bottles and cans until they've stored up a few cases and then take the empties back to the store.

Alternatively, you can take your empties purchased from various stores to a redemption center set up for exactly that purpose. Some states say it is illegal to take an empty from one state and return it to another. In practice, this is seldom enforced because most bottles and cans are stamped as being returnable in more than one state, and there is no way to enforce such a requirement. For example, in the northeast, empties may be stamped as follows:

Nationally distributed containers:
    NY-MA-OR-ME 5¢ MI 10¢
    IA-VT-CT-DE 5¢
    CA CASH REFUND
National companies, regionally bottled:
    ME-VT-CT-MA-NY
    REFUND 5¢

Locally bottled and distributed containers may only be stamped with their home state.

If your state has enacted a bottle bill, you probably know this already and are wondering why I'm taking the time to explain it. I'm explaining it because, though it may have been a part of your life for many years, most states still haven't enacted one and most people reading this book haven't the foggiest idea what a bottle bill is!

If you're not sure whether your state has enacted a bottle bill, there are two ways to tell.

Go to any big city and watch the homeless population. Do you see anybody in month-old clothing pushing a stolen shopping cart full of dirty cans and bottles? Chances are your state has enacted a bottle bill.

The other way to tell is to buy a can of cola for $.99. Did the clerk charge you $1.04? If you're not a numbers person, read the side of the container. It will either tell you in which states the container is redeemable, or it will say, "No Deposit No Return—Please Recycle" or words to that effect.

Can Collecting Basics

Even if your state (or target state) has enacted a bottle bill, you've probably already figured that it takes a good many empties to buy a pepperoni and cheese pizza. Therefore, can collecting for the average, upstanding citizen is not a worthwhile undertaking. But if you've disappeared in a puff of smoke recently and forgot to take your wallet, the empty six-pack thrown out of some teenager's car window will buy you a box of macaroni and cheese. This drive-by gift will tide you over while you're working out your next move.

For those of you who already knew about bottle bills but read through this whole section anyway, here's something you may not have already known.

Stretching Your Redemption Dollar

Occasionally, a redemption center will offer an increased redemption rate. Sometimes the state is having a "Keep Our State Clean" recycling drive, trying to raise awareness about the bottle bill, or conditioning people to participate in the bottle bill scheme. Other times, a new redemption center opens up and it wants to get your attention. Whatever the reason, you may wish to be on the lookout for such events. The drives here in New York usually offer six or seven cents for a five-cent container.

Anonymous Redemption

A company named ENVIPCO has invented a reverse vending machine. You put your empties in the machine and the machine gives you the appropriate sum of money. No need to deal with snotty clerks.

Become a Redemption Center

If you're not overly concerned about keeping a low profile, you may wish to start your own redemption center. If you live in a centralized location, you may qualify under a state redemption plan. A redemption center receives a handling fee for every can it collects; that's how they get paid.

Also, some states annually apportion proceeds from unredeemed cans among recognized redemption centers. For example if your state has a surplus of $10 million, $2.5 million may be allocated to redemption centers and beverage dealers. If your small redemption center is responsible for .1 percent of annual volume, you will receive a check for $2,500.

Bum

My subletting friend mentioned later under the real estate subheading once hired a guy to help him move one of his tenants. He saw the guy on the sidewalk with a sign that said "Will work for food." This particular "bum" admitted averaging $260 per day—yes, that's per *day*.

Even though the sign said "Will work for food," the bum knew most people would pay him cash because they felt sorry for him. Out of guilt, most people paid him quite well.

Casinos

It's impossible to beat the casinos. The only exception to this rule is blackjack. A well-disciplined person, willing to settle for modest winnings on a regular basis rather than "hitting it big" in one night, can make a living at blackjack. My father taught me the actual card counting schemes and techniques, which are beyond the scope of this book. I cannot personally recommend any books or videos because I've never needed them. However, I do know that there are books, videos, and "courses" available on the subject You'll have to determine on your own which ones are right for you.

The techniques employ easy counting schemes to detect when the house is at a disadvantage. When the house is at an advantage, keep your bets low. When the house is at a disadvantage, bet heavier. This is similar to the "one for bad, two for good" scheme used in the movie *Rainman*. At the end of *most* nights, you will be ahead. It's a tedious process, but it does work.

If you are gifted in the concentration and numbers departments, you may wish to develop your own, more sophisticated counting schemes after learning the basic principles of the game. If your gifts are exceptional, you will make even more money at blackjack. In any case, don't expect to win big—that will only do you in.

Contractor

This sphere of employment is very informal. You can show up at a job site, sometimes without tools, and ask to work. If there's an opening, the foreman will try you out for a day, usually on cleanup or lugging detail. If he likes you, you'll be asked to work as an independent contractor. You can use any name you like, even a business name.

The above holds true more often for small job sites. But I've worked on local housing projects, which are usually good-sized jobs, without having to give anybody my real name. Often you are paid in cash.

But the real money in contracting is when you're your own boss . . .

Pick One Skill and Specialize

Many of us are skilled in at least one area of home improvement. Perhaps you once built a deck for your grandmother or helped your neighbor with a roofing job. I developed my personal "specialty" after helping a friend vinyl-side a house he was rehabbing.

Even if you're not a skilled carpenter, you can get a job as a runner or laborer for someone who is. Ask questions. Offer to help with construction for a reduced wage in exchange for pointers. Learn one, simple trade such as vinyl siding and offer yourself to the public as a "specialist" in that field. Are you a specialist? If that's all you do, then you specialize in it, right? Okay then, you're a specialist.

Licenses and Permits

Many states have no licensing requirement for many types of construction. Even where a license is required, it's still pretty easy to get work without one.

Local construction permit requirements are more of a problem. Just about anything except painting and wallpapering requires a construction permit. There are two ways around this:

- Have the owner pull the permit.
- Don't pull a permit.

Having the owner pull the permit is a common practice in the industry. In this way, contractors move liability from themselves onto the owner. Many owners go along with this if your price is right. More important for the identity changer, you don't have to go to city hall with a contractor's license.

Not pulling a permit happens about a thousand times a day. If you get caught, simply tell the owner that the nice inspector man stopped by and requested the owner get a permit at town hall first thing in the morning.

Contracts: Getting Paid up Front

Every job you do should be in writing. This protects your interests because most people are afraid to violate contracts. Even though the hard-core identity changer would probably not want to sue under his or her alias, just the threat of a contract-backed suit keeps most people in line. Also, due to the statute of frauds, a contract is required if you intend to file a mechanic's lien against a property you've worked on or supplied materials for but were not paid for.

But the real beauty of a contract is that it gives you the opportunity to plainly spell out payment terms. There were a couple of times in my life where I had to "specialize" in vinyl siding. I created my own job security by adding a week's pay to my materials estimate. On big jobs I would add two or more weeks' pay. My contract required the owner to pay up front for materials. This meant that before I even started the job, I had at least a week's pay in the bank.

Because my vinyl siding business was small (I often worked alone), an average job would take me two weeks to complete. Thus, my contract stated that the second payment of half the remaining balance was due after one week and the final payment was due on completion. If the middle payment didn't come, I would have stopped working, knowing that I'd already been paid for my time. If the last payment didn't come, I would've written it off, figuring I'd already paid myself. Luckily this never happened, but having job security kept me relaxed about my financial affairs.

Becoming a Donor

Becoming a donor doesn't exactly sound like a way to make money, I know. But there are some types of donations for which you can be paid.

Blood

These days it's hard to make money donating blood. There are so many good folks out there givin' the stuff away that one can seldom find a paying "blood drive." Besides, it's physically impossible to donate often enough to make a living at it—even if you find a blood bank that does pay. A better bet is donating plasma.

Plasma

There are labs scattered throughout the country that pay reasonably well for your donated plasma. You can make between $120 and $200 per month, depending on the lab.

You can make more money donating plasma because more places will pay you for it, and you can do it frequently. The process takes about an hour, for which you are compensated $15 to $20 at the time of this writing. Since your red blood cells are returned to you after the plasma is extracted, you can repeat the process every three to four days.

The process is safe, and if you live close enough to one of these facilities, you can make a good supplemental income donating plasma.

Sperm

Sorry, ladies. Obviously not an option for you. However, there are egg donor and surrogate mother programs that pay very well—much better, in fact

Here's how the typical sperm donating scenario plays out. Since I know you're all wondering, I'll tell you up front: yes, you do have to masturbate. No, a nurse won't do it for you. Okay?

Shortly after your first contact with a sperm bank, you will be interviewed by telephone. The interview is to determine whether you fall within the bank's predetermined "standards." What they are really screening for is to make sure you are reasonably monogamous, not a drug addict, and have attained at least a high school diploma or college degree, depending on the bank. If you pass the phone interview, you will be invited to the bank to complete a comprehensive questionnaire, whereby you will be asked questions about yourself, your siblings, parents, and grandparents.

The bank will review the questionnaire and, if it's acceptable, invite you back for sample donations. They will usually set up two appointments just two or three days apart and do sperm counts on your samples. They are testing to see how fast you regenerate sperm and how well your sperm survives freezing. It's best if you eat right, exercise, and wear boxer shorts before and during the testing period.

If they still like you after checking all that, their staff MD will give you a complete physical examination. If all is well, they will draw more blood and semen samples and perform a battery of tests.

If all the results are acceptable, you will become a regular, paid, anonymous donor. You are required to agree to remain a donor for some specified minimum length of time (usually around one year) and required to make donations as many as three times a week. You will be expected to undergo periodic blood testing and return for final blood testing six months after you stop donating.

This might sound like a lot to go through, but for the privacy seeker it's all how you look at it. Initially you may say, "Privacy? How can anything be *less* private?" But you are not dealing with a public hospital; you are dealing with a private company that will destroy its records after five or so years, unless you request otherwise. The tests the company performs, while invasive, are worth thousands of dollars and invaluable to your sense of well-being. What better than to know from qualified, *financially interested* physicians that your blood and semen are free of disease and impurity?

Pay ranges from $35 to $75 for acceptable donations, depending on the facility. Urban facilities pay better than rural ones.

Unless you request otherwise, most banks will destroy your records a set number of years after your last donation. The recipient of your sperm will never be allowed to learn your true identity (if indeed you ever gave it). Likewise, you will never know the identity of the recipients or of any children you may have spawned.

Medical Prostitution

Another way your body can "work" for you is as a guinea pig for the medical profession. Yes, it's true. After medicines have been tested on rats and monkeys, the Food and Drug Administration (FDA) still requires testing on humans before the drug can be brought to market. Such studies are always FDA approved, and human volunteers are always in demand. Look through the Sunday classifieds sometime. You'll see occasional ads that read something like:

HAVE AN ULCER?

Healthy nonsmoking men aged 18 to 55 wanted for FDA-approved drug study. Earn $260 for visits.
Call for details: 111-1111

DEPRESSED?

Depression study at Virginia University. Men and women Aged 25–45. FDA-approved drug.
Ten weekends $1655. Call Tanya: 611-4567

There are many such opportunities. Some require one two-hour outpatient visit for as little as four weeks, while others require you to be sequestered for two weeks at a time. The latter types pay much better, but you best like to read!

Be Considerate

One final note: if you donate blood, plasma, or sperm under a new identity, please leave a way for the facilities to contact you in case of an emergency, even if by anonymous e-mail or a mail drop.

What kind of emergency could arise? In the case of sperm donation, the child may develop a medical condition, and doctors may need some additional information from you that could save her life. In the case of blood or plasma donation, the doctors may find something in your blood that you need to know about—something that might save *your* life.

Find Money

Unless you have extremely minimal living expenses, you will not be able to support yourself by finding money. But keeping an eye peeled in the right places at the right time could supplement your monthly income.

Most of us have accidentally happened upon a $1, $5, $10, or $20 bill at one time in our lives. These bills are in wide circulation and therefore more subject to becoming lost. I've never tried to be an active money finder, but even so, in my lifetime I've found:

- Probably a dozen $1 bills
- Three $5 bills near gas stations
- One $5 bill in a supermarket
- One $10 bill outside a supermarket
- One $10 bill outside a donut shop
- Three $5 bills rolled up with a $1 bill outside a bar
- One $20 bill outside a bar
- One $20 bill in the street
- $146 in an envelope next to an ATM
- An 18 karat gold chain outside a college
- An LCD watch with alarm function at the beach

It's certainly not a huge income when spread out over the course of a lifetime, but even this short list establishes an obvious pattern of where people are likely to lose money.

Two of the three fivers I found near gas stations were found the same day about 10 feet apart. I found the first one quite accidentally but immediately figured it blew over from the gas station across the street. So I backtracked a bit and continued walking with the intent of finding more. This was the only time in my life where I actually tried to find money. And it worked. In less than a minute, I found another one. The other fiver I found many years later when using a red box (See *Electronic Circuits and Secrets*, Chapter 4) at a gas station pay phone. The bill was right beneath the phone box, so I stepped on it. Nobody seemed to notice, care, or be looking for anything, so I scooped it up.

Given the above information, it stands to reason that an identity changer just starting out may wish to keep his or her eyes peeled around gas stations, stores, restaurants, and bars where people are in a rush (or drunk) and still in the process of pocketing their change. Money finders may wish to scour circuses, carnivals, flea markets, fairs, and campgrounds in search of easy income.

Horse and dog racetrack parking lots are also a big hit. My uncle used to take me to the see the dogs when I was little. He'd have me and my cousin searching the floor for possible winning tickets anytime an "inquiry" was called. Once, after the announcer had screamed, "And it's Sidewinder by a nose!" about 300 drunk people threw down their tickets in disgust. A second later when the "inquiry" light came on, my uncle had us scuttling between angry legs to pick up tickets off the sticky, beer-drenched racetrack floor. We all moved to a quiet closed-circuit screen inside and waited for the announcement. It turned out that Sidewinder didn't win after all but that the announcer needed a new pair of goggles. This was before the machine-readable days, and we were holding half a dozen winning tickets quite possibly owned by angry mobsters. We cashed out fast and decided to call it a day.

I never did find out how much my uncle made, but he gave us each two "sawbucks" and a "fin," which was the first time I ever heard those words used that way. Twenty-five buckeroonies was a lot of money for a kid back then. I suspect my uncle took in upward of a grand at least.

Using a Metal Detector

A metal detector takes money finding to new levels. You will not make a great hourly wage, but if you love doing it, it will certainly pay for itself. Best places to search are beaches, old carnival grounds, amusement parks, and construction sites.

Flea Markets

Many people make money by buying space at a weekend flea market and dealing in goods that they are knowledgeable about. It's very inexpensive to rent space, and in most cases nobody will ask to see your ID.

Flea market traders are like watered-down antique brokers, only their job is less risky. Because they have a general knowledge of what sells at flea markets and for how much, weekend traders will shop yard sales, estate sales, and classifieds for popular items but pay no more than half their flea market value. The business is quite profitable and, of course, tax free.

Other weekend traders specialize in a particular area of expertise. For example, you'll always find at least one stamp collector and one coin collector at any given flea market, although they are often the same person. About half of the fleas will have someone dealing in used musical instruments and accessories. The latest flea market specialty, however, is computers and periphery. These people are making a killing selling shined up, outdated personal computer packages to newcomers who aren't aware that computer prices have fallen dramatically as technology has advanced.

You can make a good, private, and anonymous living in this business working only part time. I know two people who do.

Game Shows

Not private. Not tax free. And ID will be required. However, an unhealthy knowledge of trivia or the uncanny ability to guess the prices of commercial products is not a bad way to make a quick $25,000 for an ID time capsule you have set to go off in, say, 12 to 18 months.

Gardening and Farming

This is not something I would recommend unless you love to do it. The hours are long, the risks are high, and it pays very little. However, the occupation offers many advantages in the way of privacy and identity changing. First and highly underrated is its closeness to nature. Working with the Earth's soil and bringing things to life which in turn sustain life is a very mind-broadening experience. If you are trying to free yourself from the reins of Corporate America, becoming one with nature is the way to do it. Bringing a garden to life and watching it die year after year really helps put things in perspective. You begin to realize all the corporate fringe benefits and Social Security in the world doesn't amount to a hill of fresh stringbeans in life's grand garden of opportunity. You truly develop a new world perspective while learning to depend on yourself.

You do not usually need to have any identification to rent land and farm it. In cases where you do, you may wish to consult Chapter 3, "How to Manufacture Professional-Quality Identity Documents."

Farm equipment can be expensive, but if you start small, you can do a lot by hand. As your business grows, you can invest some of your earnings in used equipment. The seller will transfer title to any name you give him and in many cases deliver the equipment right to your door. As long as you don't take the equipment on public roads, you will not have to register it.

If you've no experience whatsoever with raising vegetables, I suggest you keep a garden for a few years and learn as much as you can before trying to live as a farmer. There are hundreds of good books on gardening and the business of farming. I am sure you'll find some useful ones at your local library. While you're learning, you can save a lot of money on your weekly grocery bill too.

Investor

If you have a little nest egg set aside for a rainy day, you may want to shoe box it for a year or so before doing your impression of David Copperfield. A nice wad of cash can produce income for you if know what you're doing.

Stock Market

Risky and not recommended unless you have at least a hundred Gs to play with. Even still, it's harder to move money under an assumed identity. If you do insist on living off stocks in your quest for privacy, just be sure to have a diverse portfolio and try to pick long-standing stocks that pay a dividend.

Mutual Funds

Mutual funds are a much safer play for many reasons. Mutual funds are, by definition, more stable. You have thousands to choose from, many of which do not charge up-front or back-end fees but rather a small percentage of the firm's annual profits. These are called "no-load" mutual funds, and the percentage they charge is usually in the range of 1 percent.

You will need to choose stable no-load mutual funds that offer so-called "check writing privileges." This does not mean you can use your mutual fund account like a checkbook, though in some cases you could. Most companies that offer check-writing privileges have minimum withdrawal requirements, limits on how often you can withdraw, and fees associated with each check you write. For example, one company may only allow you to withdraw a minimum of $100 no more than twice a month at a 1.5 percent service charge.

This may not sound like such a big advantage. That's because, financially speaking, it's not. However, it is much easier to move your money around when you are compelled to do so. If, for some unimaginable reason, you need $2,000 from that account in a hurry, you can write yourself a $2,000 check. No need to call the mutual fund company, speak to a service representative, get the procedure, and have forms sent to you, which in most cases will have to be "signature guaranteed" before you can ever lay finger on your own money.

When researching mutual funds, ask the customer service rep what the procedure is for closing the account. If you hear the word "signature guarantee," scream "Oh God, no!" and hang up the phone. If a signature guarantee is required to cash out your account, you'll have to wait to have forms sent to you, then you'll have to take those forms to a bank and convince the bank manager to guarantee your signature. You probably won't get very far unless you have an account with the bank. Even if you have an account, you will need to produce some ID. In this case, a library card ain't gonna cut it. The manager who's putting out her neck for you will want to see a driver's license and will scrutinize the license well. You will sweat. It will not be fun. It may not work.

Not that a signature guarantee is impossible to obtain under a new identity. Certainly there are techniques outlined in this book that will allow you to obtain signature guarantees and notary signatures when the situation arises. But why unnecessarily impose such uncomfortable risks on yourself? Simply find a fund that doesn't require a signature guarantee.

Insider Trading

The Securities Exchange Commission is pretty clear on its policy of insider trading. But what if you live near some insiders who don't care about the SEC? What if you parked your van on Wall Street and scanned cellular telephone frequencies? (See *Circuits and Secrets*, Chapter 5.) What if these insiders just loved to talk? And if you should happen to learn that Ex Why Zee Corporation has reached a favorable, yet to be announced, out-of-court settlement . . . what? Like you're *not* going to buy a few thousand shares because the SEC might find out? I'd be in my broker's office before the insiders hung up their phones.

Landscaper

Besides being anonymous, tax free, and outdoorsy, a landscaping business is one of the easiest to establish. The biggest hurdle is acquiring the necessary equipment to do a good, yet quick, job. Once this is done, however, you can have as much work as you desire.

There are a few reasons for this. Americans are living longer and the trend is toward a more white-collar work force. This means there are many older people out there who need yard work done and fewer young people willing to do it.

The quickest way to get started is by advertising that you do lawn mowing rather than the more general "landscaping." People who specialize in lawn mowing are even scarcer than landscapers. This is because most people who start mowing businesses immediately find better opportunities doing lawn and sprinkler installations, mulching, and tree removal, which are considerably more profitable.

Once you get some clients, be dependable and give them at least two good seasons before moving onto bigger and better things. There are so many people out there used to fly-by-night landscapers that these clients will spread your good name around, telling all their elderly friends that you are a landscaping god.

Equipment

At the very minimum you will need a lawn mower. Many people have actually started a landscaping business with nothing more. The only problem with this minimum setup is that pushing a lawn mower all day long is *hard* work!

Even the completely destitute can be successful landscaping upstarts because used lawnmowers are ridiculously cheap. In fact, get up early some trash day and take a drive before the garbagemen come. There's a good chance you'll find a working lawn mower in somebody's trash. The chances are greater in the spring and fall when people buy new lawn mowers. If possible, try to get one with a bagger on it. This cuts down on your raking time.

Gas Trimmer

Actually I did get away with using an electric trimmer, aka "weed whacker," for the first solo landscaping contracts I ever had. I'd won the trimmer in a vinyl siding sales contest. At the time I was more concerned with making money and less concerned with impressing customers, so I just used it. But if you're going to go out and buy a trimmer, make it a gas one. That way you don't have to look like a jerk by asking your customer to find an outlet and toss your extension cord out a window that's painted shut or otherwise inaccessible.

Besides, the main reason for the trimmer is to make some professional-sounding noises when you are done mowing the lawn. Gas trimmers make a lot of noise. Homeowners love that. It makes them feel as though somebody's taking care of them.

A trimmer is also a great gadget for getting in those tricky spots (e.g., inside flower beds, around the jungle gym), and it does help to put that professional finishing touch around the edges of the yard and house.

Oh yeah: no ID or professional license required!

Lottery

My college buddy, Fink, had a crazy lottery scheme. I won't get into why we called him Fink, but as crazy as his scheme was, it got him enough to buy a pizza and six-pack three out of four weekends a month. The scheme was based on a simple four-digit daily lottery, but I suppose it could be used on other kinds as well. It went something like this.

Fink would get the lottery results nightly. He'd only pay attention to the last number. When he noticed that one number hadn't hit for more than ten days, he'd start playing it for $1 a night. The liquor store dude thought he was a sicko—at first. Then he realized this sicko was, more often than not, paying for beer with winning lottery tickets.

And while he was there, *any* number that hadn't hit for ten days he'd play for a dollar. If there were three numbers that hadn't appeared in the last position for ten days, he'd play all three. Now, because of the way lotteries work, a player betting $1 could only win about $8. This is because the odds are one-in-ten, and the state needs to make a few bucks.

But even if Fink had to play a number five nights in a row, he'd still make $3. Maybe he was lucky, I don't know. But I saw this scheme work time and time again.

Mail-Order Business

A mail-order business can be established from a mail drop or a post office box. A mail drop, of course will let you use a natural-sounding street address (*MIC*, Chapter 4), which is usually better for business.

A mail-order business can provide you with tax-free income, privacy, anonymity, and flexible work hours. Here's a short list of good-mail order businesses for the privacy seeker and identity changer.

Resident Agent Services

A resident agent is somebody to whom process can be served against a corporation. Any corporation doing business outside its home state must appoint a resident agent in that state.

As mentioned later in this chapter, most of these outfits try to sell you more than you really need and charge way too much money doing it. My suggestion: move to Nevada or Wyoming and offer only corporate resident agent, nominee, and bank account services for people who don't mind doing the paperwork and filing themselves.

Want a competitive edge? Include minimal phone and mail service for a nominal charge above your standard fee. This is something the other services don't do. They either don't provide it or they charge big bucks for the service. I would suggest five pieces of mail per month and one phone message per week for $5 plus the cost of stamps and phone calls.

This job is obviously more suited to the privacy seeker than the hard-core identity changer, but it can produce a substantial income for a minimal investment of time, labor, and startup capital. Anybody who starts such a business (legitimately) may advertise it on my Web sites (www.phreak.co.uk/sxc or www.sxc.8m.com) for free at my discretion.

Book Distributor

Buy your favorite books in quantity and resell them at a profit. You can do this anonymously from the Web. Most publishers will want to see a tax resale certificate, which can be in your business name. Many publishers, however, especially established ones, will require you to fill out a credit reference form as well. You *might* be able to avoid this if you pay cash up front and never try to return unsold books. If need be, your business can establish credit with a local bank, wholesaler, or another business owned by a "friend" (read: alternate ID). Just pay your bills on time and refrain from using these tactics to defraud book publishers and you're probably not doing anything too illegal.

Survival Kit Distributor

Send ads for a *Bankruptcy Survival Kit* to people who've recently filed for bankruptcy. This information is public record. You can sell your advice package for $19.95.

Send a *Divorce Survival Kit: How to Come Out Holding the Big Stick* ad to people who have just filed for divorce. You'll get two potential customers with each public record you look up!

Bankruptcies can be gleaned from county deed registries, and divorce records can be looked up at probate court. Some deeds registries may not list bankruptcy cases outright. In this case, look for dispositions of judgments, often abbreviated DISP JGMT. Open the file and see if the disposition was in fact a bankruptcy. It usually is.

Just some ideas I've seen. You get the picture.

Paperboys and Papergirls

Paperboys and papergirls are becoming a thing of the past. With all the child predators roaming the streets these days, few parents allow their children to become paperpeople.

These days you have the paper guy. You know, he's the guy that you hear pull his car up outside your bedroom window every morning at 4 A.M. You used to see a cute kid at your door every week saying "collecting." Now you get an impersonal bill in the mail demanding 13 weeks' payment before your subscription is renewed or a small manila envelope folded in your Sunday paper that accusingly says "$6.40 PAST DUE!" in green ink from a leaky pen.

Well, you can be a paper guy, too. No ID required. You're an independent contractor, and the job completely sucks. Why? Because you have to do it every single day, rain, snow, sleet, or shine, Christmas, New Year's, and Groundhog Day—no exceptions. Well, some of that may be changing . . .

Because overweight, hungover, butt-smoking paper guys are less resilient than 12-year-olds, distributors can't find many willing to commit to a daily routine. So many distributors are offering shared routes where you do only one day or more every week. Some people share an entire route and do every other week. Others just do weekends or weekdays.

In places with a dense population, you can pull in about $800 per month if you work four hours every morning. Once you become known as the paper person, the cops will leave you alone. Before that, it's important to make your paper person status as obvious as possible. Be sure to put the *Daily Post Examiner Times Globe Inquirer* bumper sticker on your car and stack the papers high in the backseat so the patrols don't think you're a 4 A.M. pervert.

If you're car-o-phobic because you don't want to get stopped and questioned, you can use a moped or bicycle if the customers are close together. All in all, a good job for identity changers just starting out.

Private Detective

They silently slide around behind unsuspecting perpetrators, have close friends on the police force willing to bend the law for them, and can commandeer a helicopter on a moment's notice. Sexy clients come out of the blue every week and fall hopelessly in love with them, and they solve every case that comes across their desk. Such is the modern detective.

Well, despite what most TV shows would have you believe, it's nothing at all like that. Perpetrators are seldom unsuspecting, people with city jobs (cops) do not risk them to do you favors, and it takes hundreds of hours of expensive training to learn how to fly helicopters. The bland fact is that a modern detective is more likely to be found in a records hall or at a computer writing boring and uneventful reports.

But the stereotypes remain. Thus, one advantage to this line of work is that you can use your occupation as a ready-made excuse for possessing false identification if you are ever questioned by authorities. People (this includes cops) *expect* you to have believable, ready-made aliases if you are a private detective. This is also a great defense if you are ever prosecuted under the False Identification Crime Control Act of 1982 or other related statutes (*MIC*, Appendix C).

Many states have licensing requirements, but there are a handful of states that don't. Licensing requirements for this profession are very easy to get around as long as you don't run a full-page newspaper ad or have a listing in the yellow pages. The sphincter police check these sources to stop unlicensed detectives from stealing their business. An easy way around state licensing requirements is given below under the heading "General Notes On Licensing Requirements."

It's a good profession, it pays well, and nobody will ask you for ID. If somebody does, hold up a handful of novelty driver's licenses and say, "Pick a card, any card."

Heir Finder

An heir finder is a special kind of detective. Those of you who know me know that I had my start in heir finding. I usually performed this service under my own name, but I didn't have to. I still do heir finding today and, to date, I've never met any of the customers or state officials with whom I've had dealings. It's all been done over the phone and through the mail. Today I no longer accept phone calls. Everything is done by fax, e-mail, or snail mail.

I once performed the service under a woman's name just to see if more people would pay me. I made all bank deposits via ATMs and never had a bank refuse to accept a properly endorsed check made out in the woman's name or any of various company names I've used.

Being an heir finder pays well, and you don't have to do it under your real name as long as you have a business or alternate ID bank account. Few states have licensing requirements. One exception is the Independent Republic of Texas, aka Capital Punishment Central.

Prostitute

Prostitution is legal in the state of Nevada. Registration requirements and periodic physical examinations are required.

Psychotherapist, Counselor

As distinguished from psychologists and psychiatrists, crisis counselors and psychotherapists are largely unregulated throughout the United States. Check your local and state laws to verify there are no licensing requirements. Some jurisdictions may require unlicensed practitioners to use specific wording or disclaimers in their advertisements.

Find a cheap office space, hang out your shingle, advertise in the phone book, and prepare to listen to a lot of complaining. Oftentimes that's all people want—to hire a shoulder to cry on. If you can offer them some advice, all the better.

Good money, usually free from government controls, low startup capital, easy-to-find customers. If things get rough, have a list of real doctors to whom you can refer seriously ill patients.

Real Estate

The real estate business offers many opportunities for the freedom oriented. Most people don't understand the industry. Even real estate professionals with whom I've worked were unclear about how it all fit together. Therefore, if you can understand it, you'll have a tremendous advantage over 99 percent of the population.

The general public perception is that the industry is a stew of legalities, boiling beyond comprehension. Most people buying a home would be lost without the real estate agent and attorney. Many folks believe that a document is not legal unless drawn up by an attorney, processed by a real estate agent, notarized, examined by the county records lawyers, and filed in a precise manner. The consensus is that one undotted I or uncrossed T can cause you to lose your life savings in real estate.

My good friends, none of these things are true. Once you learn how the industry really works, you can make a boatload of money doing any or all of the below. To begin unraveling the intricacies of this profession, read this book: *Real Estate Fundamentals, Fourth Edition Revised* by Wade E. Gaddy, Jr. and Robert E. Hart, Dearborn Publishing Group, Chicago, 1996. This is the book you will get if you sign up for a real estate licensing course, which is recommended. I also recommend studying general contract law. There should be plenty of material at your local library on both of these subjects.

Condominium Associations

By owning a controlling interest in or being a trustee of a condo association, you can pretty much decide who gets awarded the various contracts the condo puts out for bid. If you happen to be acquainted with certain landscaping, snow removal, cleaning, painting, contracting, locksmith, accounting, insurance, and property management companies, you may wish to award contracts to them. If you happen to own all these companies in trust, through corporations or under assumed identities, you best keep that information to yourself.

203K Loans

A 203K loan is a special loan awarded to homebuyers by the government. If you're buying a home in a low-income area that requires significant rehabbing, you may be eligible for such a loan.

For example, you may be paying $20,000 for a burned-out three-family apartment building located in a not-so-happy neighborhood. The fair market value of the building, if reconstructed, is $99,000. The government may give you a loan for $80,000: $23,000 for the purchase price and associated closing costs and $57,000 to be paid out to contractors you hire to fix your home.

Homeowners cannot charge for labor if they decide to do the work themselves. However, a company hired (read: set up and owned) by the homeowner will be paid according to the terms of the contract.

When the apartment building is fixed up, the owner sells it at a further profit. If it sells for a full $99,000 (in this example), then the owner makes $19,000 in addition to what the contracting companies made. People make ridiculous gobs of money like this everyday.

Be aware of constantly changing regulations. Just be sure you don't break any laws. If things change in the future, you may need a "friend" to hold title to the contracting companies. Some people do this anyway to avoid answering uncomfortable questions that may arise.

Home Inspector

A home inspector is hired by real estate purchasers to inspect the integrity of a home in which they are interested. Many states have no licensing requirement for home inspectors. You don't even need a contractor's license. The inspection report is not part of the final contract, nor is it recorded anywhere. Business can be advertised in the yellow pages or by word of mouth, and you can leave pamphlets in real estate offices. If they have a pamphlet from one company in their lobby, they must carry yours, too, or risk conflict-of-interest charges.

To make it in this business, you'll need a lot of general construction and mechanical knowledge, which I suspect many of you reading this have. Check out what other home inspectors are doing—what forms they use, how much they charge, where they advertise, etc.—and do the same. You will receive between $300 and $600 for your services, never be asked for credentials, and, with properly worded contracts, incur no liability for errors and omissions in your inspection reports. Have fun!

Real Estate Agent

Since the licensing exam only requires you to show a picture ID and not necessarily a driver's license, this is an easy profession to enter under a new identity. I still recommend bringing a driver's license with you to the testing center anyway. Chapter 3 will help you acquire a driver's license, and with it you won't have to answer the proctor's inevitable questions, "You don't drive? How did you get here?" If you're not up to making a license, refer to the section in Chapter 10 entitled "Why Don't You Have a Drivers' License?" for some ready-made answers to intrusive questions.

I hold a valid real estate broker's license and have been a salesperson in the past. Personally, I thought it sucked. I hated selling, still do, and always will. But I was surprised by how many of my fellow salespeople told me how much they loved the business. Truth be told, you can make some very good money, and if you don't mind selling you apparently can have a lot of fun at it. But if you're like me and spend two years selling houses only to discover you hate it, you can at least use your license to scout good locations for phony lock boxes (see Chapter 10, "Banking Privacy"), phantom mail drops (see *MIC*), and even phantom phone hookups (see Chapter 6, "Telephone Privacy").

My broker's license still comes in handy even though I don't work in a real estate office. Because they know I have some real estate experience, friends and family members usually come to me when they're looking to buy or sell a property. I then call an established real estate broker and work out a deal that benefits all parties involved, including myself. Typically, I end up receiving ten to twenty percent of the final commission without ever having to lift a finger. It's well worth renewing my license for an occasional $400 to $2,000. Even though mine is a broker's license, you could do the same thing with a salesperson's license.

Subletting

I have a friend who once leased a four-bedroom apartment. He only paid for half of it because a certain working alien needed a U.S. address but not the actual living accommodations.

When my friend lost his job, he placed a "Room for Rent" ad in the paper. He eventually rented out each room for $120 per week for a total of $1,560 per month. The contract rent for his lease was only $800 per month, which should have given him a gross profit of $760 per month, which is pretty good for a guy with no job. But because he was fortunate enough to know the resident alien (admittedly not a typical arrangement), my friend grossed $1,160 instead. After paying the electric and gas bill, he averaged about $950 per month—more than enough to buy food and an occasional bag of ganja.

He became very excited by his new-found venture and told me of his plans to lease property all over the city and then sublet rooms for income. Initially I had my doubts because it seemed like an awful lot of work, but he's still doing this today and making a good living at it.

Since he doesn't have to live in them, he sublets four rooms per apartment instead of three. I don't think he ever found one of those resident alien deals again, but he does try to find heated apartments with new wiring to keep overhead low.

I don't want to mislead you. Doing this with even one apartment is a lot of work and fraught with hassles. I remember one of his tenants stopped paying rent altogether. The tenant then got a restraining order against my friend. My friend couldn't so much as knock on the bedroom door to collect rent!

If you go this route, be careful and screen your tenants. Get a full month's security deposit in advance, and require rent to be paid weekly. That way, you have early warning if someone starts missing payments.

Road Samaritan

A road samaritan is a person who drives around and helps others who are broken down or otherwise in need of road assistance. A typical setup consists of a station wagon, van, or pickup truck stocked with equipment and supplies useful in a roadside emergency.

You can get underway with just a pair of jumper cables and a can of gasoline (heed state storage and transportation laws for gasoline). Bring some water, oil, and antifreeze, too. Here's a list of things you can acquire as your business grows.

Supplies

- Flares
- Five-gallon container of gasoline, preferably plastic with stowaway nozzle
- Jumper cables
- Antifreeze
- 50/50 water coolant mixture
- Oil (10W40 and 5W30 most common)
- Automatic transmission fluid (Dextron III should handle most situations)
- Windshield wash and squeegee
- Rags
- Paper towels
- Twelve-volt compressor, bicycle pump, compressed tire sealant such as Fix-A-Flat
- Hydraulic floor jack for quick, easy repairs
- Jack stands in case you need to get under the vehicle
- Four-way lug wrench
- Lubricant such as WD40 or 3-in-1 oil
- Lock deicer
- Lockout kit ("slim jim", etc.), available from Foley Belsaw and other locksmith companies
- Road maps to provide directions
- Blankets
- Metric and standard socket wrench sets with 1/4″, 3/8″, and 1/2″ ratchets with extensions
- Common taillight bulbs, twin and single filament
- Sealed container of spring water
- Epinephrine kit for bee sting victims *
- Bronchial inhaler for asthma sufferers *

- Aspirin and other analgesics ⋆
- Basic bandage and splint materials ⋆

⋆ You may wish to omit the medical supplies because administering them could open you up to huge liability. If you organize yourself as a nonprofit corporation or trust (see "Apparent Sources of Income" later in this chapter) and carry sufficient insurance, then providing medical care may not be such a concern. Many jurisdictions limit suits against nonprofits to around $20,000. Do some research to learn if your area of operation imposes such limits.

Van and Truck Equipment

- Flashing light assembly (yellow or other color legal in your area)
- Fog lights
- Spotlight
- CB radio tuned to channel 9 and 19
- Police scanner
- Cell phone
- Laptop PC
- Tow dolly
- Professionally painted logo saying "Samaritan" or the name of your business

A nonprofit corporation is the best way to organize this type of business. It derives its income from motorist contributions. When finished assisting motorists, you hand them a "performance survey" that the customer must fill out and send back to the main office. The bottom of the survey mentions, of course, that donations are graciously accepted.

You will also need to fill out some quick paperwork to "show your grant writers," which includes getting the customer's name and address and date and time of service. The customer can fill this out while you work.

More often than not, you will be given a donation right on the spot. If not, you now have the customer's name and address so you can send him or her a letter during your next pledge drive to keep your valuable service going.

Take down plate numbers and database them in your on-board computer. After you've been doing it a while, you can then run the plate numbers of disabled vehicles before stopping to offer assistance. If one should come back to a nonpaying "customer," you can blow by and flip them the bird or whatever makes you happy. I realize this is not in the true spirit of a "nonprofit" endeavor, but I have flaws, I'm imperfect, and I'm not recommending any of it. In fact, such behavior could cause the IRS to revoke your 501(c)(3) status.

The Road Samaritan business is not recommended for the hard-core identity changer because of the high road exposure (see Chapter 12, "Freedom on the Road").

Street Vendor

Pretty self-explanatory. Sell slush, ice cream, iced tea and coffee, cold soft drinks, and hotdogs in the summertime. Get a permit from the local board of health and set up by lakes, beaches, parks, and so forth.

Substitute Teacher

No degree at all required in most jurisdictions. Put your name on the substitute teacher list and wait to get called. Many places never even ask you to show ID. You're lucky if you can get the bureaucrats to give you directions to your room. Have a novelty driver's license ready just in case. If a school wants to know too much, go elsewhere.

Trash Picking

One man's trash is another man's treasure. One lady's problem is another lady's pleasure. Okay,

I'm not a big fan of trash picking either, but in some areas of the country "Dumpster diving" has become a high art. Setting aside for a second the perfectly edible food you can get in bins behind supermarkets and bakeries, people often can find working appliances, books, back issues of magazines like *National Geographic*, furniture, skis and other sporting goods, and perfectly good clothes. Such pickings are particularly good in college towns where students are constantly in search of the latest, coolest stuff and therefore ditching their "old" items. I know of more than one group of people who host weekly garage sales selling "junk" they've salvaged from Dumpsters.

If you don't want to host weekly yard sales, there are some items in general demand that can be redeemed for cash at scrap-metal yards and surplus dealers.

Aluminum and Heavy Metals

At the time of this writing, scrap yards were offering $.30 a pound for aluminum. Cast iron is much less per pound; you can get about $10 for full-size plow blade. Copper pays much better, but it's harder to come by.

Aluminum is easiest to find because people just throw the stuff away. Spring and fall are the best times because that's when most people clean house. You can also cruise industrial parks for companies going out of business or relocating. Oftentimes it's easier for them to just throw stuff away.

Here's a list of things worth picking up if you do it regularly:

- Gas barbecue grills. It may pay to just take the covers unless the bottom part comes off easily. Stands are sometimes aluminum, too. If so, take the whole thing. An average grill has 10 to 15 pounds of aluminum. It's like finding a $4 bill.
- Lawn mower bases.
- Bicycle frames.
- Storm doors. The local scrap yard pays $2 per door, but you don't have to separate the aluminum.
- TV antennas.
- Certain engine blocks.

Industrial Parks

I once pulled a $2,000 modular cabinet out of the trash in an industrial park. I needed a truck and a helper, of course, because it weighed a few hundred pounds. But for a few hours' work I got $400 from a place only 20 miles away that specialized in used industrial goods. Had I taken the time to find the right buyer in the right place I could've gotten more. I just wanted the fast money.

I also got a $300 industrial-grade TV antenna from the same park. I could've gotten about $10 for the scrap value or sold it at a flea market for $50. But it was in perfect condition and I decided to keep it. The thing picks up the Voyager II spacecraft, I swear!

These were just a few opportunities I seized during my life that happened to be profitable. It was never a regular business. While at the industrial park, though, I saw young men and old dudes alike who obviously made a very good living at scavenging aluminum, PC boards (for the gold), office equipment, and more.

Webmaster

Big bucks to be made here. If you can do it, employers could care less who you are. If you'd like to become a Webmaster, begin by learning HTML and JavaScript. Make a few demo pages of your skills. If you charge a reasonable fee, you can find clients just about anywhere you choose to live. Everyday, a thousand office managers somewhere are saying, "Man, I gotta get on that Internet." Go rescue them!

Writer

Now I *know* there are writer wanna-be's out there. It seems any time I tell somebody I'm a writer, I get the inevitable, "Yeah, I always wanted to be a writer" or the "I always wanted to write a book" or—

the one that tempts me to dash from the room—"Oh yeah? I have this idea for a book . . ." So I know for sure that many of you reading this have, at one time or another, had the notion to write.

Admittedly, the average writer does not make a lot of money. But if you live a simple life and can go without the Porsche and oceanfront estate, you can get by just fine.

Being a writer, surprisingly enough, is also a fairly private and anonymous existence. Not every writer needs to attend book signings and daytime TV talk shows to sell books. Some books sell fine without a lot of promotion. And there are other things to write besides books.

Magazine Articles

Everybody has a niche. And for every niche, there is at least one magazine. What's your specialty? What magazines do you read? Ever thought of writing for them? For some people, writing magazine articles is their sole source of income. If you have a good business relationship with just a few magazines, you can make a good living writing for them. It's a lot of work, but you get to work for yourself and mostly on your own terms.

Poetry

Hard to sell, and it doesn't pay very well, but if you are an exceptional poet, you can make some spending cash submitting poetry to magazines that have a (usually limited) use for it. For instance, a poem about a child may be of interest to a parenting magazine. Similarly, a poem about playing in the garden may be of use to an outdoor-type magazine.

Product Manuals

If you're knowledgeable about certain products, such as computer hardware or software, you can approach startup companies about writing their manuals for them. New companies are so busy engineering and refining their product trying to get it to market that their manuals are usually thrown together at the last minute by someone who doesn't want the job. If you approach them soon enough, many will be more than happy to have this pesky detail taken out of their way so they can concentrate on more important matters.

"How To" Books

If you have a particular sphere of interest in which you are comfortable and knowledgeable, you may wish to consider writing a "how to" book about it. These books are typically sold before they are written. Contact publishers who publish books that you've read in the subject area, especially if you know you can do a better job. Find out the name of the editor-in-chief and send him or her a letter explaining your qualifications, gaps you've seen in material they've published, and how you will fill them. But be tactful, though. Stick to the facts without maligning the other writers, who may in fact have developed close friendships with the editor.

Don't be discouraged by rejection letters. For every contract you win, you will likely have two dozen or more rejection letters. It's part of the business. It doesn't mean you're a bad writer or you have a bad idea. It just means that your idea is not needed by that publisher at that time. Keep trying and keep refining your approach.

Doing It Right

If you're going to make a serious attempt at this rewarding and anonymous career, there are a number of good books out there to help you. To sell your work, it is imperative that you have a current copy of *Writer's Digest*. This book lists thousands of publishers by size and category that may be interested in your work. It's an exceptional value at double the price, but you can often obtain it at a reduced price or for free by joining book clubs such as the Writer's Digest Book Club. *Writer's Digest Magazine* is a good magazine for the beginning writer, and Writer's Digest books are a wonderful source of education for the beginning or advanced writer.

Privacy, Freedom, and Identity Advantages

Writers can work from the privacy of their own home. As a writer, there are few, if any, people you must deal with in person. In fact, I've never been face to face with the person who edited any of my books, including this one. And I've never even spoken to the man responsible for publishing them!

This has advantages for people who feel they may be adversely judged by a personal encounter with their "employer." Perhaps someone has a nervous condition that causes uncontrollable stammering when speaking with someone face to face, yet they are eloquent and precise with the pen. Such a person would be much more comfortable as a writer, I would imagine.

A freelance writer can choose his or her own working location. This place can change from year to year, season to season, or even day to day. With the advent of laptop and notebook PCs, even a computer-dependent person can work from a lakeside resort, beach, hotel room, automobile, research location, or prison.

The independent wordsmith makes his or her own hours. As a professional writer, you need not worry about alarm clocks and rush-hour traffic to get to work "on time." If your child needs a ride to soccer, if you have an unexpected visit, or if some emergency arises, you can easily shift your schedule to accommodate the anomaly.

Everybody needs a vacation sometime. The problem with traditional employment is that you must plan your vacation in advance. Most people pick the summer. But what if it's the middle of January and you *really need* a vacation to preserve your sanity? What if your dog just died? What if you're depressed from those long, dark winter days and really, really need to go to the tropics? As a traditional employee, it's tough cookies—you've already allocated your "fun" to the second week of July. But as a freelance writer, you can drop your pen or shut off your PC, pack a bag, and head out into the wilderness.

However, don't make the mistake many neophyte writers make. Don't for a second believe a career as a writer is constant playtime. Discipline is required. In fact, working for yourself in any capacity requires more discipline than working for someone else. When you work for someone else, they tell you what to do and when to do it. If you don't comply, you're fired. Since most people need that paycheck at the end of the week, they simply fall into a routine and stick with it. As a freelance anything, you must make *and keep* your own schedule. Failure to meet your self-imposed deadlines will mean failure as a writer.

Writing is one of the few occupations where the people you deal with aren't the least bit fazed if you use an assumed name. Imagine someone interviewing for a bank teller position and informing the interviewer that he prefers to remain anonymous and therefore will be dealing with the bank under an assumed name. Are you laughing yet? The interviewer is.

But most publishers will be happy to deal with you under any name you choose. There are a lot of weirdos out there, and publishers don't want the liability of forcing you to publish under your own name only to have one of those weirdos track you down and move into your house when you're on vacation—or worse.

To cash royalty checks, a writer can set up a trust under his or her assumed name (see *MIC*, Chapter 5). For example, if I were writing under an assumed name, I would have my real identity (or real "new" identity) set up an account using a trust document entitled "Declaration of Trust of Sheldon X. Charrett" and naming myself, Johnny Doe, as trustee. The clerk at the bank will be forced to title the account "Sheldon X. Charrett TR, Johnny Doe, TTEE," using standard abbreviations or actually spelling out the words "trust" and "trustee" depending on how many letters the bank's computer program allows.

Then, anytime I receive a royalty in the name of Sheldon X. Charrett, I simply go to the bank and make the deposit. You can also use the ATM deposit tricks described in Chapter 10, "Banking Privacy," to avoid having to sign the check. Now *that's* privacy!

Instant Clout

Just a few centuries ago, writers were pretty much at the bottom of the food chain, right above the traveling players of the time. (The players were actors who traveled from village to village putting on brief skits and expecting money. The practice was seen as little more than begging.) Even fine writers used *nom de plumes* (literally, "pen names") to avoid the embarrassment associated with such an abhorrent career. But with the advent of newspapers, radio, television, and now the Internet, writers are promoted and their works are revered.

Just a few weeks ago, I was watching a late-night news broadcast about global warming. They had on four special guests to offer their opinions about the current state of affairs. Their occupations were as follows: a scientist, a doctor, a lawyer and . . . guess what? An author who'd recently released a book on the subject of global warming.

No credentials were given for any of the guests other than their occupations. The writer could very well have been somebody without formal education, such as the scientist, doctor, and lawyer must have had. Yet because she wrote a book that turned out to sell well, people just assumed she was "qualified" to write it and comment about it. Was she? Sure, she was. But wouldn't every paper-collecting bureaucrat who saw her that night be stunned to learn she had made something of herself without going through the "proper channels!"

GENERAL NOTES ON LICENSING REQUIREMENTS

Certain states and local jurisdictions may have licensing requirements for some of the trades and professional occupations listed above. Incorporating or claiming to be incorporated in a state that does not have a licensing requirement may sometimes keep the patrols off your back. In other cases, unlicensed practice is a problem common to the area, and an unscrupulous person may get away with an ongoing unlicensed venture for years. When caught, the unscrupulous person reestablishes the business across town under a new name. Of course, many identity changers partial to certain occupations have been known to obtain professional licenses under their new ID.

Privacy seekers wishing to engage in a business that requires licensure often set up a corporation and list a licensee as its resident manager. The licensee is responsible for corporate violations of the licensing provisions and typically requires a yearly stipend to provide this service. You may be able to advertise and find a properly licensed person to act as resident manager for your corporation.

A similar thing happens every day on a much smaller scale. Lucky Larry lands a $25,000 home improvement contract but does not have a contractor's license. Therefore he cannot pull the necessary permits or schedule the required inspections. What does Larry do? He calls his old boss, needy Ned, who just put his daughter on a plane headed to Harvard Law School. Ned is more than happy to "run the job" for a set fee of $500 or 10 percent of the profits. This, my friends, happens at least a thousand times a day in this country.

Local Business License

Most cities and towns require all businesses domiciled in their town to file a DBA ("doing business as") or fictitious name statement, which alerts the public that an individual or other entity is doing business under a trade name. Every year thousands of fly-by-nighters and legitimate businesses alike "forget" to file their DBA or let their DBA lapse. It is very difficult for cities and towns to enforce this requirement. If they do contact you, you can always change the name of your business or simply tell them you've become disenchanted and no longer run the business—or that your dog died and you got really depressed and quit working, or whatever you wanna tell 'em. They'll go away if you keep talking.

If you have the necessary documentation, usually an address and two forms of ID, you can go to the city clerk's office, file a DBA, and be done with it. Other jurisdictions don't even require that. All they require is a notarized fictitious name statement. If you bring them one, they file it. Most jurisdictions do not require you to file a DBA if you are conducting business in your own name, since your own name is not fictitious (as far as they know).

APPARENT SOURCES OF INCOME

Many of you reading this have no need to seek actual employment but would like to be associated with a company. Possible reasons for this include:

- Having a ready answer to that annoying party question, "What is it that you do?"
- Having a way to distribute saved or looted funds to a new identity
- General privacy from the IRS and nosy-neighbors
- Having a place of business where you can receive phone calls from business associates, dates, and people you meet
- Having various entities maintain title to your holdings (real estate, bank accounts, stocks, etc.)
- Having companies to accept contracts from condo associations and 203K homeowners (see above)

Many corporate shell-shuffling tricks were covered in *The Modern Identity Changer*. To be true to the no-rehash rule, I'll refer interested parties to that text and keep this section short.

Limited Liability Companies

Because they were new, controversial, and unsupported by statute, limited liability corporations (LLCs) did not make the cut for my first book. They are now coming into wide acceptance, however, and I believe they are here to stay, mostly because lawyers and crooked politicians love them. Briefly, here's how they work.

You'll remember from *MIC*, Chapter 5, that corporations protect officers and shareholders from civil liability such as business debts. The downside of corporations is you expose yourself to double taxation, as you *and* the corp must pay income tax. Well, forming a limited liability company, or LLC, lets business owners get the best of two worlds—the liability protection offered by a corporation and the tax benefits of a partnership. The latest IRS rules allow the long-awaited one-person LLC. This lets sole proprietors join in the LLC fun. LLC owners decide for themselves how they wish to be taxed (i.e., as a partner or as a sole proprietor).

More on Nevada Corporations

Everybody seems to be asking about Nevada corporations. Many readers have asked me about Delaware and Wyoming corporations as well. I touched briefly on Nevada and Delaware corporations in my first book (*MIC*, Chapter 5), but further demand necessitates further explanation.

MIC lists two main advantages of forming a Nevada corporation. Here, I will elaborate on those points and introduce some others that I've discovered. Almost everything said below about Nevada corporations may also be said about Wyoming corporations. Delaware corporations are best suited to Fortune 500 companies but also will be explained.

First of All, Is It Worth It?

State incorporation fees and resident agent services can put quite a dent in your wallet. Companies that set up Nevada corporations can charge anywhere between $300 to $3,000 for setup fees and first-year management. Even unassisted incorporation will cost you $125 minimum in Nevada. So, is it worth it? For those interested in privacy, the answer is yes.

Some people will spend over $1,000 a year on cigarettes and booze. That's fine; it's their thing. If your thing is privacy, then the cost of establishing and maintaining a Nevada corporation is well worth the privacy benefits. And, as I will explain, if you have money, assets, or business income to protect, incorporating in Nevada will actually *earn you money*.

Here is a short list of Nevada corporation advantages (source: Corporate Service Center, Inc., 1475 Terminay Way, Suite E, Reno, NV, 89502):

- Nevada has no state corporate taxes.
- Nevada has no franchise tax.

- Nevada has no tax on corporate shares.
- Nevada has no personal income tax.
- Nevada provides total privacy of shareholders.
- Nevada is the only state without a formal information-sharing agreement with the IRS.
- Nevada is the only state that allows for the issuance of "bearer shares."
- Nevada has minimal reporting and disclosure requirements.
- Nevada has nominal annual fees.
- Nevada allows for a one-man corporation.
- Nevada has established case law that prevents easy piercing of the corporate veil.
- Corporate officers and directors can be protected from any personal liability for their lawful acts on behalf of the corporation.
- Stockholders, directors, and officers need not live or hold meetings in Nevada or even be U.S. citizens.
- Only the names of the officers and directors are on public records. No other information, listings, or minutes of meetings are filed with the state.
- There is no minimum initial capital requirement to incorporate.
- Nevada corporations may issue stock for capital, services, personal property, or real estate. The directors alone may determine the value of any such transactions, and their decision is final.

TABLE 8.2
Comparison of Nevada, Wyoming and Delaware Corporations
(Source: Laughlin Associates)

Corporate Attribute	Nevada	Wyoming	Delaware
State corporate tax?	NO	NO	YES
State personal income tax?	NO	NO	YES
Annual filing list of officers?	YES	NO	YES
Franchise tax?	NO	YES *	YES
Minimum capital required to incorporate?	NO	NO	NO
Minimum directors?	1	0 **	NO
Annual filing of assets?	NO	YES	NO
Officers and directors shielded from judgment liability and lawsuits?	YES	YES	YES
Shareholders public record?	NO	NO	NO
Reporting requirement for issued shares?	NO	NO	YES
Reporting requirement for offices domiciled out of state?	NO	NO	YES
Reporting requirement for stockholder/director meeting times and dates?	NO	NO	YES
State shares information with IRS?	NO	NO	YES

* Minimal tax based on assets located within the state of Wyoming. ** If fewer than 50 shareholders.

If you study the above information, you might begin to imagine how a Nevada corporation could be used in your pursuit of privacy. But perhaps the best feature of Nevada corporations has been omitted from the chart. While the names of certain corporate officers must be disclosed to the Nevada state secretary's office (and therefore become a matter of public record), it is not necessary for the incorporators to hold those officer positions. In Nevada, it is legal to appoint one nominee to hold all officer and director positions of a corporation, a corporation that you ultimately control. Also, it is the nominee's Social Security number that will appear on IRS Form SS-4 when the corporation applies for its tax identification number, or TIN (*MIC*, Chapter 5).

If you have a friend in Nevada who would be willing to act as your resident manager and nominee, you can establish a Nevada corporation for $125 plus $85 per year. Certainly you could see fit to give your friend $100 a year for his signing an occasional document on your behalf. If you have an ex-husband or wife whose attorney is desperately seeking your assets, a corporate bank account, legally established with your nominee's signature and corporate TIN, will not pop up in any database searches.

If you don't have any friends or family in Nevada, there are many companies in Nevada that will provide resident agent and nominee services for your corporation. One such company is Laughlin Associates. Laughlin provides every possible corporate service you can imagine, including setting up the corporation, filing your SS-4, providing resident agent and nominee services, and opening up your corporate bank or brokerage account. For a free pricing and information package, write to:

Laughlin Associates, Inc.
2533 N. Carson Street
Carson City, NV 89706
E-mail: info@laughlinassociates.com
Web: www.laughlinassociates.com

Two other companies:

Val-U-Corp Services, Inc.
Web: www.val-u-corp.com
E-mail: val-u-corp@val-u-corp.com

Nevada Corporation Specialists, LTD.
4601 W. Sahara, Suite L
Las Vegas, NV 89102
Web: www.nevadacorp.onevegas.com
E-mail: nevadacorp@onevegas.com

The information in this section was sent to me upon request by the various companies as indicated or found at their Web sites. I have never used any of these services and neither encourage you to, nor discourage you from, contacting any of them. Each of them provides roughly the same services, though prices vary widely.

Laughlin Associates responded quickly and professionally to my letters and e-mails and provided as much information as possible without my actually retaining their services. Val-U-Corp responded to my e-mail promptly and professionally.

LIVING INEXPENSIVELY

An often overlooked facet of income is outgo. One's ability to survive or thrive in the material world is consistently linked with income. But what is income? If your living expenses are $2,000 per month and you have an "income" of $2,000 per month, are you really better off than Mr. Jones next door who has an "income" of only $1,200 per month but expenses of $950? If you can reduce your outgo, you can free yourself from the material world trap of perpetually needing more income. There are some simple and effective ways to do this.

Carry Little or No Mortgage on Your Principal Residence

We've all heard investment advisors tell us that to be successful, we must "leverage" or "use other people's money." This is often required to get a business or investment property scheme off the ground, true enough. But what about those of us who measure success by how well we live as opposed to how much we earn? Maybe you just want an extra hundred bucks a month to dine out, see more plays, and live an easier life? I say consider these things when purchasing your home.

Typically we're advised to use a minimal down payment to leverage the largest mortgage possible. In fact, banks do us the "favor" of prequalifying us for a loan. We are told we can afford a $120,000 home. We then make the mistake of giving this information to a real estate agent, who assures us we'll spend that amount and then some. "Surely your parents will loan you the extra $10,000 you'll need for *this* fine home," they tell us. Most of us become swept up in the fantasy of sitting on the deck with a hot morning coffee watching the sun rise over our beautiful lawn . . .

Well, four months, 400 headaches, and $4,000 in extra closing costs later, a half-crazed, mostly depressed, superstressed incarnation of someone who used to be you is sitting on that deck saying, "How did I get myself into this? Sixty hours a week and still can't make ends meet . . . I'll never be able to pay my parents back."

If this hasn't happened to you yet, do yourself a favor and keep reading.

If you have a nice chunk of change for a down payment on a small home or condo, I say use it. Find out what you "prequalify" for and spend half. Stick to your guns no matter what the bastard real estate agent tries to suck you into. Better yet, if you can buy your principal residence for cash, I say it makes sense to do so.

Why?

Because your principal residence should *not* be considered an "investment." Of course, financially speaking it is. But, more important for the enlightened individual with a new world perspective, it's your home first! Do you really want your home to be a constant source of worry and concern? Wouldn't it be nice to know that you could have a bad month and not have to worry about the bank's attorney knocking on your door? Aren't taxes, insurance, and condo fees enough?

Don't Throw Your Money Away

Corporate America constantly tries to sell us stuff we don't need. There are some products that are obviously useless, such as fuzzy dice or the U.S. Postal Service's commemorative stamp collection, that most of us have the good sense not to waste our money on. There are, however, other, less obvious products that most Americans needlessly overspend to buy. This is because the product itself actually does have a use; that much they tell you. What they don't tell you is that the product is merely a repackaged version of an inexpensive, widely available chemical. The following table illustrates some common examples.

TABLE 8.3: Product Composition, Price and Cost

Product	Retail Price	Composition *	Home Brew Cost
Widow Cleaner	$1.99–$3.79	99.9% water, 1% ammonia	$.06/gallon
Mouthwash	$2.69	79% water, 20% grain alcohol, 1% flavoring	$.20/liter

Product	Retail Price	Composition *	Home Brew Cost
Toothpaste	$2–$4/tube	Chalk, seaweed, flavorings	Baking soda: $.30. One box will last you a year. Peroxide: $.40.
Cleansers (kitchen, bath)	$1–$5/pound	Baking soda, bleach	$.40/pound.
Windshield cleaner	$1–$2/gallon	Methanol, water	$.25/gallon
Detergents	$3–$6/gallon	Various soaps	Use plain soap, baking soda and bleach: $.80/gallon.
Cereal	$2–$5/16 oz. box	Oats, honey	$1 for every 16 ounces you make.
Milk	$2–$3/gallon	Milk	Buy soy beans in bulk and make soy milk for about $.50 a gallon. **.
Bread	$1–$4/loaf	Flour, water, yeast, butter, salt	You can make your own for about $1 a loaf—healthier, heartier, and tastier.
Vitamin C	$3–$5/bottle (50 grams)		Ascorbic acid. Buy 50 grams of ascorbic acid from a chemist for about $.80.

* Excludes marketing chemicals such as coloring and other inert chemicals used to make the formulae patentable.
** This is about a thousand times healthier, too. Mix solid leftovers from processing with honey for an excellent "hard tack" desert or survival food.

When restoring the Statue of Liberty for its rededication in 1986, a team of engineers labored for expensive hours over how to clean a hundred years of gunk from inside the statue. After trying many different solvents, it was finally decided that sodium bicarbonate (baking soda) was the best choice for the job.

WARNING: Never mix ammonia and bleach! The toxic fumes will kill you!

Buy Generic

Generic and store-brand products cost 25 to 60 percent less than brand names. For example, my local grocery carries a 24-ounce box of its store brand Toasted Oats adjacent to the commercially recognizable Cheerios™. Toasted Oats costs $1.99 per box; Cheerios cost $4.70 per box. The ingredients are exactly the same. It's the same product packaged two different ways. It's amazing how many people will buy the Cheerios because they feel it must be a better quality or they're ashamed to buy a store brand. That's how intense corporate conditioning is, folks. Think about it.

Here is a table of common store-brand products and their equivalent counterparts. There are hundreds more, I'm sure. Most stores are eager to sell their own brand so they place it right next to the big-name item. Many stores go so far as to use the same color scheme and typesetting as the name brand. I have never been in a store that actually drops a brick on your head to show you that their product is the *same freakin' thing* as the nationally recognized one, and hopefully it won't come to that.

Buy the store brand or generic. Don't throw your money away!

TABLE 8.4: Product Brand Names and Prices

Product	Retail Price	Store Brand	Store Brand Price
Advil	$8.97/100 ct.	Ibuprofen	$3.99
Benadryl	$5.49/20 ct.	Diphenhydramine-HCL	$2.49/20 ct.
Cheerios	$4–$6/box	Toasted Oats	$1.99
Tylenol	$8.69/100 ct.	Acetaminophen	$3.79
Tostitos	$3.50/bag	Corn chips	$1.99/bag
Saran Wrap	$3/box	Plastic wrap	$1–$2/box
Smartfood Popcorn	$3–$4/bag	Cheddar popcorn	$1.99/bag, or buy popcorn and put your own cheddar on it for about $1

Nonprofit Organizations

When establishing a business entity to aid your quest for privacy, you may wish to consider the option of a nonprofit corporation or trust. I'm sure many of you crafty individuals will readily see how having one can benefit your privacy as well as your pocketbook.

The biggest reason to operate your business as a nonprofit (assuming it qualifies) is so it doesn't have to pay taxes on its earnings. What earnings? I thought we were talking about nonprofits? True enough. But contrary to what many people believe, "nonprofit" does not mean your business doesn't make money. Nor does it mean you can't pay yourself for running the business. It means that the money your business makes is used in some way to benefit the common good or the good of a certain group of people. It is also worth mentioning that nonprofit groups do not have to pay property tax on certain real property, such as office buildings.

Title 26, Section 501(c)(3) of the IRS code holds that contributions to an organization are tax exempt if the organization is operated exclusively for charitable, religious, educational, or scientific purposes. To qualify, an organization must be a corporation, community chest, fund, foundation, or trust. Individuals and partnerships do not qualify.

The great majority of nonprofit organizations must apply to the IRS (Form 1023) to be recognized as tax exempt. However, churches and organizations grossing under $5,000 annually are not required to file.

Just about anybody can say they're a "Church of _____" and it would be very difficult for the IRS to prove otherwise. For example the "Church of Scientology" is recognized by the IRS as a nonprofit church. Case closed.

If you choose option two and decide to gross under $5,000 per year, then by default you will also be able to avoid filing an annual Form 990 tax return, leaving your little venture paperwork free.

If you donate money to your organization, you cannot seek remuneration for services performed. In other words, you cannot take the $7,500 Aunt Hilda left you in her will, "donate" it to your "charity," and then work for your charity as an employee, disbursing the funds to yourself over the next three years to reduce your personal income tax.

Of course there's this little gem called "anonymous donors" that I'd like to discuss in detail but really can't because I'll get in a boatload of trouble. Let me just say that the beautiful thing about charity is it's done from the heart. Nobody does it 'cuz they want brownie points—nooooo—they do it out of love for humanity. In fact, many of them do so privately and anonymously and, hell, they don't even take the tax deduction. After all, no law says you *must* take a tax deduction. Thus there is this uncomfortable byproduct of the system amounting to hundreds of millions of unaccounted "donations" slipping past the IRS every year. Oh, well.

And there you have it.

I'm not going to suggest anybody break the law. And if I spell it out for you—if I say, "Make anonymous donations to your nonprofit organization's bank account that has an EIN instead of your SSN so your spouse's lawyer can't find the funds that you later disburse to yourself as manager of the organization"—well, then that would be tantamount to suggesting you break the law, wouldn't it? So I'm not going to say it. You're on your own this time.

I have a page on my Web site that expounds somewhat on this information. You can also check out the IRS Web site as well as its publication 590 if you want the gory details. But for a real quick education, turn to the appendix and read through the Articles of Organization for nonprofits as suggested by none other than the IRS itself. If you follow my suggestions above, you'll need not file organizing articles with anyone but yourself. And it's all 100 percent probably sorta-kinda legal.

Identity, Privacy, and Personal Freedom

Social Security

*Here is wisdom: Let him that hath understanding count
the number of the beast, for it is the number of a man.*
Revelation 13:18

In 1935 when the Social Security number was invented, politicians and bureaucrats promised us the number would be used only for Social Security Administration (SSA) accounting purposes. They further reassured us the SSN would never become a national identifier.

Within a decade, an executive order *required* all components of the federal government to use the SSN as an identifier whenever an identifier became necessary, but this did not fit their definition of "national identifier."

Federal bureaus eagerly followed the order, with the Civil Service Commission, IRS, Treasury Department, Medicare, Veterans Administration, and Defense Department, among others, each adopting the SSN as its identification number of choice. But it didn't stop at federal bureaus.

By 1970, the federal government required banks—private institutions, mind you—to obtain the SSNs of all their customers. Two years after that, the SSN cancer spread to our public school systems, enumerating children as they enrolled.

But even that wasn't good enough for the Beast. Today, if you expect to claim your children as dependents on your income tax, the IRS requires them to have an SSN if they are older than six months.

The SSN, which our government promised would never become a national identifier, is now tagged on every citizen, against their will, almost from birth. Sorta kinda sounds just a little like a national identifier, doesn't it? If an identification number tagged on every citizen from birth is not considered a national identifier, then I live in fear of what our government's definition of a national identifier actually is.

Hey, I know. Maybe we should just consider tattooing an SSN bar code on the sole of every baby's foot immediately after birth. After all, the tattoo would be out of sight most of the time, so how could citizen's complain? When we are pulled over by the police, it would only be a minor inconvenience to remove our shoe and get scanned—certainly faster than handing them a license, which they then have to take back to their cruiser and radio in. So why not? The bar code tattoo would be fraud-resistant and help fight crime, return runaways back to their parents, and immediately identify hoodlum teens who seldom carry ID. What's wrong with that?

Can you say *Nazi Germany*?

COLLECTING SOCIAL SECURITY UNDER A NEW IDENTITY

I had a few readers write me wondering what they should do about collecting Social Security under a new ID. In most cases, you shouldn't. Either there's no reason to do so or it's simply not possible. Besides, there are plenty of alternatives to collecting Social Security. Let me begin by explaining how Social Security works as far as paying benefits is concerned.

Basically, if you don't put anything in, you can't get anything out. That does not mean, however, that what you put in you can take out dollar-for-dollar upon retirement. The system, like most government systems, is far from being that simple.

Social Security is based on credits. Each year the SSA establishes an earnings amount that entitles you to one Social Security Credit. For example in 1999 the amount needed to tally one Social Security Credit was $740. This means you will earn one credit for each $740 *up to a maximum of four credits per year*. In other words, if your neighbor made $2,960 in 1999, she got four credits for her service to the country that year. If you made $6,000,000 in 1999, you also got four credits. If, after your very successful year of 1999, you decide to take the rest of your life off, you will not be eligible for any Social Security benefits. This is true even though you paid in $8,481 in Social Security and $160,689 in Medicare in 1999!

You are only eligible for Social Security benefits after you have earned 40 credits. This means you have to work for 10 years. If you make $6,000,000 a year and only work nine years, you will not be eligible for Social Security under these guidelines. That's the system.

Now back to the question of identity changers collecting Social Security.

If you establish a new identity, you will still have to work for 10 years to even have a shot at collecting Social Security. No matter what age you are when you establish your new identity, you won't be able to collect anything until you're 62. Before you can receive one dime, you'll have to present to the SSA a Social Security card with a valid account number (not a borrowed or made up one) and an actual birth certificate that can be verified (not one you made on your computer). These are the *minimum* requirements at the time of this writing. This severely restricts your new ID options, and you'll have to spend your whole new life wondering if the SSA clerk you visit when you're 62 will believe you are who you say you are.

That said, you will probably have noted it's not completely impossible to pull the wool over the eyes of the SSA. You're right. With a valid birth certificate, SSN, 10 years of hard labor, and a hurried SSA clerk, you can begin collecting benefits under your new ID when you are 62. My question: why strive for this pittance when life has so much more to offer?

Social Security is just another social welfare program, another excuse for Big Brother to track us and keep us in line. Then, when our age precludes us from being a threat to the Big Machine, they throw us a monthly bone until we die. Chomp, chomp, chomp.

Why create a new identity only to continue being a slave of the system? Isn't the whole idea to rid yourself of Big Brother and his countless controls? Sure, you can create a new ID, get a job, pay into Social Security, retire, and collect a Social Security check. But that's what you're doing now! What will you have accomplished? You'd just be the same slave in a different skin.

There's a Better Way

Using any of the methods described in Chapter 10, you can establish a bank, mutual fund, or brokerage account and put your hard-earned cash there. All it takes is a little discipline. After all, Social Security is nothing more than a semiforced retirement account. Why let Big Brother force you when you can force yourself? Just set up the account, decide not to touch it until your retirement, and there you'll have it. Not only will you have retirement funds, but a decent stock or mutual fund will grow into a much bigger payout than Social Security could ever provide. And, if you do it right, it will all be completely private!

SOCIAL SECURITY ADMINISTRATION HISTORY

I've gotten several requests for the historical background of the SSA and how it affects identity changers. In my first book I mentioned several times that knowledge is power. The more you know about any subject, the more of a command you'll have over it. I guess many of you took that to heart.

Figure 9.1 gives a chronology of the SSA's evolution. By studying it, you'll be able to see how Social Security and Big Brother have evolved together over the years. This public-domain chart has been provided courtesy of the Social Security Administration.

FIGURE 9.1
Social Security Chronology

1935

The Social Security Act (P.L. 74-271) is enacted. It does not expressly mention the use of SSNs, but it authorizes the creation of some type of record keeping scheme.

Treasury Decision 4704, a Treasury regulation in 1936, requires the issuance of an account number to each employee covered by the Social Security program.

The Social Security Board considers various numbering systems and ways (such as metal tags, etc.) by which employees can indicate they have been issued a number.

1936-1937

Approximately 30 million applications for SSNs are processed between November 1936 and June 30, 1937.

1943

Executive Order 9397 (3 CFR (1943-1948 Comp. 283-284) requires:

- All federal components to use the SSN "exclusively" whenever the component finds it advisable to set up a new identification system for individuals.
- The Social Security Board is to cooperate with federal uses of the number by issuing and verifying numbers for other federal agencies.

1961

The Civil Service Commission adopts the SSN as an official federal employee identifier. Internal Revenue Code amendments (P.L. 87-397) require each taxpayer to furnish an identifying number for tax reporting.

1962

The IRS adopts the SSN as its official taxpayer identification number.

1964

The Treasury Department, via internal policy, requires buyers of Series H savings bonds to provide their SSNs.

1965

Internal Revenue amendments (P.L. 89-384) enact Medicare. It becomes necessary for most individuals age 65 and older to have an SSN.

1966

The Veterans Administration begins to use the SSN as the hospital admissions number and for patient recordkeeping.

1967

The Department of Defense adopts the SSN in lieu of the military service number for identifying armed forces personnel.

1970

Bank Records and Foreign Transactions Act (P.L. 91-508) requires all banks, savings and loan associations, credit unions, and brokers/dealers in securities to obtain the SSNs of all of their customers. Also, financial institutions are required to file a report with the IRS, including the SSN of the customer, for any transaction involving more than $10,000.

1971

An SSA task force report is published that proposes that SSA take a "cautious and conservative" position toward SSN use and do nothing to promote the use of the SSN as an identifier. The report recommends that SSA:

- Use mass SSN enumeration in schools as a long-range, cost-effective approach to tightening up the SSN system.
- Consider cooperating with specific health, education, and welfare uses of the SSN by state, local, and other nonprofit organizations.

1972

Social Security amendments of 1972 (P.L. 92-603):

- Requires SSA to issue SSNs to all legally admitted aliens at entry and to anyone receiving or applying for any benefit paid for by federal funds.
- Requires SSA to obtain evidence to establish age, citizenship, or alien status and identity.
- Authorizes SSA to enumerate children at the time they first enter school.

1973

Buyers of Series E savings bonds are required by the Treasury Department to provide their SSNs.

The report of the Department of Health, Education, and Welfare (HEW) Secretary's Advisory Committee on the Automated Personal Data System concludes that the adoption of a universal identifier by this country is not desirable; it also finds that the SSN is not suitable for such a purpose, as it does not meet the criteria of a universal identifier that distinguishes a person from all others.

1974

Privacy Act (P.L. 93-579) enacted effective September 27, 1975, to limit governmental use of the SSN:

- Provides that no state or local government agency may withhold a benefit from a person simply because the individual refuses to furnish his or her SSN.
- Requires that federal, state, and local agencies that request an individual to disclose his/her SSN inform the individual whether disclosure is mandatory or voluntary. This is the first mention of SSN use by local governments.

1975

Social Services Amendments of 1974 (P.L. 93-647) provide that:
- Disclosure of an individual's SSN is a condition of eligibility for AFDC (Aid to Families with Dependent Children) benefits.

- The Office of Child Support enforcement Parent Locator Service may require disclosure of limited information (including SSN and whereabouts) contained in SSA records.

1976
Tax Reform Act of 1976 (P.L. 94-455) includes the following amendments to the Social Security Act:

- Allows use by the states of the SSN in the administration of any tax, general public assistance, driver's license, or motor vehicle registration law within their jurisdiction and authorizes the states to require individuals affected by such laws to furnish their SSNs to the states.
- Makes misuse of the SSN for any purpose a violation of the Social Security Act.
- Makes disclosure or compelling disclosure of the SSN of any person a violation of the Social Security Act.
- Amends section 6109 of the Internal Revenue Code to provide that the SSN be used as the tax identification number (TIN) for all tax purposes. While the Treasury Department had been using the SSN as the TIN by regulation since 1962, this law codified that requirement.
- The Federal Advisory Committee on false identification recommends that penalties for misuse should be increased and evidence requirements tightened and rejects the idea of a national identifier and does not even consider the SSN for such a purpose.

1977
Food Stamp Act of 1977 (P.L. 96-58) requires disclosure of SSNs of all household members as a condition of eligibility for participation in the food stamp program.
Privacy Protection Study Commission recommends that:

- No steps be taken toward developing standard, universal labels for individuals until safeguards and policies regarding permissible uses and disclosures are proven effective.
- Executive Order 9397 be amended so that federal agencies could no longer use it as legal authority to require disclosure of an individual's SSN (no action taken).

The Carter administration proposes that the Social Security card be one of the authorized documents by which an employer could be assured that a job applicant may work in this country but also states that the SSN card should not become a national identity document.

1978
SSA requires evidence of age, citizenship, and identity of all SSN applicants.

1981
The Reagan administration states that it "is explicitly opposed to the creation of a national identity card" but recognizes the need for a means for employers to comply with the employer sanctions provisions of its immigration reform legislation.

The Omnibus Budget Reconciliation Act of 1981 (P.L. 97-35) requires the disclosure of the SSNs of all adult members in the household of children applying to the school lunch program.
Social Security Benefits Act (P.L. 97-123):

- Section 4 adds alteration and forgery of a Social Security card to the list of prohibited acts and increases the penalties for such acts.
- Section 6 requires any federal, state, or local government agency to furnish the name and SSN of prisoners convicted of a felony to the secretary of Health and Human Services (HHS) to enforce suspension of disability benefits to certain imprisoned felons.

The Department of Defense Authorization Act (P.L. 97-86) requires disclosure of the SSNs to the Selective Service System of all individuals required to register for the draft.

1982

The Debt Collection Act (P.L. 97-365) requires that all applicants for loans under any federal loan program furnish their SSNs to the agency supplying the loan.

All Social Security cards issued to legal aliens not authorized to work in the United States are annotated "NOT VALID FOR EMPLOYMENT" beginning in May.

1983

The Social Security amendments of 1983 (P.L. 98-21) require that new and replacement Social Security cards issued after October 30 be made of banknote paper and (to the maximum extent practicable) not be subject to counterfeiting.

The Interest and Dividend Tax Compliance Act (P.L. 98-67) requires SSNs for all interest-bearing accounts and provides a penalty of $50 for all individuals who fail to furnish a correct TIN (usually the SSN).

1984

Deficit Reduction Act of 1984 (P.L. 98-369):

- Amends the Social Security Act to establish an income and eligibility verification system involving state agencies administering the AFDC, Medicaid, unemployment compensation, food stamp programs, and state programs under a plan approved under title I, X, XIV, or XVI of the Act. States are permitted to require the SSN as a condition of eligibility for benefits under any of these programs.
- Amends Section 6050I of the IRC to require that persons engaged in a trade or business file a report (including SSNs) with the IRS for cash transactions over $10,000.
- Amends Section 215 of the IRC to authorize the secretary of HHS to publish regulations that require a spouse paying alimony to furnish the IRS with the TIN (i.e., the SSN) of the spouse receiving alimony payments.

1986

The Immigration Reform and Control Act of 1986 (P.L. 99-603):

- Requires the comptroller general to investigate technological changes that could reduce the potential for counterfeiting Social Security cards.
- Provides that the Social Security card may be used to establish the eligibility of a prospective employee for employment.
- Requires the secretary of HHS to undertake a study of the feasibility and costs of establishing an SSN verification system.

The Tax Reform Act of 1986 (P.L. 99-514) requires individuals filing a tax return due after December 31, 1987, to include the TIN—usually the SSN—of each dependent age 5 or older.

The Commercial Motor Vehicle Safety Act of 1986 (P.L. 99-750) authorizes the secretary of transportation to require the use of the SSN on commercial motor vehicle operators' licenses. Higher Education Amendments of 1986 (P.L. 99-498) requires that student loan applicants submit their SSN as a condition of eligibility.

1987

SSA initiates a demonstration project on August 17 in the state of New Mexico enabling parents to obtain Social Security numbers for their newborn infants automatically when the infants' births are registered by the state. The program was expanded nationwide in 1989. Currently, all 50 states participate in the program, as does New York City, Washington, D.C., and Puerto Rico.

1988

The Housing and Community Development Act of 1987 (P.L. 100-242) authorizes the secretary of Housing and Urban Development (HUD) to require disclosure of a person's SSN as a condition of eligibility for any HUD program.

The Family Support Act of 1988 (P.L. 100-485):

- Section 125 requires, beginning November 1, 1990, a state to obtain the SSNs of the parents when issuing a birth certificate.
- Section 704(a) requires individuals filing a tax return due after December 31, 1989, to include the TIN—usually the SSN—of each dependent age 2 or older.

The Technical and Miscellaneous Revenue Act of 1988 (P.L. 100-647):

- Authorizes a state and/or any blood donation facility to use SSNs to identify blood donors (205(c)(2)(F)).
- Requires that all Title II beneficiaries either have or have applied for an SSN in order to receive benefits. This provision becomes effective with dates of initial entitlement of June 1989 or later. Beneficiaries who refuse enumeration are entitled but placed in suspense.

The Anti-Drug Abuse Act of 1988 (P.L. 100-690) deletes the $5,000 and $25,000 upper limits on fines that can be imposed for violations of Section 208 of the Social Security Act. The general limit of $250,000 for felonies in the U.S. Code now applies to SSN violations under Section 208 of the Social Security Act. Also, penalties for misuse of SSNs apply as well in cases where the number is referred to by any other name (e.g., taxpayer identification number).

1989

The Omnibus Budget Reconciliation Act of 1989 (P.L. 101-239) requires that the National Student Loan Data System include, among other things, the names and SSNs of borrowers.

The Child Nutrition and WIC Reauthorization Act of 1989 (P.L. 101-147) requires the member of the household who applies for the school lunch program to provide the SSN of the parent of the child for whom the application is made.

1990

The Omnibus Budget Reconciliation Act of 1990 (P.L. 101-508):

- Section 7201 (Computer Matching and Privacy Protection Amendments of 1990) provides that no adverse action may be taken against an individual receiving benefits as a result of a matching program without verification of the information or notification of the individual regarding the findings with time to contest.
- Section 8053 requires an SSN for eligibility for benefits from the Department of Veterans Affairs (DVA).
- Section 11112 requires that individuals filing a tax return due after December 31, 1991, include the TIN—usually the SSN—of each dependent age 1 or older.

The Food and Agricultural Resources Act of 1990 (P.L. 101-624), Section 1735:

- Requires an SSN for the officers of food and retail stores that redeem food stamps.
- Provides that SSNs maintained as a result of any law enacted on or after October 1, 1990, will be confidential and may not be disclosed.

1994
The Social Security Independence and Program Improvements Act of 1994 (P.L. 103-296):

- Section 304 authorizes the use of the SSN for jury selection.
- Section 314 authorizes cross-matching of SSNs and employer identification numbers maintained by the Department of Agriculture with other federal agencies for the purpose of investigating both food stamp fraud and violations of other federal laws.
- Section 318 authorizes the use of the SSN by the Department of Labor in administration of federal workers' compensation laws.

1996
The Personal Responsibility and Work Opportunity Reconciliation Act of 1996 (P.L. 104-193) (Welfare Reform):

- Section 111 requires the commissioner of Social Security to develop and submit to Congress a prototype of a counterfeit-resistant Social Security card that is made of durable, tamper-resistant material (e.g., plastic); employs technologies that provide security features (e.g., magnetic stripe); and provides individuals with reliable proof of citizenship or legal resident alien status.
- Section 111 also requires the commissioner of Social Security to study and report to Congress on different methods of improving the Social Security card application process, including evaluation of the cost and workload implications of issuing a counterfeit-resistant Social Security card for all individuals and evaluation of the feasibility and cost implications of imposing a user fee for replacement cards.
- Section 316 requires HHS to transmit to SSA, for verification purposes, certain information about individuals and employers maintained under the federal Parent Locator Service in an automated directory. SSA is required to verify the accuracy of, correct, or supply to the extent possible, and report to HHS the name, SSN, and birth date of individuals and the employer identification number of employers. SSA is to be reimbursed by HHS for the cost of this verification service. This section also requires all federal agencies (including SSA) to report quarterly the name and SSN of each employee and the wages paid to the employee during the previous quarter.
- Section 317 provides that state child support enforcement procedures require the SSN of any applicant for a professional license, commercial driver's license, occupational license, or marriage license be recorded on the application. The SSN of any person subject to a divorce decree, support order, or paternity determination or acknowledgement would have to be placed in the pertinent records. SSNs are required on death certificates.
- Section 451 provides that, in order to be eligible for the Earned Income Tax Credit, an individual must include on his or her tax return an SSN that was not assigned solely for nonwork purposes.

The Department of Defense Appropriations Act, 1997 (P.L. 104-208) (Division C (Illegal Immigration Reform and Immigrant Responsibility Act of 1996) (Immigration Reform):

- Sections 401-404 provide for three specific employment verification pilot programs in which employers would voluntarily participate. In general, the pilot programs allow an employer to confirm the identity and employment eligibility of the individual. SSA and the Immigration and Naturalization Service (INS) would provide a secondary verification process to confirm the validity of the information provided. SSA would compare the name and SSN provided and advise whether the name and number match SSA records and whether the SSN is valid for employment.
- Section 414 requires the commissioner to report to Congress every year the aggregate number of SSNs issued to noncitizens not authorized to work but under which earnings were reported. It also requires the commissioner to transmit to the Attorney General a report on the extent to which SSNs and Social Security cards are used by noncitizens for fraudulent purposes.
- Section 415 authorizes the attorney general to require any noncitizen to provide his or her SSN for purposes of inclusion in any record maintained by the attorney general or INS.
- Section 656 provides for improvements in identification-related documents (i.e., birth certificates and driver's licenses). These sections require publication of regulations that set standards, including security features and, in the case of driver's licenses, require that an SSN appear on the license. Federal agencies are precluded from accepting as proof of identity documents that do not meet the regulatory standards.
- Section 657 provides for the development of a prototype Social Security card. The requirements are the same as in Section 111 of the welfare reform legislation (described above) with the exception that the comptroller general is also to study and report to Congress on different methods of improving the Social Security card application process.

1997

The Department of Defense Appropriations Act, 1997 (P.L. 104-208) (Division C—Illegal Immigration Reform and Immigrant Responsibility Act of 1996) (Immigration Reform):

- Section 1090 requires an applicant for an SSN under age 18 to provide evidence of his or her parents' names and SSNs in addition to required evidence of age, identity, and citizenship.

The Report to Congress on "Options for Enhancing the Social Security Card" is released on September 22, 1997.

Some Interesting Notes

It's interesting to note that the 1971 task force report recommended a "cautious and conservative" approach to using the SSN while doing nothing to promote its use as a national identifier. My opinion: of course not! How could mass SSN enumeration in public schools and health programs *possibly* cause the SSN to become a national identifier? I dunno. I just write government task force reports . . .

1976 was a banner year for Big Brother. The Tax Reform Act seemed to allay public concerns of totalitarianism by limiting states' administrative use of the SSN only to "individuals affected by such laws." This, apparently, applies only to that narrow sect of the population that owes taxes or wishes to drive. Everybody else can skate. Thank you Big Brother.

POCKETBOOK NUMBERS

Many of you have inquired about pocketbook SSNs. What are they? Why didn't I mention them in my last book? Don't worry, we'll get to all that. First, a brief story about the most misused SSN of all time, courtesy of the Social Security Adminstation.

The Most Misused SSN of All Time

The most misused SSN of all time was 078-05-1120. In 1938, the E. H. Ferree Company, a wallet manufacturer in Lockport, New York, decided to promote its product by showing how a Social Security card would fit into its wallets. A sample card, used for display purposes, was inserted in each wallet. Company Vice President and Treasurer Douglas Patterson thought it would be a clever idea to use the actual SSN of his secretary, Mrs. Hilda Schrader Whitcher.

Woolworth and other department stores sold the wallet all over the country. Even though the card was only half the size of a real card, was printed all in red, and had the word "specimen" written across the face, many purchasers of the wallet adopted the SSN as their own. In the peak year of 1943, 5,755 people were using Hilda's number. SSA acted to eliminate the problem by voiding the number and publicizing that it was incorrect to use it (Mrs. Whitcher was given a new number). However, the number continued to be used for many years. In all, over 40,000 people reported it as their SSN. As late as 1977, 12 people were found to still be using the SSN "issued by Woolworth."

Mrs. Whitcher recalled coming back from lunch one day to find her fellow workers teasing her about her newfound fame. They were singing the refrain from a popular song of the day, "Here comes the million-dollar baby from the five and ten cent store."

Although the snafu gave her a measure of fame, it was mostly a nuisance. The FBI even showed up at her door to ask her about the widespread use of her number.

The New York wallet manufacturer was not the only one to cause confusion about Social Security numbers. More than a dozen similar cases have occurred over the years, usually when someone publishes a facsimile of an SSN using a made-up number. But the Whitcher case is by far the worst involving a real SSN and an actual person.

One embarrassing episode was the fault of the Social Security Board itself. In 1940, the board published a pamphlet explaining the new program and showing a facsimile of a card on the cover. The card in the illustration used a made-up number of 219-09-9999. Sure enough, in 1962 a woman presented herself to the Provo, Utah, Social Security office complaining that her new employer was refusing to accept her old Social Security number (219-09-9999). When it was explained that this could not possibly be her number, she whipped out her copy of the 1940 pamphlet to prove that yes indeed it was her number!

TABLE 9.1
Known "Pocketbook" SSNs

There are now over 200 different pocketbook SSNs, each caused by some organization displaying an actual number in its advertising.
This chart depicts some of the better known examples.

022-28-1852
141-18-5941
212-09-7694
042-10-3580
165-15-7999
219-09-9999
062-36-0749
155-18-7999

Identity, Privacy, and Personal Freedom

306-30-2348
078-05-1120
165-20-7999
308-12-5070
095-07-3645
165-22-7999
468-28-8779
128-03-6045
165-24-7999
549-24-1889
135-01-6629
189-09-2294
937-65-4320

Okay, enough anecdotes. I know all you privacy seekers and identity changers out there are wondering how to turn these cute little numbers to your advantage.

Using Pocketbook SSNs

These numbers exist. They no longer belong to anybody. And they can come in handy in a pinch. Memorizing a few of these numbers will get the privacy seeker past that annoying "SSN: ___-__-____" line on pseudobureaucratic applications. Does a video store, Internet service provider, or dental office really need to know your SSN? Do you feel like going through the hassle of explaining why you shouldn't have to give it to them? Neither do I, most of the time. So, when some little snot-nosed receptionist says, "Your Social Security number . . ." Just rattle off one of the pocketbook numbers you memorized and keep the "screw you" part to yourself.

If, for some reason, you get into a jam because the bureaucrat decides to run your SSN, you have a couple of advantages by using the pocketbook number. First, it won't end up belonging to some cop or FBI agent, who would then be notified and request an interview with you. And second, you can always claim ignorance, explaining it was one of those wallet inserts you memorized as a kid. You can then go on to explain, "After my head injury, I've forgotten a lot of things and made many stupid mistakes such as this. One time when I was pulled over, I handed the police officer my ATM card instead of my license. Golly gee, golly gee."

The biggest disadvantage for any serious use of a pocketbook SSN is that the SSA has a database of them. That's not to say they can't be used to open up an occasional bank account by mail (see Chapter 10, "Banking Privacy"), but don't be surprised if you receive an IRS Form W9, Request for Taxpayer Identification and Certification, with your bank statement at some point after establishing the account.

If you get such a form from the bank, don't panic. This has happened to me, or rather, a passing acquaintance of mine, on at least one occasion, and I, or rather, the acquaintance, simply ignored the W9. All that happened is the bank began to withhold federal income tax on the interest.

DOES THE LAW REQUIRE A SOCIAL SECURITY NUMBER?

There is no language in the Social Security Act requiring a person to have an SSN. So I decided to ask Social Security if I needed one. Their response is printed below (I did not use my real name to request the info).

Dear [Mr. Charrett]:

The Social Security Act does not require a person to have a Social Security number (SSN) to live and work in the United States, nor does it require an SSN simply for the purpose of having one. However, if someone works without an SSN, we cannot properly credit the earnings for the work performed.

Other laws require people to have and use SSNs for specific purposes. For example, the Internal Revenue Code (26 U.S.C. 6109 (a)) and applicable regulations (26 CFR 301.6109-l(d)) require an individual to get and use an SSN on tax documents and to furnish the number to any other person or institution (such as an employer or a bank) that is required to provide the Internal Revenue Service (IRS) information about payments to the individual. There are penalties for failure to do so. The IRS also requires employers to report SSNs with employees' earnings. In addition, people filing tax returns for taxable years after December 31, 1994, generally must include the SSN of each dependent.

The Privacy Act regulates the use of SSNs by government agencies. They may require an SSN only if a law or regulation either orders or authorizes them to do so. Agencies are required to disclose the authorizing law or regulation. If the request has no legal basis, the person may refuse to provide the number and still receive the agency's services. However, the law does not apply to private sector organizations. Such an organization can refuse its services to anyone who does not provide the number on request.

This response letter was unsigned. For the sake of convenience, I'll call the respondent Sadaam. Sadaam's references to 26 U.S.C. 6109 (a) and 26 CFR 301.6109-l(d) are for the most part accurate. But there are some very important things to keep in mind:

- The IRS code only applies to persons required to file a "return, statement or other document" with the IRS. If you are not required to file a tax return, you are not required to apply for an SSN.
- The same code requires a sole proprietor to use an EIN (employer identification number). Therefore if you work for yourself and hire yourself out as an independent contractor, you are required to furnish your hirer (not "employer") with your EIN. Therefore, if you always work this way, you'll never need an SSN.

Even if you are required to apply for and furnish your employer with an SSN, your employer may not compel you to provide it. When you are hired, your employer will ask you to fill out an IRS Form W4. Here's the relevant regulation, with my emphasis in italics:

> CFR 301.6109-l(c)
> Requirement to furnish another's number.
> . . . The taxpayer identifying number of any person furnishing a withholding certificate . . . shall also be furnished *if it is actually known* to the person making a return, statement, or other document . . . If the person making the return, statement, or other document *does not know* the taxpayer identifying *number* of the other person . . . *such person must request* the other person's number. The request should state that the identifying number is required to be furnished under authority of law. *When the person making the return,* statement, or other document does not know the number of the other person, and *has complied with the request* provision of this paragraph (c), *such person must sign an affidavit* on the transmittal document forwarding such returns, statements, or other documents to the Internal Revenue Service, *so stating.* A person required to file a taxpayer identifying number shall correct any errors in such filing when such person's attention has been drawn to them.

In shorthand: if the person making the return does not know your taxpayer number (SSN), such person must request it from you. If you refuse to provide it, they must sign an affidavit stating they tried to get it from you. That's the law.

Just be careful to not disclose your SSN during the application process. Many people are afraid that omitting their SSN from a job application will negatively affect their chances of getting the job. That's a reasonable fear. If an application requests your SSN, simply use a pocketbook number. The application is not a government document, and you probably aren't breaking any laws. You can also use an invalid SSN or an SSN that has yet to be issued. (For examples of pocketbook, invalid, and yet-to-be-issued SSNs, see Tables 9.1 through 9.4.)

Table 9.2
THE MOST COMPREHENSIVE AREA-OF-ISSUE CHART AVAILABLE

Every privacy and ID book has an area-of-issue chart to help privacy seekers invent legitimate-sounding SSNs. Unfortunately, many of these charts are either outdated or were watered down to begin with. Here, then, is the most comprehensive and up-to-date area-of-issue chart currently available.

Area Number	Issuing State or Territory
001–003	New Hampshire
318–361	Illinois
520	Wyoming
004–007	Maine
362–386	Michigan
521–524	Colorado
008–009	Vermont
387–399	Wisconsin
525 & 585	New Mexico
010–034	Massachusetts
400–407	Kentucky
526–527, 600–601	Arizona
035–039	Rhode Island
408–415	Tennessee
528–529	Utah
040–049	Connecticut
416–424	Alabama
530	Nevada
050–134	New York
425–428	Mississippi
531–539	Washington
135–158	New Jersey
429–432	Arkansas
540–544	Oregon
159–211	Pennsylvania
433–439	Louisiana
545–573	California
212–220	Maryland
440–448	Oklahoma

Area Number	Issuing state or Territory
574 *	Alaska
221–222	Delaware
449–467	Texas
575–576	Hawaii
223–231	Virginia
468–477	Minnesota
577–579	Washington, D.C.
232–236	West Virginia
478–485	Iowa
580	Virgin Islands
232–30-xxxx **	North Carolina
486–500	Missouri
580–584	Puerto Rico
237–246	North Carolina
501–502	North Dakota
585	New Mexico
247–251	South Carolina
503–504	South Dakota
586 & 587	Guam, Samoa and Philippines
252–260	Georgia
505–508	Nebraska
587–588	Mississippi (new issue)
261–267	Florida
509–515	Kansas
589–595	Florida
268–302	Ohio
516–517	Montana
602–626	California
303–317	Indiana
518–519	Idaho
700–728	Railroad Retirement Board

* From April 1975 through November 1979, Southeast Asian refugees were assigned SSNs from areas 574, 580, and 586.
** Group 30 in Area 232 has been transferred from West Virginia to North Carolina.

So What's with the Railroad Retirement Board?

I've often wondered that myself. After reading two dozen ID books and not getting the answer, I decided to do some further investigation.

The economic conditions of the 1930s demonstrated the need for retirement plans on a national basis, because few of the nation's elderly were covered under any type of retirement program. While the Social Security system was in the planning stage, railroad workers sought a separate retirement system which would continue and broaden the existing railroad programs under a uniform national plan. The proposed Social Security System was not scheduled to begin monthly benefit payments for several years and would not give credit for service performed before 1937, while conditions in the railroad industry called for immediate benefit payments based on prior service.

Legislation was enacted in 1934, 1935, and 1937 to establish a railroad retirement system separate

Identity, Privacy, and Personal Freedom

from the Social Security program legislated in 1935. Such legislation, taking into account particular circumstances of the rail industry, was not without precedent. Numerous laws pertaining to rail operations and safety had already been enacted since the Interstate Commerce Act of 1887 (source: Railroad Retirement Board).

The short story is that the RR retirement melds somewhat with the Social Security program, but the retired RR workers and their survivors are entitled to extra benefits. Essentially, they get a pension on top of their standard Social Security allowance.

Looking at Table 9.5, you'll note the last group issued to RR workers was 14 in area 728. You'll also note by looking at the chart in Appendix A that the last number was issued in 1956.

This means that unless exactly 9,999 RR workers applied for a number that year, there are a few (and probably more than a few) unused SSNs that will pass the high-group charts used by banks, creditors, and your friendly neighborhood pharmacist—not to mention the IRS. If you were age 59 or older in 1999, you may find some privacy in these numbers. NOTE: I happen to know that 9987 to 9999 have already been borrowed by identity changers.

Invalid SSNs

Watch out! When inventing SSNs for privacy, personal freedom, or new identity, don't unintentionally create an invalid SSN. If you know what you're doing, an invalid SSN can be useful on job applications, when dealing with low-level bureaucrats, or even when opening up a bank account. But unconsciously throwing around an invalid SSN can spell trouble with certain officials, such as registry cops.

So, how do you know which SSNs are invalid? You check it against Table 9.3, that's how.

TABLE 9.3
Chart of Invalid SSNs

Area	Group	Pre-1965 Group	Serial No.
Any number beginning with the following is invalid	Any number with these middle two digits is invalid	Any number with these middle two digits could not have been issued before 1965	Any number with this serial number is invalid
000	00	02 through 08	0000
729 through 999	Any group not yet issued by the given area	11 through 99	
700 through 728 could not have been issued after 1963			

The above table is a quick reference for SSNs that are always invalid. You may be wondering what is meant by the second entry in the group column. To be valid, an invented SSN must have a group number equal to or lower than the highest group issued for that area. The phase "equal to or lower" is misleading, though, because the SSA does not assign group numbers in sequential order. The chart below shows the order in which group numbers are issued.

TABLE 9.4
SSA Group Order of Issue

1. 01	34. 66	67. 35
2. 03	35. 68	68. 37
3. 05	36. 70	69. 39
4. 07	37. 72	70. 41
5. 09	38. 74	71. 43
6. 10	39. 76	72. 45
7. 12	40. 78	73. 47
8. 14	41. 80	74. 49
9. 16	42. 82	75. 51
10. 18	43. 84	76. 53
11. 20	44. 86	77. 55
12. 22	45. 88	78. 57
13. 24	46. 90	79. 59
14. 26	47. 92	80. 61
15. 28	48. 94	81. 63
16. 30	49. 96	82. 65
17. 32	50. 98	83. 67
18. 34	51. 02	84. 69
19. 36	52. 04	85. 71
20. 38	53. 06	86. 73
21. 40	54. 08	87. 75
22. 42	55. 11	88. 77
23. 44	56. 13	89. 79
24. 46	57. 15	90. 81
25. 48	58. 17	91. 83
26. 50	59. 19	92. 85
27. 52	60. 21	93. 87
28. 54	61. 23	94. 89
29. 56	62. 25	95. 91
30. 58	63. 27	96. 93
31. 60	64. 29	97. 95
32. 62	65. 31	98. 97
33. 64	66. 33	99. 99

Table 9.5 below shows the highest groups issued as of May 31, 1999. Use Table 9.4 to determine which groups were issued before the current highest group and which groups have yet to be issued.

TABLE 9.5
Highest Group Issued
as of April 1, 1999

Note: * indicates group change since last month.

001 92	002 92	003 92*	004 98	005 98	006 98
007 96	008 82	009 82	010 82	011 82	012 82
013 82	014 82	015 82	016 82	017 82	018 82
019 82	020 82	021 82	022 82	023 82	024 82*
025 80	026 80	027 80	028 80	029 80	030 80
031 80	032 80	033 80	034 80	035 66	036 66
037 66	038 66	039 64	040 98	041 98	042 98
043 98	044 98	045 98	046 98	047 96	048 96
049 96	050 88	051 88	052 88	053 88	054 88
055 88	056 88	057 88	058 88	059 88	060 88
061 88	062 88	063 88	064 88	065 88	066 88
067 88	068 88	069 88	070 88	071 88	072 88
073 88	074 88	075 88	076 88	077 88	078 88
079 88	080 88	081 88	082 88	083 88	084 88
085 88	086 88	087 88	088 88	089 88	090 88*
091 88*	092 88*	093 88*	094 86	095 86	096 86
097 86	098 86	099 86	100 86	101 86	102 86
103 86	104 86	105 86	106 86	107 86	108 86
109 86	110 86	111 86	112 86	113 86	114 86
115 86	116 86	117 86	118 86	119 86	120 86
121 86	122 86	123 86	124 86	125 86	126 86
127 86	128 86	129 86	130 86	131 86	132 86
133 86	134 86	135 04	136 04	137 04	138 04
139 04	140 04	141 04	142 04	143 04	144 04
145 04	146 04	147 04	148 04	149 04	150 04
151 04	152 04	153 04	154 04	155 04	156 04
157 04*	158 02	159 78	160 78	161 78	162 78
163 78	164 78	165 78	166 78	167 78	168 78
169 78	170 78	171 78	172 78	173 78	174 78
175 78	176 78	177 78	178 78	179 78	180 78
181 78	182 78	183 78	184 78	185 78*	186 78*
187 76	188 76	189 76	190 76	191 76	192 76
193 76	194 76	195 76	196 76	197 76	198 76
199 76	200 76	201 76	202 76	203 76	204 76
205 76	206 76	207 76	208 76	209 76	210 76
211 76	212 55*	213 53	214 53	215 53	216 53
217 53	218 53	219 53	220 53	221 90	222 90
223 83	224 83	225 83	226 83	227 83	228 83*
229 81	230 81	231 81	232 47*	233 45	234 45
235 45	236 45	237 89	238 89	239 89	240 89

241 89	242 89	243 89	244 89	245 89	246 89*
247 99	248 99	249 99	250 99	251 99	252 99
253 99	254 99	255 99	256 99	257 99	258 99
259 99	260 99	261 99	262 99	263 99	264 99
265 99	266 99	267 99	268 04	269 04	270 04
271 04	272 04	273 04	274 04	275 04	276 04
277 04*	278 02	279 02	280 02	281 02	282 02
283 02	284 02	285 02	286 02	287 02	288 02
289 02	290 02	291 02	292 02	293 02	294 02
295 02	296 02	297 02	298 02	299 02	300 02
301 02	302 02	303 21	304 21	305 21	306 21
307 21	308 21	309 21*	310 19	311 19	312 19
313 19	314 19	315 19	316 19	317 19	318 96
319 96	320 96	321 96*	322 96*	323 94	324 94
325 94	326 94	327 94	328 94	329 94	330 94
331 94	332 94	333 94	334 94	335 94	336 94
337 94	338 94	339 94	340 94	341 94	342 94
343 94	344 94	345 94	346 94	347 94	348 94
349 94	350 94	351 94	352 94	353 94	354 94
355 94	356 94	357 94	358 94	359 94	360 94
361 94	362 23	363 23	364 23	365 23	366 23
367 23	368 23	369 23	370 23	371 23	372 23
373 23	374 23	375 23	376 23	377 23	378 23*
379 21	380 21	381 21	382 21	383 21	384 21
385 21	386 21	387 19	388 19	389 19*	390 17
391 17	392 17	393 17	394 17	395 17	396 17
397 17	398 17	399 17	400 53	401 53	402 53
403 53	404 53	405 53	406 53	407 53*	408 85
409 85	410 85	411 85	412 85	413 85	414 83
415 83	416 49	417 49	418 49	419 49	420 49
421 49*	422 47	423 47	424 47	425 85	426 85
427 85	428 85	429 97*	430 95	431 95	432 95
433 99	434 99	435 99*	436 97	437 97	438 97
439 97	440 13	441 13	442 11	443 11	444 11
445 11	446 11	447 11	448 11	449 99	450 99
451 99	452 99	453 99	454 99	455 99	456 99
457 99	458 99	459 99	460 99	461 99	462 99
463 99	464 99	465 99	466 99	467 99	468 35
469 35	470 35	471 35	472 35	473 35	474 35
475 35*	476 33	477 33	478 29	479 27	480 27
481 27	482 27	483 27	484 27	485 27	486 15
487 15	488 15	489 15	490 15	491 15	492 15
493 15	494 15	495 15*	496 13	497 13	498 13
499 13	500 13	501 25	502 25	503 29	504 29
505 39	506 39	507 39	508 39	509 17	510 17
511 15	512 15	513 15	514 15	515 15	516 33
517 33*	518 55	519 55	520 39	521 99	522 99
523 99	524 99	525 99	526 99	527 99	528 99
529 99	530 99	531 41	532 41	533 41	534 41
535 41	536 41	537 41	538 41	539 41*	540 55

Identity, Privacy, and Personal Freedom

541 55	542 55*	543 53	544 53	545 99	546 99
547 99	548 99	549 99	550 99	551 99	552 99
553 99	554 99	555 99	556 99	557 99	558 99
559 99	560 99	561 99	562 99	563 99	564 99
565 99	566 99	567 99	568 99	569 99	570 99
571 99	572 99	573 99	574 27	575 83	576 83
577 31	578 29	579 29	580 33	581 99	582 99
583 99	584 99	585 99	586 39	587 83	589 81
590 81	591 81	592 81	593 81*	594 81*	595 79
596 60	597 60	598 58	599 58	600 87	601 87*
602 13*	603 11	604 11	605 11	606 11	607 11
608 11	609 11	610 11	611 11	612 11	613 11
614 11	615 11	616 11	617 11	618 11	619 11
620 11*	621 11*	622 11*	623 11*	624 11*	625 11*
626 11*	627 66*	628 66*	629 66*	630 66*	631 64
632 64	633 64	634 64	635 64	636 64	637 64
638 64	639 64	640 64	641 64	642 64	643 64
644 64	645 64	646 46	647 44	648 18*	649 16
650 10*	651 09	652 09	653 09	654 05	655 05
656 05	657 05*	658 03	667 05	668 05*	669 05*
670 03	671 03	672 03	673 03	674 03	675 03
680 14*	700 18	701 18	702 18	703 18	704 18
705 18	706 18	707 18	708 18	709 18	710 18
711 18	712 18	713 18	714 18	715 18	716 18
717 18	718 18	719 18	720 18	721 18	722 18
723 18	724 28	725 18	726 18	727 10	728 14

Notes on Using Invalid SSNs

If you are claiming to have had the SSN for any length of time, the group number should not be a recently issued one. For example if the high group for your area is 52 and you invent an SSN such as xxx-50-xxxx or even xxx-48-xxxx, a savvy bureaucrat may realize that these groups could not have been issued more than a few years ago. If the bureaucrat is staring into the face of a 60-year-old man claiming he was issued the SSN as a teenager, she'll be pressing frantically on the magic red button beneath her desk.

Being able to determine the approximate year of issue for a given area-group combination would be very helpful for privacy seekers. Some ways of doing this were given in my first book. Rather than repeat those methods here, I'll offer a couple of different solution.

The Modern Identity Changer refers readers to an Eden Press book entitled *Social Security Number Fraud* that has in it a 25-page table of geographic and chronological distribution of SSNs from 1951 to 1978. This table should suffice for all but the youngest of privacy seekers. I still highly recommend this book for the excellent insight it offers into the inner workings of the SSA and how it goes about detecting fraud. But as a labor of love, I have reproduced the SSA table in Appendix A as a spreadsheet document. It took me two days to enter in all the data, and I damn near hacked my ear off about halfway through the second day. Since that solution did not bode well for Mr. Van Gogh, I decided to take a break and finish the task after a big dinner and a night's sleep. I felt I owed this to privacy seekers, freedom fighters, and identity changers around the world.

If you were under the age of 21 in 1999, you will immediately realize that this table, extending only to 1978, is useless to you. In my previous book I mentioned that I have yet to come across a complete SSN area-group chronology. I have since learned the reason for this.

I wrote the SSA demanding that, since credit bureaus have access this information, then I, as a citizen of the United States, should also have the same access. Their reply:

Dear [Mr. Charrett]:

Thank you for your inquiry regarding Social Security numbers (SSN).

The Social Security Administration can only tell you when an individual SSN was issued by looking at our records. We also provide a "High Group Listing" that provides the SSN area and group numbers that are in the process of being issued.

If an agency had a computer program that updated this information monthly, they would then be able to tell when an SSN was issued. This, to our knowledge, would be the only way.

The last line of this response falls just a bit south of being completely forthright. Upon further investigation, I learned that the big three credit bureaus managed to hook into the SSA's computer for a few years. Then, after public complaint, a federal judge kicked them out. The credit bureaus, however, were allowed to keep the info they already had (which was just about all they needed—convenient isn't it?)

So what are you youngsters to do?

Well, you can use the tables in this book, follow population trends, and estimate the high group for your birth year in your target area. Or, you could use any of the methods outlined in my previous book.

Banking Privacy

I am not a number! I am a free man!
Patrick McGoohan in *The Prisoner* television series

The more I deal with banks, the more I realize how pitifully useless they are. Due to supermergers that take place almost daily, the number of banks is shrinking and the industry itself has, in fact, already become a monopoly. Interest rates are roughly the same from one bank to the next. Charges, overdraft penalties, ATM transaction fees, and even business hours vary little from bank to bank. Tight federal regulations, ostensibly implemented to protect the public, effectively eliminate open competition between banks. If you need a bank, you might as well pick the one closest to you because they're all the same.

Later in this chapter I'm going to describe why bank accounts are not needed and why the general public should boycott them (if the above reasons aren't enough). But if you absolutely must have bank accounts, there are a few things you should know about opening them — especially if you're an identity changer.

OPENING A BANK ACCOUNT WITHOUT A SOCIAL SECURITY NUMBER

You'd never know it by the way bank bureaucrats act, but it's perfectly legal to open a bank account without using your Social Security number. Under current U.S. law, the IRS only requires the *name and address* of each person to whom interest of more than $10 is paid in any given year:

> 26 USC, Section 6049
> (a) Requirement of reporting
> Every person—
> (1) who makes payments of interest (as defined in subsection (b)) aggregating $10 or more to any other person during any calendar year, or
> (2) who receives payments of interest (as so defined) as a nominee and who makes payments aggregating $10 or more during any calendar year to any other person with respect to the interest so received,
> shall make a return according to the forms or regulations prescribed by the Secretary, setting forth the aggregate amount of such payments and the *name and address* of the person to whom paid.

While it's true the section leaves open the possibility for the Secretary to promulgate regulations (as you'll see below), the courts typically hold that regulations may not be more restrictive than actual law. Therefore, if you want to spend the time and aggravation to fight them, you can force a bank to open an account for you. Of course, they'll resist. But you can corner them by having a ready-to-launch attack plan for each turn of their resistance. Or, you can do it the easy way.

The Easy Way

The easy way is to open a non-interest-bearing account in the name of your sole proprietorship, which can be your given name alone or your name DBA your company name (DBA means "doing business as"). When the clerk asks for your taxpayer identification number, give the number assigned to you by the IRS.

Bank clerks often have great difficulty dealing with anything out of the ordinary. The clerk is used to opening regular personal bank accounts and may become confused that yours is a business account. Out of habit, the clerk may ask for your SSN. But give the TIN anyway. If you use the typical SSN rhythm (xxx-xx-xxxx), the clerk won't even notice what you've done. Let me explain.

The TIN is a nine-digit number just like a Social Security number. However, the IRS breaks it down thusly: xx-xxxxxxx. But when the clerk mistakenly asks for your SSN, you will save a lot of hassle by saying, "blah, blah, blah (pause), blah, blah (pause), blah, blah, blah, blah," just as if you were rattling off an SSN. The clerk will write the number into the application without missing a beat, so to speak.

You will have done nothing illegal. The IRS in fact *requires* sole proprietors to use a TIN. All you'll have done is avoided the tedious process of explaining to the clerk the difference between SSNs and TINs, which would have only resulted in a series of long, dumb looks followed by a call to the bank manager, who will have ultimately confirmed your explanation.

Of course, the SSN rhythm trick may come in handy for less magnanimous purposes. Be aware, however, that writing a TIN with the incorrect "rhythm" is actually illegal in some circumstances.

The Less Easy Way

This is the same method as above, except that a layer of bureaucratic difficulty has been added with the reward of an additional benefit. When the clerk asks you for your TIN, tell her that you just applied for it. She'll give you a blank stare as her finger frantically stabs for the big red button under her desk. Or she'll excuse herself to go talk to her supervisor. Her supervisor will come out and ask you the same question. Upon your reply, he'll say, "Ahhh," hold up a finger, and walk out back to call the main branch. While you wait, the clerk at the main branch will run and ask the district manager if he's ever heard of such a thing . . . blah, blah, blah.

Eventually, someone (probably someone else) will come over and write "applied for" next to the little TIN box on the application. Then the original clerk will come back and finish filling in the other boxes.

So, What's the Advantage?

I thought you might ask that. The advantage is, you now have a bank account without any SSN, TIN, or other identifying number on it! But . . . what? What's that you say? You told the clerk the TIN was "applied for." Won't the bank wonder where it is? I thought you might ask that too. Now for the fun stuff.

The following has been excerpted from the Code of Federal Regulations Title 31, Volume 1, Part 103, and is accurate as of July 1, 1998. I have added all emphasis (italic, bold). Legal permutations not relative to (or affecting) our purposes have been omitted as indicated by an ellipsis (. . .).

TITLE 31
MONEY AND FINANCE: TREASURY

CHAPTER I
MONETARY OFFICES, DEPARTMENT OF THE TREASURY

PART 103
FINANCIAL RECORDKEEPING AND REPORTING OF CURRENCY AND
FOREIGN TRANSACTIONS

Subpart C—Records Required To Be Maintained

Sec. 103.34 Additional records to be made and retained by banks.

(a)(1) With respect to each certificate of deposit sold or redeemed after May 31, 1978, or each deposit or share account opened with a bank after June 30, 1972, a bank shall, within 30 days from the date such a transaction occurs or an account is opened, secure and maintain a record of the taxpayer identification number of the customer involved;
(. . .)
[If] a bank has been unable to secure . . . the required identification, it shall nevertheless *not* be deemed to be in violation of this section **if (i) it has made a reasonable effort** to secure such identification, **and (ii) it maintains a list** containing the names, addresses, and account numbers of those persons from whom it has been unable to secure such identification, and makes the names, addresses, and account numbers of those persons available to the Secretary as directed by him.
(. . .)
(2) **The 30-day period** provided for in paragraph (a)(1) of this section **shall be extended where the person** opening the account **has applied for a taxpayer identification or social security number on Form SS-4 or SS-5**, until such time as the person maintaining the account has had a **reasonable opportunity** to secure such number and furnish it to the bank.

First of all, the bank has 30 days before it has to worry about being in violation of the above section. During that time it will have opened dozens of accounts and gone happily about its business while effectively turning you into just another number on its screen. So, when some computer program recognizes your account as a potential violation of 31CFR103.34, you will be sent a form letter and an IRS Form W9, Request for Taxpayer Identification Number and Certification.

You can ignore these interminably, and the bank's only recourse is to add you to a "list" pursuant to the above section, which will protect it from liability under this "law." The bank may continue to send W9s on a regular basis. It's probably just a computer system doing this, so just continue to ignore them. I've done this myself (as well as for clients), and it has seldom been a problem. The subheading below, "Fight 'em Tooth 'n' Nail," will teach you how to tame banks that don't take no for an answer. But first, here are a few hassle-free ways around the TIN requirement worth mentioning. If you get the feeling that aliens have more privacy rights than U.S. citizens, you're right.

Sec. 103.34 Additional records to be made and retained by banks.
(3) A taxpayer identification number required under paragraph (a)(1) of this section need not be secured for accounts or transactions with the following:
(v) **aliens temporarily residing in the United States** for a period not to exceed 180 days;

(viii) a person **under 18** years of age **with respect to** an account opened as a part of **a school thrift savings program**, provided the annual interest is less than $10;

(ix) a person opening a Christmas club, vacation club and **similar installment savings programs** provided the annual interest is less than $10; and

(x) **non-resident aliens** who are not engaged in a trade or business in the United States.

Aliens (or alien identities) who meet the above requirements need not submit a TIN, but be prepared to present a passport or, my favorite, a provincial (Canadian) driver's license. The bank is pretty much stuck here. Canadians do not need passports to enter the United States. If they are nonresident aliens, they would also not have an alien registration card. Thus, the bank is forced to accept an easily manufactured (and difficult to verify) provincial driver's license as ID. Since the border patrol requires border-crossing Canadians to have a birth certificate, you may be asked to present one. But a college ID will usually suffice in its place (See Chapter 3, "How to Manufacture Professional-Quality Identity Documents").

A Christmas or vacation club account is a great place to hoard your cash. Just be sure to get a non-interest-bearing account if you plan to maintain an average monthly balance of more than a few hundred dollars. Here's a quick reference chart.

Average Balance	Interest Rate	Annual Interest
$300	3.0%	$9.12
$500	1.9%	$9.58
$1,000	1.0%	$10.05 (over the limit!)

Also note the above subsection (ix) does not define "similar installment savings programs." Therefore, you could argue that a passbook savings account, to which you intend to allocate regular deposits for a specific purpose, also qualifies under this section. Whether it actually does or not is irrelevant. It's not worth the bank's time to fight with you (see below).

Fight 'Em Tooth 'n' Nail

Tom Scambos at www.tax-freedom.com has put together a pretty nifty kit based, in part, on the above laws. The kit helps U.S. citizens force banks to open a non-SSN/TIN bank account for them. It comes complete with boilerplate letters that effectively handle just about any response or rejection a bank might send your way.

The kit provides valid legal arguments to help you fight any bank that suggests collection of an SSN/TIN is mandatory. It isn't. Each boilerplate letter references current laws, court decisions, or Constitutional rights, including rights of religious freedom, that specifically prohibit any bank from forcing a number out of you. Even if the bank does not agree with the letters, you'll dredge up enough legal muck to send its law department into convulsions. The kit includes:

- Cover letter to the bank
- Statement of citizenship in duplicate
- Legal notice and demand to any bank for compliance with the law
- Potential response letters and exhibits—approximately 35 pages complete

In the end the bank will quietly give you what you want. If it doesn't, you will sue it for a lot of money. I have reviewed the SSN kit and have found it to be accurate, worthy, thorough, and well thought out. You can order it at:

R SAFE
P.O. Box 7720
Arlington, VA 22207
Or online at:
www.tax-freedom.com
scambos@erols.com

The cost is $15 for cash, check, or money order, $20 if you use a credit card.

The tax-freedom.com web site (and others like it) is fun to visit and can be intellectually stimulating. But do take the time to research the legal references so you know what you're talking about if you ever decide to stop paying taxes.

OPENING ALTERNATE ID BANK ACCOUNTS

As Big Brother tightens bank regulations and assigns more police power to financial institutions, casual privacy seekers may justifiably fear losing the option of alternate ID bank accounts.

Now, I can't tell you to run out the door this minute and open a private bank account, because I may get in trouble. What I will say is this: casual privacy seekers wishing to open an alternate ID bank account should think about it first, take several deep breaths, and, well, don't wait too long. Otherwise you may soon need to create a hard-core new identity just to fill that purpose.

The easiest way to open an alternate ID bank account is through the mail. It is not, however, the quickest way.

Mail-Order Bank Accounts

Many banks will allow you to open an account through the mail. Send a letter to the bank explaining that you are planning to move to its lovely town and would like an account set up in advance for a smooth transition. Identity changers would use their mail drop as a return address. Oh, and the more money you "expect to deposit" the less hassles you'll have.

Choose a bank that offers an ATM card on a national network, preferably for a minimal fee. You'll need the card sent to your mail drop so it will be available for "traveling emergencies" as you trek across the country to the bank's lovely state.

A rural setting for your new home (or at least for the bank) will simplify things. Many rural banks will send you a nice welcome letter explaining how they look forward to you becoming a member of their community. Of course, they will need to see a photocopy of your driver's license and Social Security card when you send in the account application. If you don't want to get involved in detailed forgeries, I'll provide some alternatives in the following section. First, I'd like to share something with you.

I have reprinted for you here a letter I wrote to a certain bank in South Carolina and its response. The names of the bank and town have been changed. There are two reasons for this: (1) I'm not going to burn out my own connections, and (2) if I publish the name of a real bank, so many people will write them the same letter they'll get suspicious and I'll get my beloved readers into trouble. Suffice to say you must find your own bank and write your own letter. The rest of the information is verbatim. Here's how it worked:

Dear First Merchants Bank:

After visiting Merrill's Corner last autumn, I was so taken by the beauty of the area and the kindness of the people I began seriously to consider moving there. The more I thought about Merrill's Corner, the more I realized my present "home" lacks the sense of community so prevalent in Merrill's Corner.

I've recently made a big decision. I'm moving to Merrill's Corner!

I am writing to you because I'd like to establish a checking account now for a smooth transition (moving is tough enough as it is).

Could you please write me with the proper procedure for accomplishing this? I'd also like information on your savings accounts, CDs, and mortgage loans.

Very probably yours,

Sheldon X. Charrett

P.S. My initial deposit may be low, but right before I move I will be transferring a substantial sum of money (about $84,500) to your bank. Would this need to be a cashier's check or is it okay just to write a regular check?

Their response:

Dear Mr. Charrett:

We at First Merchants Bank are happy to hear that you will be moving soon to the Merrill's Corner area, and banking with us. We have several types of accounts including the regular checking account, as well as interest bearing checking accounts, such as the Money Market account, Advantage Checking and the Now account. I have enclosed a brochure indicating the various accounts we offer.

I am also enclosing a signature account [sic] and a new customer information sheet for you to complete. There is a self-addressed stamped envelope for your convenience. When you return your opening deposit, please include the following:

1) Copy of your picture I.D.
2) Copy of your social security card
3) Deposit (money order or cashier's check)

Once I receive this information, I will have your starting kit checkbook and a receipt sent to you. Mr. Charrett, I look forward to meeting you, and our officers and staff will do everything possible to merit the confidence you have shown by coming to our bank.

Sincerely,

Mary Williamson
Customer Service Representative

Enclosures

The enclosures were, in fact, a new customer information sheet as indicated and a signature card (not a signature account as written). Included also was a booklet entitled *About Your Account*, which described the various accounts and answered my question about the $84,500 deposit that I never made.

The signature card was marked with an X in two spaces. Stapled to it was a hand-printed letter stating, "Just sign your name." What could be more simple?

When I wrote Mary back with the appropriate documentation, I left the "Just sign your name" note stapled to the signature card to jog her memory and to keep her suspicions at bay. Here then, was my follow-up letter:

Dear Ms. Williamson:

Thank you for the information you sent and for all your help. Enclosed is the material you requested as well as a check for $100 to open the account.

I'll keep an eye out for my receipt and starting kit checkbook. By the way, the pamphlet you sent did not mention anything about your mortgage loans. If your bank does mortgage loans, could you please include that information in your mailing?

Otherwise, I hope all is going well for you and I look forward to meeting you after I relocate.

Thank you,

Sheldon X. Charrett

Just a few quick notes about my follow-up letter. It may seem as if I just threw it together, but certain words were chosen with great care. For example, the first sentence sets an amicable tone and reminds Mary that she's already worked with me and that I, as a customer, am satisfied with her performance. An unrecognized attempt to set up an account through the mail would normally be a red flag. Instead, she sees a new friend.

The second sentence uses the word "material" rather than "ID," "documents," or some other bureaucratic word. I do not need to remind friendly Mary that she is, in fact, a bureaucrat. Furthermore, since I am merely a person attempting to relocate (and not a fraudster), I did not want to appear fixated on the identity aspects of what I'd enclosed. After all, I'd also enclosed a check as well as an account application and a friendly cover letter. If I'd used the word "ID," Mary may wonder why I was so drawn to that portion of my mailing.

By requesting information on mortgage loans, I'm not only reinforcing the idea that I'm an honest-to-goodness immigrant to Mary's state but also tickling her sales bone. Suddenly I'm not just some schmuck who wants to open a checking account—now she might win brownie points or a commission when her bank writes my mortgage.

Quick and Dirty Docs

When opening a bank account by mail, it is not necessary to invest the time it takes to manufacture believable identity documents. Remember what Mary told us? All she needed were photocopies of a picture ID and Social Security card.

You will need to take some time to construct a photo ID, but it need not have a hologram, printing on the back, or even be a one-piece ID (see Chapter 3, "How To Manufacture Professional-Quality Identity Documents"), which reduces your time considerably. The ID need not even be in color, which makes it possible to construct one using cut-and-paste photocopy tricks, provided you do a good job. A modest work or student ID can be pasted together and laminated with wide scotch tape.

The final photocopy (the one you send to the bank) should "accidentally" be a bit too dark (but not unreadable). There's your picture ID.

For a Social Security card, follow this procedure:

1. Photocopy your own Social Security card.
2. White-out the name and SSN on the photocopy.
3. Type in your new name and SSN.
4. Photocopy the alterations.

This last photocopy is the one to send to the bank.

If the bank you are dealing with requires a driver's license instead of simply a photo ID, you may want to keep in mind that security features need not be exactly in place for photocopies. Out-of-state holograms can be bypassed altogether.

Handling the "Friendly Follow-up"

If, by chance, your letters moved Mary so much that she is compelled to write asking why you haven't moved yet (and therefore why you haven't made your big deposit or applied for a mortgage), here is a quick response you can fire off.

> *Dear Mary:*
>
> *My move has been delayed due to a family health emergency. I'd like to keep the account set up because I will be moving as soon as my grandmother kicks off.*
>
> *Best wishes,*
>
>
> *Your Name*

This will usually keep her off your back forever. Also, keep in mind there's no law against maintaining a long-distance bank account.

Bank Accounts: Phoning Them In

Many banks offer a toll-free number so people can open an account over the phone. You will need a name with a verifiable SSN because banks that offer this service are large, well-established, and thorough. Basically they do not *need* you as a customer, so your identity has to check out.

I had a bad phone experience that shook me up so much I had to abandon an identity I was rather fond of. The problem with being on the phone is that you have no time to prepare for the unexpected. All it takes is a prolonged stammer on one unexpected question and the phone rep can file a Suspicious Activity Report on you (see Chapter 1, "Big Brother Banking").

Another annoyance is those long pauses the account rep takes between questions. You don't know if the rep is pausing because your information seems dubious, because something popped up on her computer screen, or because she is just typing something or waiting for the computer to do its thing. All you hear is silence—no feedback. Even if all goes well, you will always be wondering if your account has been flagged.

Occasionally, you get a friendly phone rep who subvocalizes everything (i.e., thinks out loud to herself). This is what you want. You will readily know from voice inflections what the rep is thinking and how the application process is going.

In Person

You may think that my general phone uneasiness would automatically preclude me from opening bank accounts in person. Apples and oranges, my friends. I have little apprehension about face-to-face confrontations with bureaucrats.

In person, you have the option of picking and choosing what banks you walk into and which people you sit and talk with. Remember, banking by phone is usually only offered by large banks, which are tantamount to federal bureaus, and it's pretty much potluck who answers the phone. Opting for the "in person" approach, you can case your target and make sure it's the warm, kindly predisposed, farsighted, semiretiree you eventually sit down with.

But kindly bankers are hopelessly difficult to come by, right? Fortunately, there are even bigger advantages to opening your bank account in person.

Psychology and Novelty IDs

When I open bank accounts in person, I am well prepared and have tested my identity documents elsewhere. I think it's the security of knowing that I have good documentation to back me up that allays my fears and reinforces my confidence.

In person, I know I have psychology on my side. Over the phone I'm just another voice, and it's very hard to display that all-important presence. If I try to intimidate over the phone, the other party is likely to get angry since they have the option of hanging up at any time.

When I'm sitting next to someone, it is much easier to maintain the imposing presence of character necessary to mold and control the bureaucrat. On my best days, even the most lemon-faced bureaucrats can't do enough for me.

Know What to Expect

By knowing what to expect from a particular institution, your account opening experiences will go much easier. You will be prepared for all questions and you will have all the necessary documents. Here are some general things you should know about banks today:

- Most banks will photocopy any ID you give them.
- Most new accounts have a waiting period before certain sums of money (even if a cashier's check) can be cleared. If they tell you this, it does not mean you've been flagged.
- Many banks now run your name through a database to see if any other banks have outstanding issues with you, such as bounced checks or unpaid overdrafts. It is basically a credit-reporting system for banking habits and must comply with the Fair Credit Reporting Act.
- You will need to sign a "signature card" so the bank can have something on file to verify your signature during future tranactions.

These are just a few things to keep in mind. The best way to know a bank's procedure is to go to a branch office and open an account in your own name. Alternatively, you can go with a friend when he opens an account. Or you can simply spy on someone opening an account. Sit in a nearby chair with a big stack of checks, a calculator, and a deposit slip. Pretend you're adding up a rather complicated deposit and checking it twice. Listen to people opening accounts. When you're done, give a bug-eyed look at your watch, hastily throw everything back in your bag, and get to that appointment you forgot about!

Having an "Out"

Anytime you are tricking bureaucrats, there is the possibility of things going awry. Perhaps you forgot some piece of information, such as a new regulation or security check you were unaware of. It would be nice if you could dismiss yourself without exacerbating the bureaucrat's suspicions.

This contingency must be planned for, and there are many different ways to handle any given situation. Here are some thoughts . . .

Always be as pleasant as possible. If the bureaucrat suspects you of something, he'll be less likely to pursue it if you otherwise seem like a nice enough person. When you first sit down with the banker to open an account, say something like, "I'm just wondering how long this will take?" After he answers, mention that you have another appointment to get to and you're running a little late.

Hopefully your experience will go smoothly, but if it doesn't and the banker asks about some discrepancy in your paperwork or decides to call the college to check your student ID, you can say, "Well, if it's a problem, I'll come back later once I find my drivers' license. I really am late for that other appointment." Just get up, take your things, and try another bank.

Why Don't You Have a Drivers' License?

Rather than stammering for an excuse when a banker or other bureaucrat asks you this, why not consider some of the following:

- *Both my parents died in a car accident.* Say this bluntly with a serious face, and when the bureaucrat says, "Gosh. I'm really sorry," end the conversation.
- *I'm an epileptic.* You'll get roughly the same reply as above. This usually makes anyone feel guilty for being so narrow-minded. He won't pursue the topic, and neither should you. If he's ignorant enough to pursue it, just keep replying, "It's personal, I'd rather not discuss it." You might wish to solidify the image by wearing one of those medical dog tags or bracelets. A nice touch.
- *It's been suspended.* Just tell the nosy bastard the cops got your license. If he pursues it, ask him if he knows Bill W. There's a good chance he does. Bill W. is the founder of Alcoholics Anonymous, and there are more members than most people know. If the bureaucrat doesn't know what the hell you're talking about, just say you've had three DUI (drunk driving) convictions and you won't have a license again for a long, long time.
- *Are you serious? Drive around here?* This one goes over well in big cities. Works well with the student ID, too. If you have an out-of-state accent, tell the bureaucrat that your home city has even worse traffic.
- *The old standby.* This one also works well in big cities and has been used successfully by identity changers for years. Just tell the nosy bureaucrat, "I've lived in New York City all my life, so I've always used public transportation." If the nosy nasty gets snitty and pursues:

Snit: "How do you get into nightclubs and order drinks without a license?"
You: "I don't drink. The body is the temple of the lord."
Snit: "How do you cash checks, then?"
You: "Lenny & Maria's on 84th Street. They've known me since I was yay high."
Snit: "And when you're out of town?"
You: "Cash and traveler's cheques."

Just remain calm and confident and be sure to use the proper accent for whatever city you're claiming to be from, especially if it's the city you're in (in which case you'd better have the accent *down pat*).

W9 Forms

If for some reason you accidentally gave the bank an invalid SSN or TIN, you will receive an IRS Form W9, Request for Taxpayer Identification Number and Certification with your bank statement within a year after establishing the account. As mentioned in Chapter 9, "Social Security," under the subheading "Using Pocketbook SSNs," you can simply ignore the form, at which point the bank will start withholding federal tax on any interest earned.

Another option is to respond by supplying another SSN, a pocketbook SSN, or an existing TIN, or by sending the bank a letter explaining you are in the process of applying for a TIN (the W9 form will have instructions for doing just that).

In any case, your account will remain open for several more months, if not years. Just don't stash huge amounts of money there unless you don't mind losing it should the account be seized by authorities.

Deposit Tricks and Safety

Try walking into a bank and depositing a check made out to a business or a trust into your personal account. More often than not, you will be told you need to open an account in the name of the business in order for them to accept the deposit.

Now take the same check and deposit it in an automated teller machine (ATM). Your account will be properly credited in a few days. Does this make sense? No. But it's worth keeping in mind.

ATM Business Deposits

If you can manage to open a sole-proprietor account through the mail using an EIN as previously described, it may be to your advantage to hire somebody else to sign all the paperwork. This is because you can also make deposits into the account without ever signing a single check. When the feds bust you, your signature will appear nowhere!

Just make sure anybody who writes you a check properly fills in your complete business name. When you make ATM deposits you can leave the checks unsigned. The bank will stamp them "Unendorsed Instrument: Deposit to Account of Payee."

But sooner or later you know it's gonna happen: someone will write a check to Sheldon's Trust Thing instead of SXC Business Trust. While reasonable variations of the business name will usually be accepted, the bank cannot deposit this check unendorsed because it has no way of knowing what Sheldon's Trust Thing is. When you get an improperly filled out check, deposit it to your personal account via ATM as described above. Your personal account should be with another bank, preferably in another city.

If you make a lot of deposits, the bank might get sick of stamping your checks for you. It would also draw unwanted attention. For frequent depositors, a better solution is to stamp the checks yourself. You can have a rubber stamp made up for about $15, or you can print the endorsement from your computer. The following will suffice:

FOR DEPOSIT ONLY
To SXC BUSINESS TRUST
Acct. # nn-nnnnnnn-n

Okay, that's enough of banking in the real world. Let's touch on something new and upcoming: banking in the fake world . . .

VIRTUAL BANKING

Virtual banking has arrived. Already there are a handful of banks that transact business over the World Wide Web, and more are springing up every day. For the privacy seeker, this could be both advantageous and disastrous.

A legitimate virtual bank with secure browser forms is very safe and very private. You can do all your banking over the Internet and even pay your bills. But before signing on with a virtual bank, you'll want to make sure it's legitimate. You must be wary of fraudsters who set up phony virtual bank Web pages just to gather vital information on you, your bank accounts, and your credit card numbers.

Visit the virtual bank on several occasions before signing up. Call the state secretary's office and verify that the bank is registered with the state. Then call the bank and verify that it indeed has a Web page at the Internet address you've found. Ask questions and check the bank's responses. If anything makes you uncomfortable, find another v-bank.

Once you're confident you're dealing with a legitimate v-bank, sign up! V-banking is easy, private, convenient, and fun!

"What about us?" I seem to hear all you hard-core identity changers saying. Don't worry, I haven't forgotten you. Yes, as you might suspect, the advent of v-banking combined with the present lack of regulations specific to the same offers hard-core identity changers a new and convenient way to establish alternate ID bank accounts.

One v-bank at which I have some account-opening experience requires the following information to establish an account:

- First name
- Middle initial
- Last name
- Social Security number
- Driver's license or state-issued ID number
- Issuing state
- Date of birth
- Mother's maiden name
- Street address
- City
- State
- Zip code
- E-mail address
- Day phone
- Evening phone

In addition to entering this information online, you must print out the application, sign it, and mail it to them before your account will be opened. This is because federal bank regulations require an actual signature on file at the bank.

The above information may look innocuous, but every line of it can be used as a security checkpoint. The SSN can be checked against "Highest Group Issued" charts (see Table 9.5) or verified directly with the SSA to see if it matches the name you've given. The driver's license can be checked against state motor vehicle records. Your mom's maiden name can be used with your name and date of birth to verify birth records. The address information and date of birth can be verified against credit bureau information. The e-mail address can be validated, and the bank may call the given phone numbers to see who answers.

Depressing, isn't it? So what's the good news? You are not required to produce any identity documents—not even photocopies. Thus a properly created identity, even if lacking one or more of the vital components (actual birth record, driver's license, credit profile, etc.), can still open a v-bank account. The bank will not check all the information you provide and, in some cases, it may verify nothing.

By tailoring your application you can also dictate to the bank which, if any, of your information should be verified. For example, if you create a child banking identity, you can omit the driver's license information, and the bank will not waste its money looking for a credit report on a child. The bank in this case may call or write the "parents" to verify they are aware their "child" is opening a bank account, and it will almost certainly check the given SSN against its high group chart.

If all you want is a private account to move some money through (not for identity purposes or permanent use), the process is even more simple. Because you need not produce actual identity documents, you can borrow another's identity and set up an account. This could be your noncustodial child, a goody-two-shoes cousin, or even a perfect stranger. No harm whatsoever will come to the other person, and he or she will never even know about it as long as you open a non-interest-bearing account and keep transactions within IRS reporting thresholds (see Chapter 1, "Big Brother Is Getting Bigger," under "Big Brother Banking").

Even if you accidentally open an interest-bearing account (there's really no need to do so on purpose), your goody-two-shoes cousin will not be harmed. However, he may get an IRS notice stating the interest he reported should be $43.98 instead of $41.02. Personally, if I got such a notice, I would say "big froinkin' deal" and throw it away. But you should be aware of its potential to tip off a particularly number-conscious (read: anal retentive) cousin or stranger.

The above method works more permanently if your "host" identity happens to be recently deceased. If it also happens that you're the executor or voluntary administrator of the estate, well, that's even better. You'll be the one informed of the deceased's "extra" account. In any case, the account must be opened shortly after death to avoid credit bureau checks turning up a "deceased as of April 1, 2000" fraud alert checkpoint.

BANK ALTERNATIVES

There's no law that says you must have a bank account, although it might not seem that way if you try to go through life without one. But if you're seriously thinking about changing the way you live (and I suspect you are since you're reading this book), you can really shrink your world until it's so small that having a bank account will seem like an extravagance.

One thing I like about my world is that I don't have to do a damn thing if I don't want to. It wasn't always this way, though. It took many years of stripping away what I thought were necessities.

The first thing I stripped out of my life was cable TV. I read an ad that said, "Stop paying for TV!" I called the dude up and said, "What's the scam?" He explained that he was in the TV antenna business. He sold and installed high-quality TV antennas and signal booster devices. Said he could set me up for about $400 and I'd never miss cable. I thanked him for the info, went to Radio Shack, and set myself up for about $150. He was right. To this day, I have absolutely no regrets about skipping out on my last three cable payments. I don't miss cable at all.

To make a long story short, I eventually chopped out fancy cars, expensive sunglasses, and all material extravagances in exchange for less expensive and more rewarding things, such as good music, day trips, books on interesting subjects, and my hobbies.

I now have three bills to pay each month: phone, electric, and mortgage. Car insurance, taxes, Internet, and kerosene are each paid twice a year. That's only 44 payments per year for my nut. Even if I was stuck having to use postal money orders (which I'm not), at $.85 each that's only $37.40 a year.

As for banks, most of them charge $5 per month for account maintenance, so that's $60 right there. And if you make a mistake and bounce a check? Your bank charges you a $25 penalty, and the store you wrote the check to will charge at least $15 for a returned check. Do this once a year and you're already up to $100 a year just to have a freakin' bank account!

While it's true that I do have a life outside paying my bills and in reality have more than 44 payments every year, I do get money orders for $.49 from the local mom-and-pop grocery store and choose to pay for most things with cash.

The foregoing demonstrates that banks are neither convenient nor cheap. In fact, about the only thing good you can say about banks is they're a safe place to keep your money—the portion of it they don't take from you, that is. It thus stands to reason that if you had some other safe place to keep your money, you wouldn't need banks. Below are just two such alternatives. I'm sure you can think of more, and I hope you do. If we can get people to stop depending on banks, maybe banks will realize they can't get away with charging their customers whatever the hell they want and treating them however poorly they'd like.

A Nice Solid Floor Safe

By the time you're done paying for checks, bounced checks, ATM cards, and monthly fees, any bank interest you might receive will be far offset by these charges. You're better off with a solid, fireproof floor safe and using a 49 cent money order to pay each bill. Even if you have many bills and end up spending more in money orders than you would've in bank charges, the privacy and anonymity you receive may be well worth the price.

A safe is also a good place to hide identity documents for other identities. I mounted my floor safe between two floor joists beneath a removable panel covered by wall-to-wall carpeting in the corner of my living room beneath my sofa. When I need access, I slide the sofa forward, peel the carpet from the corner, lift the panel, dial the combo, and do my thing.

Lock Boxes

Being in real estate, I've always enjoyed using lock boxes as temporary hiding places for spare keys and emergency money. Lock boxes are like tiny safes used by real estate agents to store house keys outside the property. If the owner is not home, the Realtor can dial a combination on the box and retrieve the house key to show the property.

You can hide small items, even a wad of cash, publicly and anonymously. First you must get a box. How? Well, you can blow 35 buckeroonies and buy one, or you can happen to accidentally acquire one. They are pretty easy to—okay, I'll say it—steal because Realtors, in my humble opinion, are not very creative, which is one reason I never joined them (I've always acted as an independent broker).

For example, if the name of a certain real estate office is Buynow Real Estate, its lock box combination will likely be BRE. Similarly, if I know the box belongs to a particular agent by the name of Jane Q. Dough, JQD would be the first combination I'd try. (This is why you should *never* allow a Realtor to place a lock box on your property!)

Once you have your lock box, invent and set a thoughtful combination for it. Then take it to the nearest condominium that has several units for sale and place it next to the other lock boxes attached to the various entry railings. Try to put your box in the company of at least two others that have been there for awhile. This will ensure that the boxes are not in violation of the condo rules, which would allow the condo to remove them. Put your mail drop address on the back of the box in case somebody wishes to contact you about it. If the condo board adopts a new regulation against lock boxes, you need to leave them a way to contact you so they don't remove it for you. Otherwise you may return to find your lock box cut away and those thirty $100 bills you had stashed there gone forever.

Lock boxes are actually quite safe once you find an acceptable location and make up a decent combination. There are 26^3, or 17,576 possible combinations on the typical lock box.

Lock boxes have a combination dial lettered from A to Z, and the codes are three digits long. Calculated out: 26^3 = 17,576 possible combinations. Few Realtors take advantage of their security, opting for easily remembered passwords such as their monogram or their office's monogram. You should choose an obscure combination that won't be confused with any office or name, such as ZIQ. Just be sure to memorize it!

Some Poor Choices

Earlier I said I hope you can think of many safe places to keep your money. To spare you potential disaster, here are some foolhardy ideas others have already proven unworthy:

Under the Mattress

- Your wife will find it when she tries to hide *her* stash there.
- It's one of the first places a burglar will look.
- Fire: enough said.

Time Capsule

- Difficult to access.
- Neighbors might think you're burying a body.
- If your container fails, worms and other organisms will turn your cash to mash.

Entrusting It to a Friend

- Tee hee, giggle: good one.
- Friend joins a cult.
- Friend blows it at the dog track.
- Friend falls in love.
- Friend decides heroin makes him feel good.

Well that should help spare you some potential embarrassment. While you're thinking up a great banking alternative, Chapters 11 and 12 will give you some other things to chew on.

Marriage Privacy (and ID tricks)

Keep the church and state forever separate.
Ulysses S. Grant

So you finally meet Mr. or Ms. Right and you decide to get married. What's the procedure? Well, if you're a man you have to buy Ms. Right a diamond and think of a fancy way to spring it on her. Then she has to tell her mother and go shopping for a wedding dress, and you both have to get involved with the church, rent a hall, hire caterers, send wedding invitations, get a marriage license, blood tests, et cetera, et cetera, et froinkin' cetera.

That's the way to go, right?

Well unfortunately it's the way most people do it. Personally, I think it's a serious waste of time and a total invasion of one's privacy. You have to involve the state and a hypocritical church in your personal affairs. You expose yourself to state bureaucrats and self-proclaimed theologians who use the opportunity to talk down to you and tell you what you must and mustn't do and what you can and cannot think, feel, and believe. And most people invite these invasions themselves—all for the sake of satisfying some age-old fairytale about having the perfect traditional wedding.

There's no law that says you have to buy a diamond or even a wedding ring. There's no statute that requires a formal ceremony in order to get married. Because marriage has been around for millennia, most of it is based in common law and, fortunately for privacy seekers, the legislature and general laws devote relatively few words to the matter of marriage.

Money-motivated marriages of celebrities and the rich are often performed quite legally in an attorneys office. State laws vary, but the basic requirements are these:

1. A willingness of both parties to marry
2. A declaration of intent to marry
3. An application for marriage license
4. A solemnization by authorized official

Bada-bing bada-boom—you're married.

Believe it or not, none of these requirements are common to all states—not even the first one. Some states will marry you even if you *don't* want to be married! Other states omit requirements for a declaration of intent or application for a marriage license. Some states do not require blood tests, and some states allow you to solemnize your own marriage and file your own certificate of marriage.

All states, however, require that proposed marriage partners be qualified. The rules typically prohibit marriage between first cousins and closer relatives of whole or half-blood. Most states prohibit same-sex marriages, and some states prohibit marriage of a stepparent to a stepchild.

Another commonality among most states is that an "imperfect" marriage is still valid as long as one or both (depending on the state) marital partners believed their actions constituted a valid marriage and the marriage has been "consummated." An imperfect marriage is one in which proper application was not made or a certificate of marriage was not filed, or one that was solemnized by an unrecognized or unlicensed official. In most states, children born of an invalid marriage (such as a marriage between first cousins) are nonetheless considered legitimate by statute.

ONE STATE AS AN EXAMPLE: COLORADO

Under current Colorado law, a couple who wishes to be married may hold their own ceremony, solemnize their own marriage, and file their own marriage certificate. The ceremony may be little more than the couple getting together to fill in the blanks.

Only one of the marriage participants must appear before the county clerk to obtain the marriage license and certificate. Birth certificates and driver's licenses are valid forms of identification and proof of age. In other words, you can walk into the county clerk's office with out-of-state documents, go home, get married, and mail the form back to the city clerk's office, preferably from a mailbox in the same town. Under these rules, it is possible to marry someone who doesn't exist, has died, or has never met you.

The next step is to have a baby.

Having Babies

The Colorado Revised Statues pertaining to birth certificates, reads in part (italics added):

> CRS 25-2-112(2)
> . . . When the birth occurs outside an institution, the certificate shall be prepared and filed by the physician in attendance at or immediately after birth, or in the absence of such a physician by any person witnessing the birth, or in the absence of any such witness *by the father or mother, or in the absence of the father and the inability of the mother by the person in charge of the premises* where the birth occurred. The person who completes and files the certificate shall also be responsible for obtaining the social security account numbers of the parents and delivering those numbers to the state registrar along with the certificate.

If for some reason you plan to file a birth certificate, but, strangely enough, there seems to be a conspicuous lack of actual offspring, there are some steps you might wish to take to backstop your little plan.

Seven or eight months before baby's due, buy some baby books and videos and, most important, subscribe to some parenting magazines. Around the same time, sign up for a Lemaze birth class.

You don't need to begin eating everything in sight or stuffing pillows under your maternity dress wherever you go. You only want to be pregnant on paper. In the event some creepy city clerk requests additional evidence of the birth after you file the certificate, respond by enclosing copies of your paid receipts for the above items along with the following note:

Dear Creepy Clerky:

Enclosed please find copies of the only records we have that may substantiate baby's existence. Our lawyer has informed us that baby's birth certificate was properly filled out and filed according to Colorado law. We are not big records people, and it is all right with us if you do not want to register baby's birth.

I trust the matter is settled.

Very goofy yours,

Mr. & Mrs. Baby's Parents

A photograph of mom struggling with an armful of newborn, wrinkled triplets would be a nice touch. You don't want to send a laser or ink-jet printout, because city clerks are mistrustful of people who have computers. Note the following equation:

Computer
+ unconventional photo
<u>+ unconventional childbirth</u>
= too many reasons to call the sheriff

Just send a regular photo.

In actuality, this birth method should require no backstopping, but as Big Brother gets bigger, this may change.

Baby on the Road

You've heard of drive-by shootings? Well, Colorado recognizes drive-by birthings. The Colorado Revised Statues pertaining to birth certificates, reads in part (italics added):

> CRS 25-2-112(1)
> A certificate of birth for each live birth . . . shall be filed with the state registrar . . . within ten days after such birth and shall be registered if it has been completed and filed in accordance with this section. *When a birth occurs on a moving conveyance within the United States and the child is first removed from the conveyance in Colorado*, the birth shall be registered in Colorado, and the place where the child is first removed shall be considered the place of birth.
>
> [. . .] Either of the parents of the child shall verify the accuracy of the personal data entered thereon in time to permit its filing within such ten-day period.

Again, if you're filing a birth certificate under this rule despite a curious lack of temper tantrums, breast feeding, and baby puke, you'll need to keep a few things in mind.

Don't toy with the city clerk by giving your baby a cute name like "Phantom," "Casper," or "The Invisible Monkey Thing."

It's probably best not to claim your baby was born on a bus, plane, or taxi. This only leaves an opening for a clerk to inquire as to witnesses (e.g., bus and plane passengers and crew, taxi driver).

It's best to pick a remote, unincorporated area where baby will be born. You must then find out which town handles the birth records for that area. Then fill out baby's birth certificate and send the following letter:

Dear Jerky Clerky:

We are requesting a blank birth certificate be sent to us at: Mr. & Mrs. Phony Name, 5 Mail Drop Plaza, Suite 16, Outta State, OS 00000. We were driving through your lovely state when baby paid us a surprise by arriving three weeks ahead of schedule.

We have been informed that baby's birth certificate must be filed in Colorado since we removed baby from the car in Unincorporated Area 725. We have also been informed that your town handles the records for UA725.

We've always loved beautiful Colorado but never imagined our child would have the honorable distinction of being born there! Blah, blah, blah.

Please use the enclosed priority envelope to expedite the certificate to us, as we do not wish to be assessed a fee for late filing.

Hardly truly yours,

Mr. & Mrs. Baby's Parents

If you already have a mail drop and phone service set up as an attorney's office, you can send the above letter "from your attorney." The town will see their having to handle this matter for UA725 as a mild bureaucratic annoyance. They will see you and your spouse as people afraid of being assessed a late fee. You will be the proud parents of a newborn bouncing baby piece of paper.

SOME FUNKY RAMIFICATIONS OF THESE LOOPHOLES

Birth and marriage certificate loopholes have been around since record keeping began. And in the past, there were more of them. I'm sure you've already thought of some nifty ways to turn these loopholes to your advantage, if only to apply for baby's SSN and open a private bank account, which will be explained later. But bear in mind that others before you also had some pretty crafty ideas. One such idea is the marketing of prepackaged, aged identities.

Prepackaged, Aged Identities

They're out there, floating around, getting moldy: identities set up years ago using the above methods. Now, I can't tell you that this is precisely how I used to make a shit-load of money. Inspector Sphincter would be all over me. And, of course, I'd have no way of knowing that an unused identity would run you between $1,500 and $25,000, depending on who's selling it, how long it's been around, how much money you have, and how much trouble you're in. Never heard of such a thing? Good. It's not supposed to be posted on billboards across the country. The feds don't care for that sort of thing.

How Do I Get One?

Maybe you don't need to. I just saved you a couple grand by telling you exactly how it's done. But maybe you'd like an identity that's significantly aged. Something closer to your own age, perhaps? Well, I've two words for you: Big Bucks. The single most salable feature of an unused prefabricated identity is how long it has been around. The longer it's been around, the more expensive it is. Why? Very low supply, ridiculously high demand. The $25,000 figure given above was just the high end of typical average costs. If you need a 56-year-old identity in a hurry, you'd better be a millionaire.

I'm a Millionaire. How Do I Get One?

I can't provide exact locations because I'd be shot within hours after this book's release if I do. I hope you understand that. But let me just say this. For starters, write down every seedy place you've avoided in every big city you've ever been in. Not poor neighborhoods, now—that's kid's stuff. I'm talking bars, nightclubs, and gambling establishments that have been associated with newspaper headlines like, "Parkway Lounge Owner, Molto Ricci, Indicted on Racketeering Charges Fifth Time."

Unless you have very good connections, nobody will do this work for you. You must visit these places yourself and *you must know the lingo*. If you look weak and desperate and act indiscreet, you will get blank looks and a lot of I-don't-know-what-the-fuck-your-talkin'-abouts. Push your luck and you'll be leaving with broken bones.

The proper lingo and etiquette varies from area to area and organization to organization. I can't teach it to you, and you can't learn it from TV. But here's some general advice. There's nothing these guys hate worse than someone who pretends to know about "the underworld" because he saw all three parts of *The Godfather* on TV the week before. Whatever you do, don't dance nervously in front of your contact making air quotation marks around the lingo words you think he's supposed to understand. You will not be taken seriously, and you may get your genitals removed on the spot. In short, Mr. Millionaire, do your homework.

Steal a Prefab

A client once suggested it would be much cheaper to steal a prefab ID than to purchase one. He was a computer software engineer and had the ingenious idea of comparing birth records, death records, and SSA records (he claimed he'd have no problem hacking into these databases, but I had my doubts).

All births from the year in which he wished to be born would be cross-referenced to all death records from that year forward. The remaining birth records were to be cross-referenced with SSA records that he could supposedly hack into. His theory was that older, unused, prefab identities would not have SSNs associated with them, since back then it was not standard procedure for parents to make application for an SSN within two years of baby's birth. Therefore the mobsters would not have bothered to do so for their prefab identities. This client also made the reasonable assumption that 99.999 percent of still-living "real" people born in his target year could not have gotten through life without an SSN.

So if only .1 percent of the remaining names did not have associated SSNs, there was a high probability that any one of them was a prefab ID still available for black market sale. He was convinced that proper research of these remaining identities would yield him a verifiable prefab that he could then slip into.

So where is this friend today?

I don't know. That's what makes this whole scenario worth mentioning. I told him his idea was crazy. That even if it worked, he would have a hard time getting an SSN at his age without any school records, driving history, and so on. I told him it was risky to steal a prefab ID. If caught, the mob would kill him. If not, the ID would most likely be sold to someone else, which would complicate matters.

I billed the guy $460.25, which was my standard fee at the time, plus 25 cents as a joke. During our discussion, he had asked to use the men's room. I said, "Sure, leave a quarter on the toilet." He said, "Bill me for it." So I did.

I heard through the grapevine that he'd turned up missing. I figured he'd done something stupid and got caught by the mob. He'd yet to pay his bill, and I figured I'd never be paid for that afternoon's work.

Well, 18 months later I received a letter postmarked from a certain U.S. territory. In the envelope was a money order for $460.25 and a small note that stated simply, "Fee and pee: $460.25. Thanks."

Baby's Bank Account

Slightly less glamorous than either of the above scenarios is to open up a bank account for baby. Be sure to apply for baby's SSN first, which will be a piece of cake with a perfectly valid birth certificate. Now you've a safe place to stash money should ex-spouses, private detectives, or divorce lawyers be checking into your assets.

You may also wish to consider trust and custodial accounts for baby. Rules vary, so do proper research in advance to make sure you still have control over the deposited funds. In these cases, you may wish to bite the bullet and pay taxes when the time comes. No sense inviting the IRS to come asking questions.

Freedom on the Road

I can't drive 55.
Sammy Hagar

Though you may often feel otherwise, your most vulnerable moment is when you're behind the wheel of your car. As an identity changer, this is doubly so. The U.S. Constitution requires cops to have a reason to detain and question you. Unfortunately, a motor vehicle provides just that. There are many things that can go wrong in traffic or with the vehicle itself that could result in unwanted police attention. Table 12.1 lists a few of the more common road hazards.

TABLE 12.1

What Can Go Wrong	How Police Get Involved
Motor Vehicle	
Light out	Gives them reason to stop you
Loud exhaust	Gives them reason to stop you
Noxious emission	Gives them reason to stop you
Loud stereo	Gives them reason to stop you
Bald tires	Gives them reason to stop you
Studded snow tires out of season	Gives them reason to stop you
Hanging or dragging parts	Gives them reason to stop you
Missing or expired stickers and plates	Gives them reason to stop you
Traffic	
Failure to stop	Gives them an excuse to pull you over
Failure to signal	Gives them an excuse to pull you over
Speeding	Gives them an excuse to pull you over
Vehicle disabled or out of gas	Allows police to "offer their assistance," at which time you may come under scrutiny

Roadblocks (highway death tolls cause people to accept these breaches of the Constitution)	Gives police a chance to profile you, smell your breath for alcohol, and inspect the vehicle for stickers, registration, etc.
Insufficient policing of police	Allows police to cross Constitutional boundaries without fear of reprimand
Insufficient pay of police	Allows police take out their anger and frustration on motorists
A large public ignorant of or afraid to assert their rights	Allows police to get used to pushing people around

If you commit any of the above road infractions or countless others, the police have full legal power to stop you, question you, run your name, check your history, and detain you for up to 48 hours without charging you with anything. Only in the good ol' US of A my friends.

Because there is so much that can go wrong on the road, even when you are completely in the right, the cops can easily "invent" an infraction if they think you fit a particular profile.

Most police and police departments are lazy. They'd rather not do actual police work, so they'll bet that traffic stops will ferret out most known and wanted criminals. And it's a pretty safe bet. All they need is a missed turning signal and they have an excuse to run your license through their computer. If you match the profile of a bad guy, there's a good chance they'll run your name through the National Crime Information Center computer. Many folks on the lam are caught exactly this way.

HOW TO AVOID MATCHING POLICE PROFILES

Profiling was discussed in Chapter 2 of *Modern Identity Changer*. I'll elaborate on the topic here by introducing some ways around matching police profiles.

Pseudo-Conformity

Perhaps the best way to avoid matching police profiles is to conform to conservative white-collar dress codes, mannerisms, habits, and lingo, at least while you're on the road. You don't have to cut your hair, but maybe there are times when it would be best to tuck it up under your hat. Luckily for us hipsters, long hair is becoming fashionable again, so hat tucking can be reserved for the stickiest of moments, such as when crossing international borders.

Keep your first two radio presets for classical music stations, especially if you drive a fancy car. If you get stopped by the fuzz for a misaligned headlight, switch to the classical station and adjust the volume to create a soft background effect. When the officer gets to the car, she'll be more likely to believe you have political influence if you're listening to classical music.

Now Hold on a Minute

I know some of you may cringe at the thought of any kind of conformity—even pseudo-conformity. Just remember: it's only a game. If played right, it's a game that *you* control. Use societal prejudices to your advantage. If the sphincter police are going to let you cross the border on the wholly arbitrary basis of your white collar, then by wearing a white collar you easily and effectively control them rather than the other way around.

It only takes a few minutes of your time to dress and act the part. But don't overdo it. Many cops are not stupid, and experienced ones will pick up on phoniness faster than you can say, "Step out of the car, please." Once you get to your destination, you can let your hair down, roll your sleeves up, and flaunt your "Cops Suck" tattoo all you want. Why? Because *you're free to do so*. Because you've played their game . . . and you've beaten them.

If you're reading this, there's a good chance you have something you're trying to protect from Big Brother. There's also a good chance you're getting away with it. Most of the time you're not playing their game, and you're having a fun time at doing your own thing. This is good. This is life. This is freedom. But sometimes, to protect your own thing, whether it's a stash of cash you don't want the IRS to hear about, a tax-free side business, or a new identity, you have to play their game. As long as you're playing it to win, and in fact winning, conformity in these circumstances is a means to an end, not a threat to your freedom.

If you're pulling the wool over their eyes most of the time, is it really going to kill you to play the game when the situation calls for it? After all, you're not giving up control. To the contrary: *you* are controlling the mind of Big Brother.

OBEY THE TRAFFIC LAWS

For the average person, a typical traffic violation will result in a ticket. For the identity changer, it could result in a federal prison sentence. Minor, temporary alterations of personal appearance and obeying traffic laws is a small price to pay in exchange for privacy, identity, and personal freedom. They are easy laws to obey, and you are ultimately protecting something that is far more precious to you. The rules of the road are straightforward. If you drive responsibly and avoid matching police profiles, you can tool around the United States and Canada safely and indefinitely.

Lose the Opportunist Mentality

If you don't have it, good. If you have it, lose it fast. Often after following someone in traffic to a predetermined location, I'm asked, "What took you so long." One time a guy bragged he'd arrived a good five minutes ahead of me taking the same route. I told him his entire argument was predicated on his fallacious belief that I was trying to get there as fast as possible. He said, "Well, weren't you?" I said, "No." He said, "But that's what everybody does." I said, "I can't speak for everybody. I can only speak for myself. I was trying to get here as *safely* as possible." The guy spent the next 10 minutes trying to convince everybody he did not feel like a complete asshole.

Opportunist Mentality Defined

A person who drives with the opportunist mentality is one who consistently speeds, passes unnecessarily, tailgates, runs yellow lights, and cuts people off just because he can "make it." If this is how you drive, you will sooner or later make a mistake and get pulled over. Maybe the yellow light will change to red when there's a cop watching. Or perhaps the cop will think you could've easily stopped for the yellow light (many people have forgotten that you should stop for a yellow light if you can). Perchance the vehicle you cut off is an unmarked police detective's patrol unit. The point is, you never know. And if you have fantasies about ever changing your identity, it's best to get in the habit of safe driving now. Otherwise you'll never make it. I guarantee it.

NUISANCE LAWS

In addition to the regular rules of the road, there are a number of things the identity changer must remember when operating in "protection mode." They aren't rules of the road in the truest sense but peripheral nuisances that can give rise to a traffic stop and unwanted questioning.

We all like to listen to the radio when we drive. Sometimes we get into a favorite song and crank it up. Sometimes we crank it up so loud we can't hear the engine running or, say, an ambulance approaching or someone beeping at us. A loud car stereo gives a police officer the right to stop you. Once stopped, the officer has the right to run your manufactured driver's license through the state's computer to see what pops up. An innocent mistake such as this and your life on the run may be over.

Here are couple more nuisance laws to watch out for:

Inspection stickers. A pain in the ass, but not difficult to get. Have the necessary work done on your vehicle and get the sticker. Many cops can spot a missing or invalid inspection sticker even when passing you at 45 mph.

Studded snow tires. Many jurisdictions don't allow studded snow tires on their roadways during certain months (April 1 to September 30 in New York, for example). Many southern jurisdictions don't allow them at all. If you're traveling across county with bells on your toes and a detective on your tail, you'd best keep standard, all-season tires on your vehicle.

I once passed a cop who literally peeled out, raced up behind me, swerved around my car to cut me off, and brought me to a stop. I figured I must've matched an armed robbery or murder suspect that just came over his radio. As it turned out, he felt the need to tell me my studded snow tires should've come off four days ago.

HOW TO AVOID SPEED VIOLATIONS
(EVEN IF YOU SPEED)

Here are some great tips to keep you from being pulled over for speed violations. First and foremost, never be the fastest one on the road. The fastest one (or sometimes two if they're racing) gets pulled over 99 percent of the time. This means that if you're the only one on the road, you have to be a good doobie or risk the consequences.

When you pass somebody, do it in a passing zone and get it done as fast as possible. If you are on the highway, never remain in the passing (aka "hammer") lane. Ever! The simplest way for a lazy cop to catch speeders is to keep an eye on the passing lane and who's staying in it. In many areas, traveling in the passing lane is a violation in and of itself. If you have to remain in the passing lane for any length of time, it's just not a good time to do your speeding.

In a line of speeding vehicles, never be the leader. Swallow your pride, pull into the granny lane, and send a few speed demons up ahead to clear the way. No matter how fast you want to go on the highway, there's always some testosterone-poisoned macho maggot on steroids who wants to go faster. Your duty: let him. Send him up ahead and keep an eye on his brake lights. Watch for movement from the passing lane to the travel lane; this could indicate the sucker has seen a cop. For the same reason, watch for truckers moving from the left lane to the right. They have radios and usually know where the cops are. Since they're not supposed to remain in the passing lane (if in fact they're supposed to be there at all), they will move over before getting to an area where cops have been spotted. Get a CB yourself and monitor channel 19, especially if you don't use a radar detector or they are illegal in your area.

Also, by keeping a "sweep" in front of you about a hundred yards, you can see if they swerve around potential dangers in the road (moose, deer, kitchen sink, etc.). You don't need to be involved in a traffic accident; this also gives cops the right to demand your papers.

If You're Tipped Off About a Speed Trap

If you're driving and someone tips you off about the cops up ahead (usually by flashing their headlights), just take the tip and go with it. Slow down to the speed limit (or speed up to it if that's the case). Look straight ahead, place both hands on the wheel, put your seatbelt on, and, most important, *don't return the favor!* In other words, don't flash your lights to other motorists to warn them of a speed trap (or for any other reason). You may just be "returning the favor" to a cop, who will pull you over and cite you for obstruction of justice.

By the way, if this ever does happen to you, just tell the nice officer that a lot of people were flicking their lights at you so you decided to make sure your headlights were on (if at night) or off (if during day) and that's why you were flicking them. As far as you know, there is no hidden or secondary meaning to this action. You may wish to hint that you feel your civil rights are being violated, but don't be too vociferous about it or you'll be charged with some other made-up infraction.

After being tipped off about a speed trap, don't look at, taunt, or wave sarcastically at the cruiser when you do spot it! Don't stick your thumb on your nose and wiggle your fingers at them.

RENTING A CAR

Most car rental agencies in the United States will not rent to a person who is under 25 years of age. Apparently, some magic thing happens to human beings at the age of 25 that suddenly makes them better drivers and safer insurance risks. So what do you do if you are under 25?

Search the yellow pages for car rental companies and cross out all the ones you've heard of before (Hertz, Avis, etc.). Then cross out all the ones who've paid for display ads larger than one column inch. If there are any left, you can try them, beginning with the ones who have no display ad at all and whose street address indicates anything but a Main Street store front (e.g., 61-R Houghton Street; 123 Third Street, Apt. 12; 4 Shyster Street behind Fred's house) One of these places may rent to you if you are under 25 or look the other way when you pass them a novelty ID.

If that doesn't work, try this:

Use the techniques of Chapter 3 to make a foreign driver's license, perhaps from a European country. Go to the airport. Carrying an inordinate amount of luggage and, wearing plaid pants and a raincoat-yellow top, present your European driver's license to any rental car agent, using the appropriate accent or pretending to be mute.

If you are pretending to be French, it would be a very good idea to pick a time when a flight from France has just arrived. Before you go to the rental agent, make sure that the French flight has not been delayed, diverted, or shot out of the sky by the Iraqis. If you fail to take this step, you may find yourself in a very embarrassing situation. Wait an hour or two after "your flight" lands before you try to rent the car. This gives you plenty of time to get your luggage and also provides you with an opportunity to "lose" your plane ticket in case it is requested as backup ID.

There is no effective way for rental car companies to verify the validity of a license issued overseas. They rent to tourists on a daily basis, and your request will come as no surprise to them. If they ask for your passport, either have one ready (see Chapter 4, "Camouflage Passports") or use one of the following excuses:

• I gave all the important papers to my wife for safekeeping once she finds a hotel room. I won't see her again until tonight. I was told all I would need is a driver's license. If I don't get a car now, I'll be sitting here for 10 hours! I have no way of getting in touch with her. Why didn't you tell me over the phone you would need my passport? What am I gonna do now! (Start sobbing, if necessary).
• Say simply, "It's at the hotel," which is occasionally effective as long as you also remember to leave your luggage at the hotel. Many clerks will ask you to come back with it, though.

Oh yeah, don't try any of these ideas if you're under 20 years old because you'll probably get busted.

STICKER SAFETY

Members of 12-step programs, such as Alcoholics Anonymous, often put program-related bumper stickers on their cars. "One day at a time" and "Honk if you know Bill W." are two that immediately come to mind. You may be tempted to place these stickers on your vehicle in an effort to demonstrate to the authorities what a reformed stand-up citizen you have become. Unless you know for sure that half the police officers in your town are recovering substance abusers, this is probably not the best idea. The typical cop attitude is "once a scumbag, always a scumbag," and he will most likely pull you over betting that you've recently fallen off the wagon.

College Decals

There's no need for them. It doesn't matter how proud you are of your accomplishments—the cold, hard truth of the matter is that nobody on the road gives a shit. You're more likely to piss off the guy behind you in the beat-up 1977 Chevy Malibu who never had a shot at college. Maybe this guy's considering suicide. Maybe he has nothing to lose by taking a few "rich kids" with him.

Many cops may have the same attitude toward snotty college grads rubbing everybody else's nose in it. Most of the cities "finest" study no more than two years of "criminology" at a community college, if they're educated at all. So if it's 6:01 P.M. in the big city and your parking meter just expired, a cop who may ordinarily look the other way might decide to stick a ticket right over your college decal while you're running your little college grad ass up the street.

Bumper Stickers

Driving around with a "Pro Choice" bumper sticker is as good as driving around with a "Pro Getting My Tires Slashed" bumper sticker. Better yet, just cross out the word "Choice" and write in "Getting Fire-Bombed."

There's absolutely no need to advertise your political beliefs or party affiliations to 35,000 angry commuters first thing in the morning five days a week. The lady behind you is *not* going to change her vote or donate money to your cause because of your bumper sticker. It's much more likely to attract the attention of extremist groups who will harass or even kill you for your beliefs.

You also may as well replace your "One Day at a Time" bumper sticker with one that says, "Officer, Check to See if I Fell off the Wagon."

A similar threat to your privacy are those who's "on board" signs that people put in their rear windows. Do you really want a black-market adoption ring member to see your "Baby on Board" sign? Or the guy with a foot fetish to know there's a "Podiatrist on Board"? Your mother was right—the world is full of whackos. Don't give them a reason to come after you.

Parking Permits

Attach your parking permit to the inside corner of your windshield with Velcro. Remove it wherever you go. If the fatal attraction you encounter in the mall should follow you to your car, there's no need for him to see your "Back Bay Resident" parking permit.

Vanity Plates

Vanity plates do nothing more than advertise information about yourself. Maybe it's your nickname or your job, or maybe it's the fact that you love your car so much you chose MY-IROC as your tag number. Whichever, it's more than you want people to know.

The only good use for a vanity plate is for the identity changer who's playing a specific role. If you want to reinforce the impression you're an accountant, then IMA-CPA might make a good license tag. But I'd recommend finding other ways to reinforce your identity.

Why? Because vanity plates are much easier to remember. If you zoom past a cop who happens to be busy with someone else at the moment, she may take a casual glance at your license plate. COPSUCK is much easier for the officer to remember than 2HNB043. Similarly, what if you unwittingly piss off some road-raged lunatic? The road-rager will more readily remember EATDUST than six or seven random digits. For $5, most states will give your name and address to anybody who takes the time to memorize your license plate.

DRIVER'S LICENSE

Several states use the Social Security number as a driver's license number. When you present your driver's license as ID for check cashing or credit card use, the greasy-haired kid behind the counter now has your SSN in addition to your bank account or credit card number. This is enough for him and his friends to gain access to your credit so they can go out and buy $400 worth of Jack Daniels.

Fortunately, these states offer you the option of choosing a random number for your driver's license number. If this applies to you, I suggest you take them up on this offer.

WHEN NATURE CALLS: THE URINATION DILEMMA

Most drivers at one time or another have had to stop to make a run into the woods. In many cases, such as on a highway, just being stopped on the side of a road is reason enough for the police to make an inquiry. Even if you're not drinking and driving, they may think you are if they see you pissing on the side of the road. Besides it's illegal, unsanitary, and dangerous to stop on the highway!

I have no idea how the ladies handle this problem, but I've found that wide-mouth containers (such as 32 oz. apple juice containers) with screw-on caps are quite handy on the road. Now I can't tell you to urinate while you drive, even though many people do exactly that, so be sure to pull safely into a parking lot, rest area, or side street. Throw a map on the steering wheel and look lost. The map also helps to cover any part of your body that may be exposed to passersby, if you know what I mean.

FINAL DO'S AND DON'TS

A good way for privacy seekers to attract authorities is to get in an accident or place themselves in some kind of danger. So don't speed in a snowstorm or try to cross rushing water during a flood.

Do dip your high beams when you're supposed to—even if you have a headlight out and you're driving toward a cop. Do replace headlights as soon as they fail, though, which may mean carrying a spare and the tools to replace it at all times. Why give them an excuse to pull you over?

Always look ahead and anticipate things in the roadway so you don't end up hitting something and becoming disabled, thereby attracting the authorities.

Do heed special traffic alert signs, work zones, etc.

Do learn how to use tire chains if you live in an area where you may need them. Practice putting them on in the snow. Get good at it. Time yourself until you can do the job in four or five minutes in the dark. When you need to actually use them, you'll be ready.

If you are followed by a police officer or fed, don't keep looking in your rearview mirror, don't pull over to let him pass, and don't take a side street just to lose him. Just do your job, stay between the lines, and stay around the speed limit (a little over is usually okay, if not better because it's more realistic).

Don't chance running too low on gas. Carry a little container with extra gas if you're that type.

Do carry emergency supplies in your trunk: flares, oil, fan/accessory belts, tools, container of gasoline (check local laws), premixed antifreeze and water, and anything listed under the "Road Samaritan" section in Chapter 8 that you have or can cheaply get your hands on. Any of these things may get your disabled vehicle off the road before the cops come to "help" you.

Don't "rubberneck" or step on the brakes after a cop passes you. Just downshift if necessary and look straight ahead. A surreptitious glance in the rearview mirror is okay, but don't turn your head. I have an ex-comrade cop acquaintance who sits in the cruiser with binoculars as his partner drives. He looks in the rearview mirrors of passing vehicles for an overanxious or guilty glance. An overly guilty look and they turn around and follow the guy. Facecrime is alive and well in the new millenium, my friends.

Do not break laws at anytime on the road—even briefly to transport your prized marijuana plant to the annual meeting of NORML (National Organization for the Reformation of Marijuana Laws) or whatever your bag is. Although you may not realize it, there will be subtle changes in your mannerisms and behaviors of which you are probably unaware but police officers are trained to detect. Have you ever heard anybody say, "Man, I never do nuthin' wrong, but yesterday I was doing such and such and I got pulled over"? Well, there's a reason for that.

Don't feel like you're home until you get home—a lot of accidents happen because people, upon pulling onto their street or into their neighborhood, feel they are "home." At this point you still have the task of driving, and it's imperative that you understand it—not just for the sake of your physical safety but also for the sake of your freedom. I've been pulled over three times in my life while on my own street!

Do stay within 5 mph of the speed limit at all times. It only takes one anxious moment of driving to invite the patrols into your life.

Don't be paranoid on the road. Just do what you're supposed to and remember that you're complying with these simple laws not out of fear and mindless conformity but to beat Big Brother at his own game.

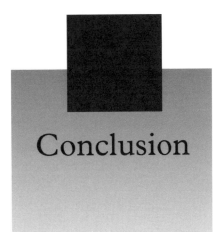

Conclusion

Everything was all right, the struggle was finished. He had won the victory over himself. He loved Big Brother.
Last three sentences from George Orwell's *1984*.

Individuals own themselves. They have the inalienable right to interact peacefully with other individuals. This was so before the concept of government ever existed, and it should be so today.

But is it?

In the dark ages, when most of the world was ruled by monarchs and dictators, people were horribly oppressed. It took many centuries and countless lives for the oppressed of the world to rise and oppose the status quo.

A small group of such people eventually made a pilgrimage to a new world. They took with them their history and drafted a plan, a constitution, that, if followed, would prevent the horrible oppression of their ancestry and allow individuals to pursue life, liberty, and happiness. It was obvious that these rights were endowed on every individual at birth, and the pilgrims fought a bloody war to secure their revolutionary ideas and to guarantee these rights to citizens of the new world forever.

This small group of people eventually died off. Each successive generation of their new government forgot more history and made more liberal interpretations of their original constitution. Now the new world is on the brink of repeating the same horrible atrocities of the dark ages.

The once fundamental concept of a free population has become a threat to those in power, from the president of the United States to the president of a condo association. People who have a compelling need to control other people's behavior, income, preferences, and even thoughts naturally gravitate to positions where they are given the authority and legal use of force to do just that.

With a legal monopoly on force, modern government controls us through harassment and threats. If you don't pay your taxes, an armed, Gestapo-clad representative of the state will break your door down and haul you to off to jail.

The other half of modern government, Corporate America, controls us with the "golden handcuffs" of salary, health care packages, dress codes, strict work schedules, and the promise of a secure retirement. All you have to do is dedicate the greater part of your life to them and piss in a cup once a week to prove you are not consuming unapproved intoxicants.

This entire system is supported by wards of the state—your fellow workers and neighbors—who are born into this dangerous methodology and ultimately buy the farm. They become complacent (if they're not already born that way) and begin to believe that condo associations and town councils *should* have the power to squelch people the majority deems icky or abnormal, such as those with long hair, aberrant thoughts, or new ideas. The masses are so blinded by the rising mushroom cloud of totalitarianism, they cannot see that the very laws empowering government to control those whom they dislike or disagree with can and most probably *will* eventually be used against others who aren't so disagreeable. Ultimately, it will be used against *them*.

Those who stand outside the masses, surrounded by people on treadmills snapping at carrots, may find it disheartening and hopeless. If this is you—and I suspect it is—I want you to know that the New Resistance is growing and in need of new members. Do not allow the tyrants to control your personal history, your everyday location, your financial records and identity. Do not allow them to track your buying habits or teach you to worship the almighty buck. When they ask you to bend over and grab your ankles, do not comply.

To some, resisting these things may seem unnatural. Before we were born, our parents, guided by Big Brother and the Corporate Machine, dreamed of how they would mold us into this system: what things we would know, what products we would use, what beliefs we would have, what schools we would attend, and what titles and positions we would hold. Those of you reading this are lucky enough to have questioned this status quo. Most, unfortunately, do not.

But now that you've recognized something is seriously wrong with the "system," now that you've taken initiative to learn how the world really operates, now that you stand outside the masses, what will you do with your newfound knowledge?

Some people get angry and forever wallow in it. They spend a lifetime throwing themselves in front of wrecking balls, shouting outside abortion clinics, or waving placards at the gates of nuclear power plants. Others immerse themselves in decade-long court battles, desperate to show others the truth. Forgetting what they'd originally found so objectionable, they ultimately bleed themselves of life.

We must remember that it's the infringement on our lives and liberties we object to. And, while activism is necessary if we are to change the world, we must first find peace with ourselves before we can be effective. You need not write a thousand hate letters to Big Brother in an effort to teach him how wrong he is. Such an exercise is futile. You will get more out of the world by recognizing its shortcomings and adopting a new worldview. You've already recognized that you see the world differently than most; now allow yourself to live in the new world that you see.

Do not wield in anger what you've learned from these pages. Do not hate that Big Brother tries to shred your humanity. Just know it and move on. Hatred will only poison your effectiveness as a freedom fighter, and this is something the New Resistance cannot afford. Once you know where you stand in relation to the Bureaucratic Machine, you can look upon it from the outside, from the sanctity of your new world. You can then use with confidence the knowledge that you gain. Use it not out of hate for Big Brother but out of love for yourself. This will consume Big Brother and cause him to rot from the inside out.

For Big Brother does not know love.

STATE	Area	1951	1952	1953	1954	1955	1956	1957	1958	1959	1960	1961	1962	1963	1964	1965	1966	1967	1968	1969	1970	1971	1972	1973	1974	1975	1976	1977	78
NH	001	26	26	28	28	28	30	32	32	32	32	34	36	36	38	40	42	42	44	46	46	48	48	54	56	56	58	60	60
NH	002	26	26	26	28	28	30	30	30	32	32	34	34	38	38	40	40	42	44	44	46	46	48	52	54	56	58	60	60
NH	003	24	26	26	26	28	28	30	30	32	32	32	34	38	38	38	40	42	42	44	46	46	48	52	54	56	58	58	58
ME	004	32	34	36	36	38	40	40	40	42	42	44	46	50	50	50	52	54	56	56	58	60	62	66	68	70	72	72	74
ME	005	32	34	34	36	38	40	40	40	42	42	44	44	48	50	50	52	54	54	56	58	60	62	64	66	68	70	72	72
ME	006	32	34	34	34	36	38	40	40	40	42	44	44	48	48	50	52	54	54	56	58	60	62	64	66	68	70	72	72
ME	007	32	32	34	34	36	38	38	40	40	42	42	44	46	48	50	50	52	54	56	58	58	60	64	66	68	70	70	72
VT	008	24	24	26	26	28	28	28	30	30	32	32	34	36	36	38	40	40	42	42	44	46	46	54	54	58	60	60	60
VT	009	22	24	24	24	26	28	28	28	30	30	32	32	34	36	38	38	40	40	42	44	46	52	54	56	58	58	58	58
MA	010	28	28	28	30	30	30	32	32	32	34	34	36	38	38	40	42	42	44	46	46	48	48	50	52	54	54	58	58
MA	011	26	28	28	30	30	30	32	32	32	34	34	36	38	38	40	42	42	44	46	46	48	48	50	52	54	54	58	58
MA	012	26	28	28	28	28	30	32	32	32	34	34	36	38	38	40	42	42	44	46	46	48	48	50	52	54	54	58	58
MA	013	28	28	28	28	30	30	32	32	32	34	34	36	38	38	40	42	42	44	44	46	48	48	50	52	54	54	58	58
MA	014	26	28	28	28	30	30	32	32	32	34	34	36	38	38	40	42	44	46	46	46	48	48	50	52	54	54	56	58
MA	015	26	28	28	28	30	30	30	32	32	34	34	34	38	38	40	42	44	44	46	48	48	50	52	54	54	54	56	58
MA	016	28	28	28	28	30	30	30	32	32	32	34	34	38	38	40	42	42	44	46	46	48	48	50	52	54	54	56	58
MA	017	26	28	28	28	30	30	30	32	32	32	34	36	38	38	40	40	42	44	44	46	48	48	50	52	54	54	56	58
MA	018	26	28	28	28	30	30	30	32	32	32	35	34	36	38	40	40	42	44	44	46	48	48	50	52	54	54	56	58
MA	019	26	28	28	28	30	30	30	32	32	32	34	34	38	38	40	40	42	44	44	46	48	48	50	52	54	54	56	58
MA	020	26	28	28	28	30	30	30	32	32	32	34	34	36	38	40	40	42	44	44	46	48	48	50	52	52	54	56	58
MA	021	26	28	28	28	30	30	30	32	32	32	34	34	36	38	40	40	42	44	44	46	48	48	50	52	52	54	56	58
MA	022	26	26	28	28	30	30	30	30	32	32	34	34	38	38	40	40	42	44	44	46	48	48	50	52	52	54	56	58
MA	023	26	26	28	28	28	30	30	30	32	32	34	34	36	38	40	40	42	42	44	46	48	48	50	52	52	54	56	58
MA	024	26	26	28	28	28	30	30	30	32	32	34	34	36	38	38	40	42	42	44	46	48	48	50	52	52	54	56	58
MA	025	26	26	28	28	28	30	30	30	32	32	34	34	36	38	38	40	42	42	44	46	48	48	50	52	52	54	56	58
MA	026	26	26	28	28	28	30	30	30	32	32	34	34	36	38	38	40	42	42	44	46	46	48	50	52	52	54	56	58
MA	027	26	26	28	28	28	30	30	30	32	32	32	34	36	38	38	40	42	42	44	46	46	48	50	52	52	54	56	58
MA	028	26	26	28	28	28	30	30	30	32	32	32	34	36	38	38	40	40	42	44	46	46	48	50	52	52	54	56	58
MA	029	26	26	28	28	28	30	30	30	32	32	32	34	36	38	38	40	42	42	44	46	48	48	50	50	52	54	56	56
MA	030	26	26	28	28	28	30	30	30	32	32	32	34	36	38	38	40	42	42	44	46	46	48	50	50	52	54	56	56
MA	031	26	26	28	28	28	30	30	30	32	32	34	34	36	38	38	40	42	42	44	44	46	48	50	50	52	54	56	56
MA	032	26	26	28	28	28	28	30	30	30	32	32	34	36	38	38	40	42	42	44	44	46	48	50	50	52	54	56	56
MA	033	26	26	28	28	28	28	30	30	30	32	32	34	36	38	38	40	42	42	44	44	46	48	50	50	52	54	56	56
MA	034	26	26	28	28	28	28	30	30	30	32	32	34	36	36	38	40	42	42	44	46	46	50	50	52	52	54	56	56
RI	035	22	24	24	26	26	26	26	26	28	28	28	30	32	32	32	34	36	36	38	38	38	40	42	44	46	46	48	48
RI	036	22	24	24	24	24	26	26	26	26	28	28	30	32	32	32	34	34	36	36	38	38	40	42	44	44	46	48	48

STATE	Area	1951	1952	1953	1954	1955	1956	1957	1958	1959	1960	1961	1962	1963	1964	1965	1966	1967	1968	1969	1970	1971	1972	1973	1974	1975	1976	1977	78
RI	037	22	22	24	24	24	26	26	26	26	28	28	28	30	32	32	34	34	36	36	38	38	40	42	44	44	46	46	46
RI	038	22	22	24	24	24	24	26	26	28	28	28	28	30	30	32	32	34	34	36	36	38	38	42	42	44	46	46	46
RI	039	22	22	24	24	24	24	26	26	26	28	30	30	32	32	34	34	36	36	38	38	42	42	44	46	46	46		
CT	040	28	28	30	30	30	32	32	34	34	34	36	38	42	42	44	46	48	48	50	52	54	56	60	62	64	68	68	68
CT	041	26	28	30	30	30	32	32	34	34	34	36	38	40	42	44	46	48	48	50	52	54	56	60	62	64	66	68	68
CT	042	26	28	30	30	30	32	32	34	34	34	36	36	40	42	44	46	46	48	50	52	54	54	60	62	64	66	68	68
CT	043	26	28	30	30	30	30	32	34	34	34	36	36	40	42	42	44	46	48	50	52	54	54	60	62	64	66	68	68
CT	044	26	28	28	30	30	30	32	32	34	34	34	36	40	42	44	44	46	48	50	52	54	54	60	62	64	66	66	68
CT	045	26	28	28	30	30	30	32	32	34	34	36	36	40	42	44	44	46	48	50	52	52	54	60	62	64	66	66	68
CT	046	26	28	28	30	30	30	32	32	32	34	34	36	40	40	42	44	46	48	50	52	52	54	58	60	64	66	66	68
CT	047	26	26	28	30	30	30	30	32	32	34	34	36	38	40	42	44	46	48	48	50	52	54	58	60	64	66	66	66
CT	048	26	26	28	30	30	30	30	32	32	34	34	36	38	40	42	44	46	48	50	50	52	54	58	60	62	66	66	66
CT	049	26	26	28	28	28	30	30	32	32	34	34	36	38	40	42	44	46	46	48	50	52	54	58	60	62	66	66	66
NY	050	28	28	30	30	30	32	32	34	34	34	36	36	38	40	42	42	44	46	46	48	50	50	54	54	56	60	60	62
NY	051	28	28	30	30	30	32	32	34	34	34	36	36	40	40	42	42	44	46	46	48	50	50	54	54	56	60	60	62
NY	052	28	28	30	30	30	32	32	34	34	34	36	36	40	40	42	42	44	46	46	48	50	50	54	54	56	60	60	62
NY	053	28	28	30	30	30	32	32	34	34	34	36	36	40	40	42	42	44	46	46	48	50	50	54	54	56	60	60	62
NY	054	28	28	30	30	30	32	32	34	34	34	36	36	40	40	42	42	44	46	46	48	50	50	54	54	56	60	60	62
NY	055	28	28	30	30	30	32	32	34	34	34	36	36	40	40	42	42	44	46	46	48	50	50	54	54	56	58	60	62
NY	056	28	28	30	30	30	32	32	34	34	34	36	36	40	40	42	42	44	46	46	48	50	50	54	54	56	58	60	62
NY	057	28	28	30	30	30	32	32	34	34	34	36	36	40	40	42	42	44	46	46	48	50	50	54	54	56	58	60	62
NY	058	28	28	30	30	30	32	32	34	34	34	36	36	40	40	42	42	44	44	46	48	50	50	54	54	56	58	60	62
NY	059	28	28	30	30	30	32	32	32	34	34	36	36	40	40	42	42	44	46	46	48	50	50	54	54	56	58	60	62
NY	060	28	28	30	30	30	32	32	34	34	34	36	36	40	40	42	42	44	46	46	48	50	50	54	54	56	58	60	62
NY	061	28	28	30	30	30	32	32	34	34	34	36	36	40	40	42	42	44	46	46	48	50	50	54	54	56	58	60	62
NY	062	28	28	30	30	30	32	32	34	34	34	36	36	40	40	42	42	44	46	46	48	50	50	54	54	56	58	60	62
NY	063	28	28	30	30	30	32	32	34	34	34	36	36	40	40	42	42	44	46	46	48	50	50	54	54	56	58	60	62
NY	064	28	28	30	30	30	32	32	34	34	34	36	36	40	40	42	42	44	46	46	48	50	50	52	54	56	58	60	62
NY	065	28	28	30	30	30	32	32	34	34	34	36	36	40	40	42	42	44	44	46	48	50	50	52	54	56	58	60	62
NY	066	28	28	30	30	30	32	32	34	34	34	36	36	40	40	40	42	44	44	46	48	50	50	52	54	56	58	60	62
NY	067	28	28	30	30	30	32	32	32	34	34	36	36	40	40	40	42	44	44	46	48	50	50	52	54	56	58	60	62
NY	068	28	28	30	30	30	32	32	34	34	34	36	36	40	40	40	42	44	44	46	48	50	50	52	54	56	58	60	62
NY	069	28	28	28	30	30	32	32	32	34	34	36	36	40	40	40	42	44	44	46	48	50	50	52	54	56	58	60	62
NY	070	28	28	30	30	30	32	32	32	34	34	36	36	40	40	40	42	44	46	46	48	50	50	52	54	56	58	60	62
NY	071	28	28	30	30	30	32	32	34	34	34	36	36	40	40	40	42	44	44	46	48	50	50	52	54	56	58	60	62
NY	072	28	28	28	30	30	32	32	32	34	34	36	36	40	40	40	42	44	46	46	48	50	50	52	54	56	58	60	62
NY	073	28	28	28	30	30	32	32	32	34	34	36	36	40	40	40	42	44	44	46	48	50	50	52	54	56	58	60	62
NY	074	28	28	28	30	30	32	32	34	34	34	36	36	40	40	40	42	44	44	46	48	50	50	52	54	56	58	60	62

STATE	Area	1951	1952	1953	1954	1955	1956	1957	1958	1959	1960	1961	1962	1963	1964	1965	1966	1967	1968	1969	1970	1971	1972	1973	1974	1975	1976	1977	78
NY	075	28	28	28	30	30	32	32	32	34	34	36	36	40	40	40	42	44	44	46	48	50	50	52	54	56	58	60	62
NY	076	28	28	28	30	30	32	32	32	34	34	36	36	38	40	40	42	44	46	46	48	50	52	52	54	56	58	60	62
NY	077	26	28	28	30	30	32	32	32	34	34	34	36	38	40	40	42	44	44	46	48	50	52	52	54	56	58	60	62
NY	078	26	28	28	30	30	32	32	32	34	34	34	36	38	40	40	42	44	44	46	48	50	52	52	54	56	58	60	62
NY	079	28	28	28	30	30	32	32	32	34	34	34	36	38	40	40	42	44	44	46	48	50	52	52	54	56	58	60	62
NY	080	26	28	28	30	30	32	32	32	34	34	34	36	38	40	40	42	44	44	46	48	50	52	52	54	56	58	60	62
NY	081	28	28	28	30	30	32	32	32	34	34	34	36	38	40	40	42	44	44	46	48	50	52	52	54	56	58	60	62
NY	082	26	28	28	30	30	30	32	32	34	34	34	36	38	40	40	42	44	44	46	48	50	52	52	54	56	58	60	60
NY	083	26	28	28	30	30	30	32	32	34	34	34	36	38	40	40	42	44	44	46	48	50	52	52	54	56	58	60	60
NY	084	26	28	28	30	30	30	32	32	34	34	34	36	38	40	40	42	44	44	46	48	50	52	52	54	56	58	60	60
NY	085	26	28	28	30	30	32	32	32	34	34	34	36	38	40	40	42	44	44	46	48	50	52	52	54	56	58	60	60
NY	086	28	28	28	30	30	30	32	32	34	34	34	36	38	40	40	42	44	44	46	48	50	52	52	54	56	58	60	60
NY	087	28	28	28	30	30	30	32	32	34	34	34	36	38	40	40	42	44	44	46	48	50	52	52	54	56	58	60	60
NY	088	28	28	28	30	30	30	32	32	34	34	34	36	38	40	40	42	44	44	46	48	50	52	52	54	56	58	60	60
NY	089	26	28	28	30	30	30	32	32	34	34	34	36	38	40	40	42	44	44	46	48	50	52	52	54	56	58	60	60
NY	090	28	28	28	30	30	30	32	32	34	34	34	36	38	40	40	42	44	44	46	48	50	52	52	54	56	58	60	60
NY	091	26	28	28	30	30	30	32	32	34	34	34	36	38	40	40	42	42	44	46	48	50	52	52	54	56	58	60	60
NY	092	26	28	28	30	30	30	32	32	34	34	34	36	38	40	40	42	44	44	46	48	50	52	52	54	56	58	60	60
NY	093	26	28	28	30	30	30	32	32	34	34	34	36	38	40	40	42	42	44	46	48	50	52	52	54	56	58	60	60
NY	094	26	28	28	30	30	30	32	32	34	34	34	36	38	40	40	42	44	44	46	48	50	52	52	54	56	58	60	60
NY	095	26	28	28	30	30	30	32	32	34	34	34	36	38	38	40	42	44	44	46	48	50	52	52	54	56	58	60	60
NY	096	26	28	28	30	30	30	32	32	34	34	34	36	38	40	40	42	42	44	46	48	50	52	52	54	56	58	60	60
NY	097	26	28	28	30	30	30	32	32	34	34	34	36	38	38	40	42	42	44	46	48	50	52	52	54	56	58	60	60
NY	098	26	28	28	30	30	30	32	32	34	34	34	36	38	38	40	42	42	44	46	48	50	52	52	54	56	58	60	60
NY	099	26	28	28	30	30	30	32	32	32	34	34	36	38	38	40	42	42	44	46	48	50	52	52	54	56	58	60	60
NY	100	26	28	28	30	30	30	32	32	32	34	34	36	38	38	40	42	42	44	46	48	50	52	52	54	56	58	60	60
NY	101	26	28	28	30	30	30	32	32	32	34	34	36	38	38	40	40	42	44	46	46	48	50	52	54	56	58	60	60
NY	102	26	28	28	28	30	30	32	32	32	34	34	36	38	38	40	40	42	44	46	46	48	50	52	54	56	58	60	60
NY	103	26	28	28	28	30	30	32	32	32	34	34	36	38	38	40	40	42	44	46	46	48	50	52	54	56	58	60	60
NY	104	26	28	28	28	30	30	32	32	32	34	34	36	38	38	40	40	42	44	46	46	48	50	52	54	56	58	60	60
NY	105	26	28	28	28	30	30	32	32	32	34	34	36	38	38	40	40	42	44	46	48	48	50	52	54	56	58	60	60
NY	106	26	28	28	28	30	30	32	32	32	34	34	36	38	38	40	40	42	44	46	46	48	50	52	54	56	58	60	60
NY	107	26	28	28	28	30	30	32	32	32	34	34	36	38	38	40	40	42	44	46	46	48	50	52	54	56	58	60	60
NY	108	26	28	28	28	30	30	32	32	32	34	34	36	38	38	40	40	42	44	46	46	48	50	52	54	56	58	60	60
NY	109	26	28	28	28	30	30	32	32	32	34	34	36	38	38	40	40	42	44	46	46	48	50	52	54	56	58	60	60
NY	110	26	28	28	28	30	30	32	32	32	34	34	36	38	38	40	40	42	44	46	46	48	50	52	54	56	58	60	60
NY	111	26	28	28	28	30	30	32	32	32	34	34	36	38	38	40	40	42	44	46	46	48	50	52	54	56	58	60	60
NY	112	26	28	28	28	30	30	32	32	32	34	34	36	38	38	40	40	42	44	46	46	48	50	52	54	56	58	60	60
NY	113	26	28	28	28	30	30	30	32	32	34	34	36	38	38	40	40	42	44	46	46	48	50	52	54	56	58	60	60
NY	114	26	28	28	28	30	30	32	32	32	34	34	36	38	38	40	40	42	44	46	48	48	50	52	54	56	58	60	60

STATE	Area	1951	1952	1953	1954	1955	1956	1957	1958	1959	1960	1961	1962	1963	1964	1965	1966	1967	1968	1969	1970	1971	1972	1973	1974	1975	1976	1977	78
NY	115	26	28	28	28	30	30	32	32	32	34	34	36	38	38	40	40	42	44	46	48	48	50	52	54	56	58	60	60
NY	116	26	28	28	28	30	30	30	32	32	34	34	36	38	38	40	40	42	44	46	46	48	50	52	54	56	58	60	60
NY	117	26	28	28	28	30	30	32	32	32	34	34	36	38	38	40	40	42	44	46	48	48	50	52	54	56	58	60	60
NY	118	26	28	28	28	30	30	32	32	32	34	34	36	38	38	40	40	42	44	46	46	48	50	52	54	56	58	60	60
NY	119	26	28	28	28	30	30	32	32	32	34	34	36	38	38	40	40	42	44	46	46	48	50	52	54	56	58	60	60
NY	120	26	28	28	28	30	30	32	32	32	34	34	36	38	38	40	40	42	44	46	46	48	50	52	54	56	58	60	60
NY	121	26	28	28	28	30	30	32	32	32	34	34	36	38	38	40	40	42	44	46	46	48	50	52	54	56	58	60	60
NY	122	26	26	28	28	30	30	32	32	32	34	34	36	38	38	40	40	42	44	46	46	48	50	52	54	56	58	58	60
NY	123	26	26	28	28	30	30	32	32	32	34	34	36	38	38	40	40	42	44	46	46	48	50	52	54	56	58	58	60
NY	124	26	26	28	28	30	30	30	32	32	34	34	36	38	38	40	40	42	44	46	46	48	50	52	54	56	58	58	60
NY	125	26	26	28	28	30	30	32	32	32	34	34	34	38	38	40	40	42	44	46	46	48	50	52	54	56	58	58	60
NY	126	26	26	28	28	30	30	30	32	32	34	34	34	38	38	40	40	42	44	44	46	50	52	54	54	54	58	58	60
NY	127	26	26	28	28	30	30	30	32	32	34	34	34	38	38	40	40	42	44	44	46	50	52	54	54	54	58	58	60
NY	128	26	26	28	28	30	30	30	32	32	34	34	34	38	40	40	40	42	44	44	46	50	52	54	54	54	58	58	60
NY	129	26	26	28	28	30	30	30	32	32	34	34	34	38	38	40	40	42	44	44	46	50	52	54	54	54	58	58	60
NY	130	26	26	28	28	30	30	30	32	32	34	34	34	38	38	40	40	42	44	44	46	50	52	54	54	54	58	58	60
NY	131	26	26	28	28	30	30	30	32	32	34	34	34	38	38	40	40	42	44	46	46	50	52	52	52	54	58	58	60
NY	132	26	26	28	28	30	30	30	32	32	32	34	34	36	38	40	40	42	44	44	46	50	52	52	52	54	58	58	60
NY	133	26	26	28	28	30	30	30	32	32	32	34	36	38	38	40	40	42	44	46	46	50	52	52	52	54	58	58	60
NY	134	26	26	28	28	30	30	30	32	34	34	34	34	36	38	40	40	42	44	44	46	48	52	52	52	54	58	58	60
NJ	135	26	28	28	30	30	32	32	32	34	34	36	36	38	40	42	44	46	46	48	50	52	56	58	58	62	64	66	68
NJ	136	26	28	28	30	30	32	32	32	34	34	36	36	38	40	42	44	46	46	48	50	52	56	58	58	62	64	66	68
NJ	137	26	28	28	30	30	30	32	32	34	34	36	36	40	40	42	44	46	46	48	50	52	56	58	58	62	64	66	68
NJ	138	26	28	28	30	30	30	32	32	34	34	36	36	38	40	42	44	44	46	48	50	52	56	58	58	62	64	66	68
NJ	139	26	28	28	28	30	30	32	32	34	34	34	36	38	40	42	44	44	46	48	50	52	56	58	58	62	64	66	68
NJ	140	26	28	28	28	30	30	32	32	34	34	34	36	38	40	42	44	44	46	48	50	52	56	58	58	60	64	66	68
NJ	141	26	28	28	28	30	30	32	32	34	34	34	36	38	40	42	44	44	46	48	50	52	56	58	58	60	64	66	68
NJ	142	26	28	28	28	30	30	32	32	32	34	34	36	38	40	42	42	44	46	48	50	52	56	58	58	60	64	66	68
NJ	143	26	28	28	28	30	30	32	32	32	34	34	36	38	40	42	42	44	46	48	50	52	56	58	58	60	64	66	66
NJ	144	26	26	28	28	30	30	32	32	32	34	34	36	38	40	42	42	44	46	48	50	52	56	58	58	60	64	66	66
NJ	145	26	26	28	28	30	30	32	32	32	34	34	36	38	40	40	42	44	46	48	50	52	56	58	58	60	64	66	66
NJ	146	26	26	28	28	30	30	32	32	32	34	34	36	38	40	40	42	44	46	48	50	52	56	58	58	60	64	66	66
NJ	147	26	26	28	28	30	30	32	32	32	34	34	36	38	40	40	42	44	46	48	48	52	56	58	58	60	64	66	66
NJ	148	26	26	28	28	30	30	32	32	32	34	34	36	38	40	40	42	44	46	48	50	52	56	58	58	60	62	66	66
NJ	149	26	26	28	28	30	30	30	32	32	34	34	36	38	40	40	42	44	46	48	48	52	56	58	58	60	62	66	66
NJ	150	26	26	28	28	30	30	30	32	32	34	34	36	38	40	40	42	44	46	48	48	52	56	58	58	60	62	66	66
NJ	151	26	26	28	28	28	30	30	32	32	34	34	36	38	38	40	42	44	46	46	48	50	52	56	58	60	62	64	66
NJ	152	26	26	28	28	28	30	30	32	32	34	34	36	38	38	40	42	44	46	46	48	50	52	56	58	60	62	64	66
NJ	153	26	26	28	28	28	30	30	32	32	32	34	38	38	40	42	44	46	48	48	50	52	54	58	60	62	64	66	66

STATE	Area	1951	1952	1953	1954	1955	1956	1957	1958	1959	1960	1961	1962	1963	1964	1965	1966	1967	1968	1969	1970	1971	1972	1973	1974	1975	1976	1977	78
NJ	154	24	26	26	28	28	30	30	32	32	32	34	34	38	38	40	42	44	46	48	48	50	52	54	58	60	62	64	66
NJ	155	24	26	26	28	28	30	30	32	32	32	34	34	38	38	40	42	44	46	46	48	50	52	54	58	60	62	64	66
NJ	156	26	26	26	28	28	30	30	32	32	32	34	34	38	38	40	42	44	44	46	48	50	52	54	58	60	62	64	66
NJ	157	26	26	26	28	28	30	30	30	32	32	34	34	38	38	40	42	44	44	46	48	50	52	54	58	60	62	64	66
NJ	158	26	26	26	28	28	30	30	30	32	32	34	34	38	38	40	42	44	44	46	48	50	52	54	56	60	62	64	66
PA	159	28	28	30	30	30	32	32	34	34	34	36	36	38	40	40	42	44	44	46	46	48	48	52	52	54	56	58	58
PA	160	28	28	30	30	30	32	32	34	34	34	36	36	38	40	40	42	44	44	46	46	48	48	52	52	54	56	58	58
PA	161	28	28	30	30	30	32	32	34	34	34	36	36	38	40	40	42	42	44	46	46	48	48	52	52	54	56	58	58
PA	162	28	28	30	30	30	32	32	34	34	34	36	36	38	40	40	42	42	44	46	46	48	48	52	52	54	56	58	58
PA	163	28	28	30	30	30	32	32	34	34	34	36	36	38	40	40	42	42	44	46	46	48	48	52	52	54	56	58	58
PA	164	28	28	30	30	30	32	32	34	34	34	36	36	38	40	40	42	42	44	46	46	48	48	52	52	54	56	58	58
PA	165	28	28	30	30	30	32	32	32	34	34	34	36	38	38	40	42	42	44	46	46	48	48	52	52	54	56	58	58
PA	166	28	28	30	30	30	32	32	32	34	34	36	36	38	38	40	42	42	44	46	46	48	48	52	52	54	56	58	58
PA	167	28	28	30	30	30	32	32	32	34	34	36	36	38	38	40	42	42	44	46	46	48	48	52	52	54	56	58	58
PA	168	28	28	30	30	30	32	32	32	34	34	34	36	38	38	40	42	42	44	46	46	48	48	52	52	54	56	58	58
PA	169	28	28	30	30	30	32	32	32	34	34	36	36	38	38	40	42	42	44	46	46	48	48	52	52	54	56	58	58
PA	170	28	28	30	30	30	32	32	32	34	34	34	36	38	38	40	42	42	44	46	46	48	48	52	52	54	56	58	58
PA	171	28	28	30	30	30	32	32	32	34	34	34	36	38	38	40	42	42	44	46	46	48	48	52	52	54	56	58	58
PA	172	28	28	28	30	30	32	32	32	34	34	34	36	38	38	40	42	42	44	46	46	48	48	52	52	54	56	58	58
PA	173	28	28	28	30	30	32	32	32	34	34	34	36	38	38	40	42	42	44	46	46	48	48	50	52	54	56	58	58
PA	174	28	28	28	30	30	32	32	32	34	34	34	36	38	38	40	42	42	44	44	46	48	48	50	52	54	56	58	58
PA	175	28	28	28	30	30	32	32	32	34	34	34	36	38	38	40	42	42	44	44	46	48	48	50	52	54	56	58	58
PA	176	28	28	28	30	30	32	32	32	34	34	34	36	38	38	40	42	42	44	44	46	46	48	50	52	54	56	58	58
PA	177	26	28	28	30	30	30	32	32	34	34	34	36	38	38	40	42	42	44	44	46	46	48	50	52	54	56	58	58
PA	178	26	28	28	30	30	30	32	32	32	34	34	36	38	38	40	42	42	44	46	46	48	48	50	52	54	56	58	58
PA	179	26	28	28	30	30	30	32	32	34	34	34	36	38	38	40	42	42	44	44	46	46	48	50	52	54	56	58	58
PA	180	26	28	28	30	30	32	32	32	34	34	34	36	38	38	40	42	44	44	46	46	48	48	50	52	54	56	58	58
PA	181	26	28	28	30	30	32	32	32	34	34	34	36	38	38	40	40	42	44	44	46	46	48	50	52	54	56	58	58
PA	182	26	28	28	30	30	32	32	32	34	34	34	36	38	38	40	40	42	44	44	46	46	48	50	52	54	56	58	58
PA	183	26	28	28	30	30	32	32	32	34	34	36	38	38	40	40	42	44	44	46	46	48	50	52	54	56	58	58	58
PA	184	26	28	28	30	30	30	32	32	34	34	34	36	38	38	40	40	42	44	44	46	46	48	50	52	54	56	58	58
PA	185	26	28	28	30	30	30	32	32	32	34	34	36	38	38	40	40	42	44	44	46	46	48	50	52	54	56	58	58
PA	186	26	28	28	30	30	30	32	32	32	34	34	36	38	38	40	40	42	44	44	46	46	48	50	52	54	56	58	58
PA	187	26	28	28	28	30	30	32	32	32	34	34	36	38	38	40	40	42	42	44	46	46	48	50	52	54	56	58	58
PA	188	26	28	28	28	30	30	32	32	32	34	34	36	38	38	40	40	42	44	44	46	46	48	50	52	54	56	58	58
PA	189	26	28	28	28	30	30	32	32	32	34	34	36	38	38	40	40	42	44	44	46	46	48	50	52	54	56	58	58
PA	190	26	28	28	28	30	30	32	32	32	34	34	34	36	38	40	40	42	42	44	46	46	48	50	52	54	56	58	58
PA	191	26	28	28	28	30	30	32	32	32	34	34	36	36	38	40	40	42	44	44	46	46	48	50	52	54	56	58	58
PA	192	26	28	28	28	30	30	32	32	32	34	34	34	36	38	40	40	42	42	44	46	46	48	50	52	54	56	58	58

STATE	Area	1951	1952	1953	1954	1955	1956	1957	1958	1959	1960	1961	1962	1963	1964	1965	1966	1967	1968	1969	1970	1971	1972	1973	1974	1975	1976	1977	78
PA	193	26	28	28	28	30	30	32	32	32	34	34	34	38	38	40	40	42	42	44	46	46	48	50	52	54	56	58	58
PA	194	26	28	28	28	30	30	32	32	32	34	34	34	36	38	40	40	42	42	44	46	46	48	50	52	54	56	58	58
PA	195	26	28	28	28	30	30	32	32	32	34	34	34	36	38	40	40	42	42	44	46	46	48	50	52	54	56	58	58
PA	196	26	28	28	28	30	30	32	32	32	34	34	34	38	38	40	40	42	42	44	46	46	48	50	52	54	56	58	58
PA	197	26	28	28	28	30	30	32	32	32	34	34	34	36	38	38	40	42	42	44	46	46	48	50	52	54	56	58	58
PA	198	26	28	28	28	30	30	32	32	32	34	34	34	36	40	38	40	42	42	44	46	46	48	50	52	54	56	58	58
PA	199	26	28	28	28	30	30	32	32	32	34	34	34	36	40	38	40	42	42	44	46	46	48	50	52	54	56	58	58
PA	200	26	28	28	28	30	30	32	32	32	32	34	34	36	40	38	40	42	42	44	44	46	48	50	52	54	56	58	58
PA	201	26	28	28	28	30	30	32	32	32	34	34	34	36	38	40	40	42	42	44	46	46	48	50	52	54	56	56	58
PA	202	26	28	28	28	30	30	30	32	32	32	34	34	36	38	38	40	42	42	44	44	46	48	50	52	54	56	56	58
PA	203	26	28	28	28	30	30	32	32	32	32	34	34	36	38	38	40	42	42	44	44	46	48	50	52	54	56	56	58
PA	204	26	26	28	28	30	30	30	32	32	32	34	34	36	38	38	40	42	42	44	44	46	46	50	52	54	54	56	58
PA	205	26	26	28	28	30	30	30	32	32	32	34	34	36	38	38	40	42	42	44	44	46	46	50	52	54	54	56	58
PA	206	26	26	28	28	30	30	30	32	32	32	34	34	36	38	38	40	42	42	44	44	46	46	50	52	54	54	56	58
PA	207	26	26	28	28	30	30	30	32	32	32	34	34	36	38	38	40	42	42	44	44	46	46	50	52	54	54	56	58
PA	208	26	26	28	28	30	30	30	32	32	32	34	34	36	38	38	40	42	42	44	44	46	46	50	52	54	54	56	56
PA	209	26	26	28	28	30	30	32	32	32	34	34	36	38	38	40	42	42	44	44	46	46	50	52	54	54	56	56	
PA	210	26	26	28	28	28	30	30	32	32	32	34	34	36	38	38	40	42	42	44	44	46	46	50	52	54	54	56	56
PA	211	26	26	28	28	28	30	30	32	32	32	34	34	36	38	38	40	42	42	44	44	46	46	50	52	54	54	56	56
MD	212	32	34	34	36	36	38	40	40	42	42	44	46	50	52	54	56	58	62	64	66	70	72	76	80	82	86	90	92
MD	213	32	34	34	34	36	38	38	40	42	42	44	46	50	52	54	56	60	62	64	68	70	72	76	80	82	86	90	92
MD	214	32	34	34	34	36	38	38	40	40	42	44	46	50	52	54	56	58	62	64	66	70	72	76	80	82	86	90	92
MD	215	32	32	34	34	36	38	38	40	40	42	44	46	50	50	54	56	58	60	64	66	70	72	76	80	82	86	88	90
MD	216	32	32	34	34	36	36	38	40	40	42	44	46	48	50	54	56	58	60	64	66	70	72	76	78	82	86	88	90
MD	217	32	32	34	34	36	36	38	38	40	42	44	44	48	50	52	56	58	62	64	66	70	72	76	78	82	86	88	90
MD	218	32	32	34	34	36	36	38	40	40	42	42	44	48	50	52	56	58	60	64	66	70	72	76	78	82	86	88	90
MD	219	30	32	32	34	34	36	38	38	40	42	42	44	48	50	52	56	58	60	64	66	68	72	76	78	82	86	88	90
MD	220	30	32	32	34	34	36	38	38	40	40	42	44	48	50	52	56	58	60	62	66	68	72	76	78	82	84	88	90
DE	221	22	22	22	24	24	26	26	26	28	28	30	30	32	32	34	36	38	40	40	42	44	46	52	54	58	60	60	60
DE	222	20	20	22	22	24	24	24	26	26	26	28	28	30	32	34	34	36	38	40	42	44	46	52	54	56	58	60	60
VA	223	42	44	46	48	50	52	54	54	56	58	60	62	66	68	70	74	76	80	82	86	88	90	96	02	06	11	15	17
VA	224	40	44	46	48	50	52	52	54	56	58	60	62	66	68	70	74	76	80	82	84	88	90	96	02	06	11	15	17
VA	225	40	44	46	46	48	52	52	54	56	58	58	60	66	68	70	74	76	78	82	84	88	90	96	02	06	11	13	15
VA	226	42	44	46	46	48	50	52	54	56	56	58	60	66	68	70	74	76	78	82	84	88	90	96	02	06	11	13	15
VA	227	42	44	46	46	48	50	52	54	54	56	58	60	64	68	70	74	76	78	82	84	88	90	96	02	06	11	13	15
VA	228	42	44	46	46	48	50	52	54	54	56	58	60	64	68	70	74	76	78	82	84	86	90	96	02	06	11	13	15
VA	229	42	44	44	46	48	50	52	54	54	56	58	60	64	66	70	72	76	78	82	84	86	90	96	02	04	08	13	15

Identity, Privacy, and Personal Freedom

STATE	Area	1951	1952	1953	1954	1955	1956	1957	1958	1959	1960	1961	1962	1963	1964	1965	1966	1967	1968	1969	1970	1971	1972	1973	1974	1975	1976	1977	78
VA	230	42	42	44	46	48	50	52	52	54	56	58	60	64	66	70	72	76	78	80	84	86	90	96	02	04	08	13	15
VA	231	40	42	44	46	48	50	52	52	54	56	58	60	64	66	70	72	74	78	80	84	86	88	02	98	04	08	13	15
WV & NC	232	54	56	58	58	60	62	64	66	68	70	70	72	76	78	80	82	84	86	88	92	92	94	02	04	06	11	13	15
WV	233	54	54	56	58	60	62	64	66	66	68	70	72	76	76	80	82	84	86	88	90	92	94	98	04	06	11	13	15
WV	234	52	54	56	58	60	62	64	64	66	68	70	72	74	76	80	82	84	86	88	90	92	94	98	04	06	11	13	15
WV	235	52	54	56	58	60	62	64	64	66	68	70	70	74	76	78	82	84	86	88	90	92	94	98	02	06	08	13	13
WV	236	52	54	56	58	60	62	62	64	66	66	68	70	74	76	78	80	84	86	88	90	92	94	98	02	06	08	11	13
NC	237	50	52	54	56	58	60	62	66	66	70	72	74	76	80	82	86	90	92	94	98	02	04	11	15	19	23	27	29
NC	238	50	52	54	56	58	60	62	64	66	68	70	74	78	80	82	86	90	92	94	98	02	04	11	15	19	23	27	29
NC	239	48	52	54	54	58	60	62	64	66	68	70	72	76	80	82	86	90	92	94	98	02	04	11	15	19	23	25	29
NC	240	50	50	54	54	58	60	62	64	66	68	70	72	78	80	82	86	88	92	94	98	02	04	11	15	19	23	25	27
NC	241	48	50	52	54	58	60	62	64	66	68	70	72	76	80	82	86	88	92	94	98	02	04	11	15	19	23	25	27
NC	242	50	50	52	54	58	60	62	64	66	68	70	72	76	78	82	86	88	92	94	98	02	04	11	15	19	23	25	27
NC	243	48	50	52	54	56	60	62	64	66	68	70	72	76	78	82	86	88	90	94	96	02	04	11	15	19	23	25	27
NC	244	48	50	52	54	56	60	62	64	66	68	70	72	76	78	82	86	88	90	94	96	02	04	11	15	17	21	25	27
NC	245	48	50	52	54	56	60	62	64	66	68	70	72	76	78	82	84	88	90	94	96	02	04	11	15	17	21	25	27
NC	246	48	50	52	54	56	58	62	64	66	68	70	72	76	78	82	84	88	90	92	96	02	04	11	15	17	21	25	27
SC	247	54	52	58	58	62	64	66	68	70	74	76	78	82	84	88	94	96	98	04	06	11	13	19	25	31	33	37	39
SC	248	54	52	56	58	62	64	66	68	70	72	76	78	82	84	88	94	96	98	04	06	11	13	19	25	29	33	37	39
SC	249	52	52	56	58	62	64	66	68	70	72	74	78	82	84	88	92	96	98	02	06	08	13	19	25	29	33	37	39
SC	250	52	52	56	58	60	64	66	68	70	72	74	78	82	84	88	92	94	98	02	06	08	13	19	25	29	33	35	39
SC	251	52	54	56	58	60	64	66	68	70	72	74	76	82	84	88	94	94	96	02	06	08	13	19	25	29	33	35	39
GA	252	52	54	56	56	58	60	64	64	66	68	70	72	76	78	82	88	88	92	94	98	02	06	15	19	23	27	29	31
GA	253	52	54	54	56	58	60	62	64	66	68	70	72	76	78	82	88	88	92	94	96	02	06	15	19	23	27	29	31
GA	254	50	52	54	56	58	60	62	64	66	68	70	72	76	78	82	88	88	92	94	98	02	04	15	19	23	27	29	31
GA	255	52	52	54	56	58	60	62	64	66	68	70	72	76	78	82	88	88	92	94	96	02	04	15	19	23	27	29	31
GA	256	52	52	54	56	58	60	62	64	66	68	68	70	74	78	80	88	88	90	94	96	02	04	15	19	23	27	29	31
GA	257	52	52	54	56	58	60	62	64	64	66	68	70	74	76	80	88	88	90	94	96	02	04	17	21	23	27	29	31
GA	258	50	52	54	56	58	60	62	64	64	66	68	70	74	76	80	88	88	90	94	96	02	04	17	21	23	27	29	31
GA	259	50	52	54	56	58	60	62	62	64	66	68	70	74	76	80	86	86	90	92	96	02	04	17	21	25	27	27	29
GA	260	50	52	54	54	56	60	62	62	64	66	68	70	74	76	80	86	86	90	92	96	02	04	17	21	25	25	27	29
FL	261	48	50	52	54	58	60	62	64	68	70	74	78	88	94	98	13	13	19	23	31	35	39	51	61	67	75	81	87
FL	262	50	50	52	54	58	60	62	64	66	70	72	80	866	94	98	13	13	19	23	29	35	39	51	59	67	75	81	87
FL	263	48	50	52	54	56	60	62	64	66	70	72	78	88	92	98	13	13	17	23	29	35	39	51	59	67	75	81	85

STATE	Area	1951	1952	1953	1954	1955	1956	1957	1958	1959	1960	1961	1962	1963	1964	1965	1966	1967	1968	1969	1970	1971	1972	1973	1974	1975	1976	1977	78
FL	264	48	50	52	54	56	60	62	64	66	70	72	78	86	90	98	13	13	17	23	29	35	39	51	59	67	75	81	85
FL	265	48	50	52	54	56	60	62	64	66	68	72	76	86	92	98	13	13	17	23	29	35	39	51	59	67	73	81	85
FL	266	48	50	52	52	56	58	60	64	66	70	72	76	86	92	98	13	13	17	23	29	35	39	51	59	67	73	81	85
FL	267	48	50	50	54	56	58	60	62	66	68	72	76	86	92	98	11	11	17	23	29	33	39	49	59	67	73	79	85
OH	268	30	32	32	34	34	36	36	38	38	40	40	42	44	46	50	52	52	54	56	58	58	60	64	66	68	72	72	74
OH	269	30	32	32	34	34	36	36	38	38	40	40	42	44	46	50	52	52	54	54	56	58	60	64	66	68	72	72	74
OH	270	30	32	32	34	34	36	36	38	38	40	40	40	44	46	50	52	52	54	54	56	58	60	64	66	68	72	72	74
OH	271	30	32	32	34	34	36	36	38	38	38	40	40	44	46	50	52	52	54	54	56	58	60	64	66	68	72	72	74
OH	272	30	32	32	34	34	36	36	38	38	38	40	40	44	46	50	52	52	54	56	56	58	60	64	66	68	72	72	74
OH	273	30	32	32	34	34	36	36	36	38	38	40	40	44	46	50	52	52	54	54	56	58	60	64	66	68	72	72	74
OH	274	30	32	32	34	34	36	36	38	38	38	40	40	44	46	50	52	52	54	54	56	58	60	64	66	68	70	72	74
OH	275	30	32	32	34	34	36	36	36	38	38	40	40	44	46	50	52	52	52	54	56	58	60	64	66	68	70	72	74
OH	276	30	32	32	34	36	36	36	36	38	38	40	40	44	46	48	50	52	52	54	56	58	60	64	66	68	70	72	74
OH	277	30	32	32	32	36	36	36	36	38	38	40	40	44	46	48	50	52	52	54	56	58	60	64	66	68	70	72	74
OH	278	30	32	32	32	36	36	36	36	38	38	40	40	44	46	48	50	50	52	54	56	58	60	64	66	68	70	72	72
OH	279	30	32	32	32	34	34	36	36	38	38	40	40	44	46	48	50	50	52	56	56	58	60	64	66	68	70	72	72
OH	280	30	32	32	32	36	36	36	36	38	38	40	40	44	46	48	50	50	52	54	56	58	60	64	66	68	70	72	72
OH	281	30	32	32	32	36	36	36	36	38	38	40	40	44	46	48	50	50	52	54	56	58	60	64	66	68	70	72	72
OH	282	30	32	32	32	34	34	36	36	38	38	40	40	48	46	46	50	50	52	54	56	58	60	64	66	68	70	72	72
OH	283	30	30	32	32	34	34	36	36	38	38	40	40	48	46	48	50	50	52	54	56	58	60	64	66	68	70	72	72
OH	284	30	30	32	32	34	34	36	36	38	38	40	40	48	46	48	50	50	52	54	56	58	58	64	66	68	70	72	72
OH	285	30	30	32	32	34	34	36	36	38	38	38	40	48	46	48	50	50	52	54	56	58	58	64	66	68	70	72	72
OH	286	30	30	32	32	34	34	36	36	38	38	40	40	48	46	46	50	50	52	54	56	58	58	64	66	68	70	72	72
OH	287	30	30	32	32	34	34	36	36	38	38	38	40	48	46	46	48	50	52	54	56	58	58	64	66	68	70	72	72
OH	288	30	30	32	32	34	34	36	36	38	38	38	40	48	46	46	48	50	52	54	56	58	58	64	66	68	70	72	72
OH	289	30	30	32	32	34	34	36	36	38	38	38	40	48	44	46	48	50	52	54	56	58	58	64	66	68	70	72	72
OH	290	30	30	32	32	34	34	36	36	36	38	38	40	48	44	48	48	50	52	54	56	58	58	64	66	68	70	72	72
OH	291	30	30	32	32	34	34	36	36	36	38	38	40	48	44	48	48	50	52	54	56	56	58	64	66	68	70	72	72
OH	292	30	30	32	32	34	34	36	36	36	38	38	40	48	44	48	48	50	52	54	56	58	58	62	66	68	70	72	72
OH	293	30	30	32	32	34	34	36	36	36	38	38	40	42	44	48	48	50	52	54	56	56	58	62	66	68	70	72	72
OH	294	30	30	32	32	34	34	36	36	36	38	38	40	44	44	48	48	50	52	54	56	58	58	62	64	68	70	72	72
OH	295	28	30	32	32	32	34	36	36	36	38	38	40	42	44	48	48	50	52	54	56	56	58	62	64	68	70	70	72
OH	296	28	30	32	32	34	34	34	36	36	38	38	40	44	44	48	48	50	52	54	56	56	58	62	64	68	70	70	72
OH	297	28	30	32	32	32	34	34	36	36	38	38	40	44	44	48	48	50	52	54	54	56	58	62	64	68	70	70	72
OH	298	28	30	32	32	32	34	34	36	36	38	38	40	44	44	48	48	50	52	54	54	56	58	62	64	66	70	70	72
OH	299	28	30	32	32	32	34	34	36	36	38	38	40	42	44	48	48	50	52	54	54	56	58	62	64	66	70	70	72
OH	300	30	30	30	32	32	34	34	36	36	38	38	40	44	44	48	48	50	52	54	54	56	58	62	64	66	70	70	72
OH	301	28	30	30	32	32	34	34	36	36	38	38	40	44	44	46	48	50	52	54	54	56	56	62	64	66	70	70	72
OH	302	28	30	30	32	32	34	34	36	36	38	38	40	44	44	46	48	50	52	54	54	56	58	62	64	66	70	70	72

STATE	Area	1951	1952	1953	1954	1955	1956	1957	1958	1959	1960	1961	1962	1963	1964	1965	1966	1967	1968	1969	1970	1971	1972	1973	1974	1975	1976	1977	78
IN	303	36	36	38	38	40	42	42	44	44	46	46	48	52	52	54	48	58	60	62	64	66	58	72	74	76	80	82	82
IN	304	34	36	38	38	40	42	42	44	44	46	46	48	52	52	54	56	58	60	62	64	66	68	72	74	76	80	82	82
IN	305	34	36	38	38	40	42	42	44	44	46	46	48	52	52	54	56	58	60	62	64	66	68	72	74	76	80	80	82
IN	306	34	36	36	38	40	40	42	42	44	46	46	48	50	52	54	56	58	60	62	64	66	68	72	74	76	80	80	82
IN	307	34	36	36	38	40	40	42	42	44	44	46	48	50	52	54	56	58	60	62	64	66	68	72	74	76	78	80	82
IN	308	34	36	36	38	40	40	42	42	44	44	46	48	50	52	54	56	58	60	62	64	66	68	72	74	76	78	80	82
IN	309	34	36	36	38	38	40	42	42	44	44	46	48	50	52	54	56	58	60	62	64	66	68	72	74	76	78	80	82
IN	310	34	36	36	38	38	40	42	42	44	44	46	48	50	52	54	56	58	60	62	64	66	68	72	74	76	78	80	82
IN	311	34	36	36	36	38	40	42	42	44	44	46	46	50	52	54	56	58	60	62	64	66	68	72	74	76	78	80	82
IN	312	34	34	36	38	38	40	42	42	44	44	46	46	50	52	54	56	58	58	62	64	66	68	70	74	76	78	80	82
IN	313	34	34	36	36	38	40	42	42	44	44	46	46	50	52	54	56	58	58	60	64	66	68	70	72	76	78	80	82
IN	314	34	34	36	36	38	40	40	42	42	44	46	46	50	52	54	54	56	58	60	62	66	68	70	72	74	78	80	82
IN	315	34	34	36	36	38	40	40	42	42	44	44	46	48	50	52	56	56	58	60	64	64	68	70	72	74	78	80	82
IN	316	34	34	36	36	38	40	40	42	42	44	44	46	50	50	52	54	56	58	60	62	64	66	70	72	74	78	80	80
IN	317	34	34	36	36	38	40	40	42	42	44	44	46	48	50	52	54	56	58	60	62	66	66	70	72	74	78	80	80
IL	318	28	30	30	32	32	34	34	34	36	36	38	38	40	42	44	46	46	48	50	52	54	54	58	60	62	64	66	66
IL	319	28	30	30	32	32	34	34	34	36	36	38	38	40	42	44	46	46	48	50	52	52	54	58	60	62	64	66	66
IL	320	28	30	30	30	32	34	34	34	36	36	38	38	40	42	44	44	46	48	50	52	52	54	58	60	62	66	66	66
IL	321	28	30	30	30	32	34	34	34	36	36	38	38	40	42	44	46	46	48	50	52	54	54	58	60	62	64	66	66
IL	322	28	30	30	30	32	32	34	34	36	36	38	38	40	42	44	44	46	48	50	52	54	54	58	60	62	64	66	66
IL	323	28	30	30	30	32	34	34	34	36	36	36	38	40	42	44	44	46	48	50	52	54	54	58	60	62	64	64	66
IL	324	28	30	30	30	32	34	34	34	36	36	36	38	40	42	44	44	46	48	50	52	52	54	58	60	62	64	64	66
IL	325	28	30	30	30	32	34	34	34	36	36	36	38	40	42	44	44	46	48	50	52	52	54	58	60	62	64	64	66
IL	326	28	30	30	30	32	32	34	34	36	36	36	38	40	42	44	44	46	48	50	52	54	54	58	60	62	64	64	66
IL	327	28	30	30	30	32	32	34	34	36	36	36	38	40	42	44	44	46	48	50	52	54	54	58	60	62	64	64	66
IL	328	28	30	30	30	32	32	34	34	36	36	36	38	40	42	42	44	46	48	50	52	52	54	58	58	60	64	64	66
IL	329	28	28	30	30	32	32	34	34	36	36	36	38	40	42	42	44	46	48	50	52	52	54	58	58	60	64	64	66
IL	330	28	28	30	30	32	32	34	34	34	36	36	38	40	42	44	44	46	48	50	50	52	54	58	58	60	64	64	66
IL	331	28	28	30	30	32	32	34	34	34	36	36	38	40	42	44	44	46	48	50	52	52	54	58	58	60	64	64	66
IL	332	28	28	30	30	32	32	34	34	34	36	36	38	40	42	42	44	46	48	50	52	52	54	58	58	60	64	64	66
IL	333	28	28	30	30	32	32	34	34	34	36	36	38	40	42	42	44	46	48	50	50	52	54	56	58	60	62	64	66
IL	334	28	28	30	30	32	32	34	34	34	36	36	38	40	42	42	44	46	48	50	50	52	54	56	58	60	62	64	66
IL	335	28	28	30	30	32	32	34	34	34	36	36	38	40	42	42	44	46	48	50	50	52	54	56	58	60	62	64	66
IL	336	28	28	30	30	32	32	34	34	34	36	36	38	40	42	42	44	46	48	50	50	52	54	56	58	60	62	64	66
IL	337	28	28	30	30	32	32	34	34	34	36	36	38	40	42	42	44	46	48	48	50	52	54	56	58	60	62	64	66
IL	338	28	28	30	30	32	32	34	34	34	36	36	38	40	42	42	44	46	48	50	50	52	54	56	58	60	62	64	66
IL	339	28	28	30	30	32	32	34	34	34	36	36	38	40	40	42	44	46	46	50	50	52	54	56	58	60	62	64	66
IL	340	28	28	30	30	32	32	34	34	34	36	36	38	40	40	42	44	46	46	48	50	52	54	56	58	60	62	64	66

STATE	Area	1951	1952	1953	1954	1955	1956	1957	1958	1959	1960	1961	1962	1963	1964	1965	1966	1967	1968	1969	1970	1971	1972	1973	1974	1975	1976	1977	78
IL	341	28	28	30	30	32	32	32	34	34	36	36	38	40	40	42	44	46	46	48	50	52	54	56	58	60	62	64	66
IL	342	28	28	30	30	32	32	32	34	34	36	36	38	40	40	42	44	46	46	48	50	52	54	56	58	60	62	64	66
IL	343	28	28	30	30	32	32	32	34	34	36	36	38	40	40	42	44	46	46	48	50	52	54	56	58	60	62	64	66
IL	344	28	28	30	30	30	32	32	34	34	36	36	38	40	40	42	44	46	48	48	50	52	54	56	58	60	62	64	66
IL	345	28	28	30	30	30	32	32	34	34	36	36	38	40	40	42	44	46	46	48	50	52	54	56	58	60	62	64	66
IL	346	28	28	30	30	30	32	32	34	34	36	36	38	40	40	42	44	46	46	48	50	52	54	56	58	60	62	64	66
IL	347	28	28	30	30	30	32	32	34	34	36	36	36	40	40	42	44	46	46	48	50	52	54	56	58	60	62	64	66
IL	348	28	28	30	30	30	32	32	34	34	36	36	36	40	40	42	44	46	46	48	50	52	54	56	58	60	62	64	66
IL	349	28	28	28	30	30	32	32	34	34	36	36	36	40	40	42	44	46	46	48	50	52	54	56	58	60	62	64	66
IL	350	26	28	28	30	30	32	32	34	34	34	36	36	40	40	42	44	46	46	48	50	52	52	56	58	60	62	64	66
IL	351	26	28	28	30	30	32	32	34	34	34	36	36	40	40	42	44	46	46	48	50	52	52	56	58	60	62	64	64
IL	352	28	28	28	30	30	32	32	34	34	34	36	36	38	40	42	44	46	46	48	50	52	52	56	58	60	62	64	64
IL	353	28	28	28	30	30	32	32	34	34	34	36	36	40	40	42	44	44	46	48	50	52	52	56	58	60	62	64	64
IL	354	26	28	28	30	30	32	32	34	34	34	36	36	40	40	42	44	44	46	48	50	52	52	56	58	60	62	64	64
IL	355	28	28	28	30	30	32	32	32	34	34	36	36	40	40	42	44	44	46	48	50	52	52	56	58	60	62	64	64
IL	356	26	28	28	30	30	32	32	32	34	34	36	36	40	40	42	44	44	46	48	50	52	52	56	58	60	62	64	64
IL	357	26	28	28	30	30	32	32	34	34	34	36	36	40	40	42	44	44	46	48	50	52	52	56	58	60	62	64	64
IL	358	26	28	28	30	30	32	32	32	34	34	36	36	38	40	42	44	44	46	48	50	52	52	56	58	60	62	64	64
IL	359	26	28	28	30	30	32	32	32	34	34	36	36	40	40	42	44	46	46	48	50	52	52	56	58	60	62	64	64
IL	360	26	28	28	30	30	32	32	32	34	34	36	36	38	40	42	44	44	46	48	50	52	52	56	58	60	62	64	64
IL	361	26	28	28	30	30	32	32	32	34	34	36	36	38	40	42	44	44	46	48	50	52	52	56	58	60	62	64	64
MI	362	34	36	36	38	38	40	42	42	44	44	44	46	48	50	54	56	56	60	62	62	64	66	72	74	76	80	82	84
MI	363	34	36	36	38	38	40	42	42	42	44	44	46	48	50	52	54	58	58	60	64	64	66	72	74	76	80	82	84
MI	364	34	36	36	38	38	40	42	42	42	44	44	46	48	50	52	54	56	60	60	62	64	66	72	74	76	80	82	84
MI	365	34	34	36	36	38	40	40	42	42	44	44	46	50	50	52	54	56	60	60	62	64	66	72	74	76	80	82	84
MI	366	34	34	36	38	38	40	40	42	42	44	44	46	48	50	52	54	56	58	60	62	64	66	70	74	76	80	82	84
MI	367	34	34	36	36	38	40	40	42	42	44	44	46	48	50	52	54	56	58	60	62	64	66	70	74	76	80	82	84
MI	368	34	34	36	36	38	40	40	42	42	44	44	46	48	50	52	54	56	58	60	62	64	66	70	74	76	80	82	84
MI	369	34	34	36	36	38	40	40	42	42	44	44	46	48	50	52	54	56	58	60	62	64	66	70	74	76	80	82	84
MI	370	34	34	36	36	38	40	40	42	42	44	44	46	48	50	52	54	56	58	60	62	64	66	70	74	76	78	82	84
MI	371	34	34	36	36	38	40	40	42	42	44	44	46	48	50	52	54	56	58	60	62	64	66	70	72	76	78	82	84
MI	372	32	34	36	36	38	40	40	42	42	44	44	46	48	50	52	54	56	58	60	62	64	66	70	72	76	78	82	84
MI	373	32	34	36	36	38	40	40	42	42	44	44	46	48	50	52	54	56	58	60	62	64	66	70	72	74	78	82	82
MI	374	34	34	36	36	38	40	40	40	42	44	44	46	48	50	52	54	56	58	60	62	64	66	70	72	74	78	82	82
MI	375	34	34	36	36	38	40	40	40	42	44	44	46	48	50	52	54	56	58	60	62	64	66	70	72	74	78	82	82
MI	376	32	34	36	36	38	40	40	40	42	44	44	46	48	50	52	54	56	58	60	62	64	66	70	72	74	78	82	82
MI	377	32	34	36	36	38	38	40	40	42	42	44	46	48	50	52	54	56	58	60	62	64	66	70	72	74	78	80	82
MI	378	32	34	36	36	38	38	40	40	42	42	44	46	48	50	52	54	56	58	60	62	64	64	70	72	74	78	80	82
MI	379	32	34	36	36	38	38	40	40	42	42	44	44	48	50	52	54	56	58	60	62	64	64	70	72	74	78	80	82

Identity, Privacy, and Personal Freedom

STATE	Area	1951	1952	1953	1954	1955	1956	1957	1958	1959	1960	1961	1962	1963	1964	1965	1966	1967	1968	1969	1970	1971	1972	1973	1974	1975	1976	1977	78
MI	380	32	34	34	36	38	38	40	40	42	42	44	44	48	50	52	54	56	58	60	62	64	64	70	72	74	78	80	80
MI	381	32	34	34	36	38	38	40	40	42	42	44	44	48	50	52	54	56	58	60	62	64	64	70	72	74	78	80	80
MI	382	32	34	34	36	38	38	40	40	42	42	44	44	48	50	52	54	56	58	60	62	64	64	70	72	74	78	80	80
MI	383	32	34	34	36	38	38	40	40	42	42	44	44	48	50	52	54	56	58	60	62	64	64	70	72	74	78	80	80
MI	384	32	34	34	36	36	38	40	40	42	42	44	44	48	50	52	54	56	58	60	60	64	64	70	72	74	78	80	80
MI	385	32	34	34	36	36	38	40	40	42	42	44	44	48	50	50	54	54	58	60	60	62	64	70	72	74	78	80	80
MI	386	32	34	34	36	36	38	40	40	40	42	44	44	48	48	52	54	54	58	60	60	64	64	70	72	74	78	80	80
WI	387	32	34	34	36	36	38	40	40	42	42	44	44	48	50	52	54	56	58	60	62	64	66	70	74	76	80	82	80
WI	388	32	32	34	34	36	38	40	40	42	42	44	44	48	50	52	54	56	58	60	62	64	66	70	74	76	80	82	80
WI	389	32	32	34	34	36	38	40	40	42	42	44	44	48	50	52	54	56	58	60	62	64	66	70	74	76	80	82	80
WI	390	32	32	34	34	36	38	40	40	40	42	44	44	48	50	52	54	56	58	60	62	64	66	70	74	76	80	80	80
WI	391	32	32	34	34	36	38	38	40	40	42	44	44	48	50	52	54	56	58	60	62	64	66	70	74	76	78	80	80
WI	392	32	32	34	34	36	38	38	40	40	42	44	44	48	50	52	54	56	58	60	62	64	66	70	72	76	78	80	80
WI	393	32	32	34	34	36	38	38	40	40	42	44	44	48	50	52	54	56	58	60	62	64	66	70	72	76	78	80	80
WI	394	32	32	32	34	36	38	38	40	40	42	44	44	48	50	52	54	56	58	60	62	64	66	70	72	76	78	80	80
WI	395	30	32	32	34	36	36	38	40	40	42	44	44	48	50	52	54	56	58	60	62	64	64	70	72	76	78	80	80
WI	396	30	32	32	34	36	38	38	38	40	42	44	44	48	50	50	54	56	58	58	60	64	64	70	72	74	78	80	80
WI	397	30	32	32	34	36	36	38	38	40	42	44	44	46	48	50	54	56	56	58	60	62	64	70	72	74	78	80	80
WI	398	30	32	32	34	34	36	38	38	40	40	44	44	48	48	50	52	54	58	60	60	62	64	70	72	74	78	80	80
WI	399	30	32	32	34	34	36	38	38	40	40	44	44	48	48	50	54	54	56	58	60	64	64	70	72	74	78	80	80
KY	400	44	46	48	50	52	54	56	56	58	60	60	62	66	68	72	74	76	78	82	84	86	88	94	98	04	06	08	11
KY	401	44	46	48	48	52	54	56	56	58	58	60	62	66	68	70	74	76	78	80	84	86	88	94	98	04	06	08	11
KY	402	44	46	48	48	50	54	54	56	58	58	60	62	66	68	70	74	76	78	80	84	86	88	92	96	04	06	08	11
KY	403	42	46	46	48	50	54	54	56	56	58	60	62	66	66	70	72	76	78	80	82	86	88	92	96	02	06	08	11
KY	404	44	44	46	48	50	52	54	56	56	58	60	62	64	66	70	72	74	78	80	82	86	88	92	96	02	06	08	11
KY	405	44	44	46	48	50	52	54	54	56	58	60	62	64	66	70	72	76	78	80	82	86	88	92	96	02	06	08	11
KY	406	42	44	46	48	50	52	54	56	56	58	60	62	64	66	70	72	74	76	80	82	84	88	92	96	02	06	08	11
KY	407	42	44	46	48	50	52	54	54	56	58	58	60	64	66	68	72	74	76	78	82	84	86	92	96	02	04	08	08
TN	408	54	56	58	58	62	64	66	66	68	70	72	74	78	80	84	86	90	92	96	98	02	06	15	19	23	27	08	29
TN	409	54	54	54	58	60	64	66	66	68	70	72	74	78	80	84	88	90	92	94	98	04	06	15	19	23	27	29	29
TN	410	54	54	54	58	62	64	66	66	68	70	72	74	78	80	84	88	90	92	94	98	02	04	13	19	23	25	27	29
TN	411	52	54	54	58	60	62	64	66	68	70	72	74	78	80	84	88	90	92	94	98	02	04	13	19	21	25	27	29
TN	412	52	54	54	58	60	62	64	66	68	70	72	74	78	80	84	86	88	92	94	98	02	04	13	17	21	25	27	29
TN	413	52	54	54	58	60	62	64	66	68	70	70	74	76	80	82	86	88	92	94	96	02	04	13	17	21	25	27	29
TN	414	52	54	54	58	60	62	64	66	68	70	72	72	76	80	84	86	88	92	94	96	02	04	13	17	21	25	27	29
TN	415	52	54	54	58	60	62	64	66	68	68	70	72	76	78	82	86	88	90	94	96	02	04	13	17	21	25	27	29

STATE	Area	1951	1952	1953	1954	1955	1956	1957	1958	1959	1960	1961	1962	1963	1964	1965	1966	1967	1968	1969	1970	1971	1972	1973	1974	1975	1976	1977	78
AL	416	44	46	46	48	50	52	54	54	56	58	60	62	64	66	70	72	74	76	78	80	82	84	90	94	96	02	04	06
AL	417	44	44	44	48	50	52	54	54	56	58	60	60	64	66	70	72	74	76	78	80	82	84	90	94	96	02	04	04
AL	418	42	44	44	48	50	52	54	54	56	58	60	60	64	66	68	72	74	76	78	80	82	84	90	94	96	98	02	04
AL	419	44	44	44	48	50	52	52	54	56	58	58	60	64	66	70	72	74	74	78	80	82	84	90	94	96	98	02	04
AL	420	44	44	44	48	50	52	52	54	56	58	58	60	64	66	68	70	72	76	76	80	82	84	90	92	96	98	02	04
AL	421	42	44	44	48	50	50	52	54	56	58	58	60	64	64	68	70	74	74	76	78	80	82	90	92	96	98	02	04
AL	422	42	44	44	46	48	50	52	54	56	56	58	60	62	64	68	72	74	74	76	78	80	82	90	92	96	98	02	04
AL	423	42	44	44	46	48	50	52	54	54	56	58	60	62	64	68	70	72	74	76	78	80	84	88	92	94	98	02	04
AL	424	42	44	44	46	48	50	52	54	54	56	58	60	62	64	68	70	72	74	76	78	80	82	88	92	94	98	02	04
MS	425	62	64	64	70	74	78	82	84	86	88	90	94	98	98	98	98	98	98	98	02	08	11	17	21	25	29	31	33
MS	426	60	64	68	70	74	78	80	82	86	88	90	92	98	98	98	98	98	98	98	02	06	11	17	21	25	29	31	33
MS	427	60	64	66	68	74	78	80	82	84	88	90	92	96	98	98	98	98	98	98	02	06	11	15	21	25	29	29	31
MS	428	62	64	66	68	74	76	80	82	84	86	90	92	96	98	98	98	98	98	98	02	06	11	15	19	23	29	29	31
AR	429	62	62	66	66	70	74	74	76	78	80	82	86	88	90	96	98	02	04	08	11	15	17	25	29	33	35	39	41
AR	430	60	62	64	66	70	72	74	76	78	80	82	84	88	90	96	98	02	04	06	11	13	17	23	27	31	35	37	39
AR	431	60	62	64	66	70	72	74	76	78	80	82	84	88	90	94	98	02	04	06	11	13	17	23	27	31	35	37	39
AR	432	60	62	64	66	68	72	74	76	76	78	82	84	88	90	94	98	02	04	06	11	13	15	23	27	31	35	37	39
LA	433	48	50	52	54	56	58	60	60	62	64	66	68	72	74	80	84	86	90	94	98	02	06	15	19	25	29	33	35
LA	434	48	50	52	52	54	56	58	60	62	64	64	68	72	74	78	82	86	90	92	98	02	06	15	19	25	29	33	35
LA	435	48	50	52	52	54	56	58	60	62	64	66	66	72	74	78	82	86	88	92	96	02	06	13	19	25	29	31	35
LA	436	48	50	52	52	54	56	58	60	62	62	64	66	72	74	76	82	86	88	92	96	02	06	13	19	23	29	31	35
LA	437	48	48	50	52	54	56	58	60	60	62	64	66	72	74	78	82	84	88	92	96	02	06	13	19	23	29	31	35
LA	438	48	48	50	52	54	56	58	60	60	62	64	68	70	74	78	82	86	88	92	96	02	06	13	19	23	27	31	33
LA	439	48	48	50	52	54	56	58	58	60	62	64	66	70	74	78	82	84	88	92	96	02	04	13	17	23	27	31	33
OK	440	34	36	36	38	38	40	42	42	44	44	46	46	48	50	52	54	54	56	58	60	62	62	66	68	70	72	74	74
OK	441	34	34	36	36	38	40	40	42	42	44	44	46	48	50	52	54	54	56	58	60	62	62	66	68	70	72	74	74
OK	442	32	34	36	36	38	40	40	42	42	44	44	46	48	50	52	54	54	56	58	60	60	62	66	68	70	72	74	74
OK	443	34	34	36	36	38	40	40	42	42	44	44	46	48	48	50	52	54	56	58	58	60	62	66	68	70	72	74	74
OK	444	32	34	36	36	38	40	40	42	42	42	44	46	48	48	50	52	54	56	56	58	60	62	66	68	70	72	72	74
OK	445	34	34	36	36	38	38	40	40	42	42	44	46	46	48	50	52	54	56	56	58	60	62	66	68	70	72	72	74
OK	446	34	34	34	36	38	38	40	40	42	42	44	44	46	48	50	52	54	54	56	58	60	62	64	68	70	72	72	74
OK	447	32	34	34	36	38	38	40	40	42	42	44	44	46	48	50	52	54	54	56	58	60	62	64	66	70	72	72	74
OK	448	32	34	34	36	36	38	40	40	42	42	44	44	46	48	50	52	52	54	56	58	58	60	64	66	70	70	72	74
TX	449	54	56	58	58	62	64	66	68	70	72	74	76	80	84	88	92	96	98	06	08	13	15	25	29	35	39	41	45
TX	450	52	56	58	58	62	64	66	68	70	72	74	76	80	84	88	92	94	98	04	06	13	15	23	29	35	39	41	45

STATE	Area	1951	1952	1953	1954	1955	1956	1957	1958	1959	1960	1961	1962	1963	1964	1965	1966	1967	1968	1969	1970	1971	1972	1973	1974	1975	1976	1977	78
TX	451	54	56	58	58	62	64	66	68	70	72	74	76	82	84	88	92	96	98	04	08	13	15	23	29	33	39	41	45
TX	452	52	56	58	58	62	64	66	68	70	72	74	76	80	84	88	92	96	98	04	08	11	15	23	29	33	39	41	45
TX	453	54	54	56	58	62	64	66	68	70	72	74	76	80	84	88	92	94	98	04	08	13	15	23	29	33	39	41	43
TX	454	52	56	56	58	62	64	66	68	70	72	72	76	80	82	88	92	94	98	04	06	13	15	23	29	33	39	41	43
TX	455	54	54	56	58	60	64	66	68	68	72	72	76	80	84	88	92	94	98	04	08	13	15	23	29	33	37	41	43
TX	456	54	54	56	58	60	64	66	68	68	70	74	76	80	84	88	92	94	98	04	06	13	15	23	29	33	37	41	43
TX	457	52	54	56	58	60	64	66	68	68	70	72	76	80	82	88	90	94	98	04	06	13	15	23	29	33	37	41	43
TX	458	52	54	58	58	60	64	66	66	68	70	72	76	80	82	88	92	94	98	04	06	11	15	23	29	33	37	41	43
TX	459	52	54	56	58	60	64	66	66	68	70	72	76	80	82	86	92	94	96	04	06	11	15	23	29	33	37	41	43
TX	460	52	54	56	58	60	64	66	66	68	70	72	74	80	82	86	92	94	98	04	06	11	13	23	29	33	37	41	43
TX	461	52	54	56	58	60	62	66	66	68	70	72	74	80	82	86	90	94	98	02	06	11	13	23	29	33	37	39	43
TX	462	52	54	56	58	60	62	64	66	68	70	72	74	80	82	86	90	94	98	02	06	11	13	23	29	33	37	39	43
TX	463	52	54	56	58	60	62	64	66	68	70	72	74	80	82	88	90	94	98	02	06	11	13	23	27	33	37	39	43
TX	464	52	54	56	58	60	64	64	66	68	70	72	76	80	82	86	90	94	96	02	06	11	13	23	27	33	37	39	43
TX	465	52	54	56	58	60	62	64	66	68	70	72	74	80	82	86	90	92	96	02	06	11	13	23	27	33	37	39	43
TX	466	52	54	56	58	60	62	64	66	68	70	72	74	80	82	86	90	94	98	02	06	08	13	23	27	33	37	39	43
TX	467	52	54	56	56	60	44	64	66	68	70	72	74	78	82	84	90	94	96	02	06	11	13	23	27	33	37	39	43
MN	468	36	38	38	40	42	44	46	46	48	48	50	52	56	56	58	62	64	66	68	70	72	74	80	82	84	84	90	90
MN	469	36	36	38	40	42	44	46	46	48	48	50	52	56	56	58	62	64	66	68	70	72	74	78	82	84	84	90	90
MN	470	34	36	38	40	42	44	44	46	48	48	50	52	54	56	58	62	64	64	68	70	72	74	78	82	84	84	88	90
MN	471	36	36	38	38	42	44	44	46	46	48	50	50	54	56	58	60	62	64	66	70	70	72	78	82	84	84	88	90
MN	472	34	36	38	38	42	44	44	46	46	48	50	52	54	56	58	60	62	64	66	68	70	72	78	82	84	84	88	90
MN	473	34	36	38	38	40	44	44	46	46	48	50	50	54	56	58	60	62	64	66	68	70	72	78	80	84	84	88	90
MN	474	36	36	38	38	40	42	44	44	46	48	48	50	54	56	58	60	62	64	66	68	70	72	78	80	84	84	88	90
MN	475	34	36	36	38	40	42	44	44	46	48	48	50	54	56	58	60	62	64	66	68	70	72	78	80	84	84	88	90
MN	476	34	36	36	38	40	42	44	44	46	48	48	50	54	56	58	60	62	64	66	68	70	72	78	80	84	84	88	90
MN	477	34	36	36	38	40	42	44	44	46	46	48	50	52	56	56	60	62	64	66	68	70	72	78	80	82	82	88	90
IA	478	36	38	40	42	46	48	50	50	52	52	54	56	62	62	66	68	70	72	74	76	78	78	84	86	88	88	94	94
IA	479	36	38	40	42	44	48	48	50	52	52	54	56	58	62	66	68	70	72	74	74	78	78	84	86	88	88	94	94
IA	480	38	38	40	40	44	48	48	50	50	52	54	56	60	62	64	66	68	70	72	74	76	78	82	86	88	88	94	94
IA	481	38	38	40	40	44	48	48	50	50	52	54	54	58	62	64	66	68	72	72	74	76	78	82	86	88	88	92	94
IA	482	38	38	40	40	44	48	48	50	50	52	54	54	58	62	64	66	68	70	72	74	76	78	82	86	88	88	92	94
IA	483	36	38	40	40	44	48	48	48	50	52	52	54	58	62	64	66	68	70	72	74	76	78	82	86	88	88	92	94
IA	484	36	38	38	40	44	46	48	48	50	52	52	54	58	62	64	66	68	70	72	74	76	78	82	84	88	88	92	94
IA	485	34	38	38	40	42	46	48	48	50	52	52	54	58	60	64	66	68	70	72	74	76	78	82	84	88	88	92	94
MO	486	38	38	40	40	42	44	44	46	46	48	48	50	52	54	56	56	58	60	62	64	66	66	70	72	74	74	80	80
MO	487	38	38	40	40	42	44	44	46	46	48	48	50	52	54	54	58	58	60	62	64	66	66	70	72	74	74	80	80

STATE	Area	1951	1952	1953	1954	1955	1956	1957	1958	1959	1960	1961	1962	1963	1964	1965	1966	1967	1968	1969	1970	1971	1972	1973	1974	1975	1976	1977	78
MO	488	36	38	40	40	42	44	44	46	46	48	48	50	52	52	56	56	58	60	62	64	66	66	70	72	74	74	80	80
MO	489	36	38	40	40	42	44	44	44	46	46	48	50	52	52	56	56	58	60	62	64	66	66	70	72	74	74	80	80
MO	490	36	38	38	40	42	44	44	44	46	46	48	50	52	52	54	56	58	60	62	64	64	66	70	72	74	74	78	80
MO	491	36	38	38	40	42	42	44	44	46	46	48	48	52	52	54	56	58	60	62	62	64	66	70	72	74	74	78	80
MO	492	36	38	38	40	42	42	44	44	46	46	48	48	52	52	54	56	58	60	62	62	64	66	70	72	74	74	78	80
MO	493	36	38	38	40	42	42	44	44	46	46	48	48	50	52	54	56	58	60	62	62	64	66	70	72	74	74	78	80
MO	494	36	38	38	40	42	42	44	44	46	46	48	48	52	52	54	56	58	60	60	62	64	66	70	72	74	74	78	80
MO	495	36	38	38	40	40	42	44	44	46	46	48	48	50	52	54	56	58	58	60	62	64	66	70	72	74	74	78	80
MO	496	36	36	38	38	40	42	44	44	44	46	48	48	50	52	54	56	58	58	60	62	64	66	68	72	74	74	78	80
MO	497	36	36	38	38	40	42	44	44	44	46	46	48	50	52	54	56	58	58	60	62	64	66	68	72	74	74	78	80
MO	498	36	36	38	38	40	42	44	44	44	46	46	48	50	52	54	56	58	58	60	62	64	66	68	70	74	74	78	80
MO	499	36	36	38	38	40	42	42	44	44	46	46	48	50	52	54	56	56	58	60	62	64	66	68	70	74	74	78	80
MO	500	36	36	38	38	40	42	42	44	44	46	46	48	50	52	54	56	56	58	60	62	64	66	68	70	72	72	78	78
ND	501	30	32	34	34	40	42	44	44	46	48	48	50	54	54	56	60	56	64	68	70	74	78	84	88	90	90	92	92
ND	502	32	32	32	34	36	40	42	44	44	46	48	50	52	54	56	58	56	62	66	70	72	76	84	86	88	88	92	92
SD	503	34	34	36	38	42	46	46	48	48	50	52	54	58	60	60	64	66	68	70	72	76	78	86	88	90	90	94	94
SD	504	32	34	36	36	40	44	46	46	48	50	50	54	56	58	60	62	64	66	68	72	74	76	84	86	90	90	92	92
NE	505	40	42	42	44	48	52	52	54	54	56	58	60	62	64	66	70	72	74	76	78	82	84	88	92	94	94	98	02
NE	506	38	40	42	44	46	50	52	52	54	56	56	58	64	64	66	70	72	74	76	78	80	84	88	92	94	94	98	02
NE	507	32	40	42	42	46	50	52	52	54	54	56	58	62	64	66	68	70	74	76	78	80	82	88	90	94	94	98	98
NE	508	32	40	40	42	46	50	50	52	54	54	56	58	62	64	66	68	70	72	74	78	80	82	88	90	94	94	96	98
KS	509	32	34	36	36	38	40	42	42	44	44	46	46	52	52	54	56	56	58	60	62	64	66	72	74	76	78	78	80
KS	510	32	34	34	36	38	40	42	42	44	44	46	46	50	52	54	54	56	58	60	62	64	66	70	74	76	78	78	80
KS	511	32	34	34	36	38	40	40	42	42	44	46	46	50	52	52	54	56	58	60	62	64	66	70	72	74	76	78	78
KS	512	32	32	34	36	38	40	40	42	42	44	44	46	50	50	52	54	56	58	60	62	64	66	70	72	74	76	78	78
KS	513	30	32	34	34	38	40	40	42	42	44	44	46	48	50	52	54	56	58	60	62	64	64	70	72	74	76	78	78
KS	514	32	32	34	34	36	40	40	40	42	42	44	46	50	50	52	54	56	58	60	62	64	64	70	72	74	76	76	78
KS	515	32	32	34	34	36	38	40	40	42	42	44	46	48	50	52	54	56	56	58	60	62	64	70	72	74	76	76	78
MT	516	36	38	40	40	42	46	46	48	48	50	52	54	56	58	60	64	66	66	70	72	74	76	86	88	90	94	94	94
MT	517	36	36	38	40	42	44	46	46	48	50	50	52	56	58	60	62	64	66	68	70	72	74	84	88	90	92	92	92
ID	518	38	38	40	40	42	44	46	48	48	50	52	54	58	58	60	64	66	68	70	72	74	76	86	88	92	94	94	94
ID	519	36	36	38	40	42	44	44	46	48	50	52	54	56	56	60	62	64	66	70	72	74	76	84	88	90	92	94	94
WY	520	36	36	38	40	42	44	44	46	46	48	50	52	56	56	58	60	62	64	66	68	70	72	80	84	86	88	90	90

Identity, Privacy, and Personal Freedom

STATE	Area	1951	1952	1953	1954	1955	1956	1957	1958	1959	1960	1961	1962	1963	1964	1965	1966	1967	1968	1969	1970	1971	1972	1973	1974	1975	1976	1977	78
CO	521	42	42	46	48	50	52	52	54	56	58	60	62	66	68	72	76	78	80	84	88	90	94	02	08	13	17	21	23
CO	522	42	42	46	46	48	50	52	54	54	56	58	60	66	68	72	74	78	80	84	86	90	94	02	06	13	17	21	23
CO	523	42	42	44	46	58	50	52	52	54	56	58	60	66	68	70	74	76	80	82	86	90	94	02	06	11	17	19	23
CO	524	42	42	44	46	58	50	52	52	54	56	58	60	64	66	72	74	76	80	84	86	90	94	98	06	11	15	19	21
NM	525	74	74	80	84	86	92	96	98	98	98	98	98	98	98	98	98	98	98	98	98	98	98	98	08	15	19	23	25	27
AZ	526	44	44	46	48	52	54	56	60	62	64	68	72	78	80	86	90	96	02	08	17	21	27	41	51	59	65	71	75
AZ	527	42	44	46	48	50	54	56	58	60	64	66	70	74	82	84	92	96	02	08	15	21	27	41	49	57	65	69	75
UT	528	44	44	46	48	50	52	54	56	58	60	62	64	68	70	72	76	80	84	88	90	92	94	06	13	17	21	23	25
UT	529	42	44	46	48	50	52	52	54	56	58	60	64	68	70	72	76	80	84	86	88	92	94	06	11	15	19	21	25
NV	530	20	22	22	24	24	26	26	28	28	30	30	32	36	36	38	42	44	46	50	52	56	58	70	74	78	82	84	84
WA	531	32	34	34	34	38	38	40	40	40	42	44	44	48	50	52	54	56	58	60	62	64	64	70	72	74	78	80	82
WA	532	32	34	34	34	36	38	38	40	40	42	42	44	48	50	52	54	56	58	60	62	64	64	68	72	74	78	80	82
WA	533	32	32	34	34	36	38	38	40	40	42	42	44	48	48	50	54	56	58	60	60	64	64	68	72	74	78	80	82
WA	534	32	32	34	34	36	38	38	40	40	42	42	44	48	48	50	54	56	56	58	60	64	64	68	70	74	78	80	82
WA	535	32	32	32	34	36	38	38	38	40	40	42	44	46	48	50	52	54	56	60	60	62	64	68	70	74	76	80	82
WA	536	35	32	32	34	36	36	38	38	40	40	42	44	46	48	50	52	54	56	58	60	62	64	68	70	74	76	80	82
WA	537	30	32	32	34	36	36	38	38	40	42	42	44	46	48	50	52	54	56	58	60	62	64	68	70	74	76	80	82
WA	538	30	30	32	34	36	36	38	38	40	40	42	44	46	48	50	52	54	56	58	60	62	64	68	70	72	76	78	80
WA	539	30	32	32	34	36	36	38	38	40	40	42	42	46	48	50	52	54	56	58	60	62	64	68	70	72	76	78	80
OR	540	36	38	40	40	44	46	46	48	48	50	50	52	56	58	60	62	64	66	68	70	74	76	80	84	88	90	92	94
OR	541	36	38	40	40	44	44	46	46	48	48	50	52	56	58	60	62	64	66	68	72	74	76	80	84	88	90	92	94
OR	542	36	38	38	40	42	44	46	46	48	48	50	52	56	56	60	62	64	66	68	72	74	74	80	84	86	90	92	94
OR	543	36	36	38	38	42	44	44	46	46	48	50	52	54	56	58	60	64	64	68	72	74	74	80	84	86	90	92	94
OR	544	36	36	38	40	42	44	44	46	46	48	50	50	54	56	58	60	64	64	66	72	74	74	80	82	86	90	90	92
CA	545	46	48	50	50	52	54	56	58	60	62	64	68	72	76	80	86	88	92	98	04	11	19	27	33	39	45	49	53
CA	546	44	48	48	50	52	54	56	58	60	62	64	68	74	76	80	84	88	92	96	04	11	19	27	33	39	45	49	53
CA	547	44	46	48	50	52	54	56	58	60	62	64	66	72	76	80	84	88	92	98	02	08	19	27	33	39	45	49	53
CA	548	46	46	48	50	52	54	56	58	60	62	64	66	72	76	80	84	88	92	96	04	11	19	27	33	39	45	49	53
CA	549	46	46	48	50	52	54	56	58	60	62	64	68	72	76	80	84	88	92	96	02	08	19	27	33	39	45	49	53
CA	550	46	46	48	50	52	54	56	58	60	62	64	68	72	76	80	84	88	92	96	04	11	19	27	33	39	45	49	53
CA	551	46	46	48	50	52	54	56	58	60	62	64	68	72	76	78	84	88	92	96	02	11	17	27	33	39	45	49	53
CA	552	46	46	48	50	52	54	56	58	60	62	64	66	72	76	78	84	88	92	96	02	08	19	27	33	39	45	49	53

STATE	Area	1951	1952	1953	1954	1955	1956	1957	1958	1959	1960	1961	1962	1963	1964	1965	1966	1967	1968	1969	1970	1971	1972	1973	1974	1975	1976	1977	78
CA	553	46	46	48	50	52	54	56	58	60	60	64	66	72	76	80	82	88	92	96	02	11	19	27	33	39	43	49	53
CA	554	44	46	48	50	52	54	56	58	58	62	64	66	72	76	80	84	88	92	96	04	11	19	27	33	39	43	49	53
CA	555	44	46	48	50	52	54	56	56	58	62	64	66	72	76	80	84	88	92	96	04	11	19	27	33	37	43	49	53
CA	556	44	46	48	50	52	54	56	56	58	62	64	66	72	74	80	84	88	92	96	04	11	17	27	33	37	43	49	53
CA	557	44	46	48	50	52	54	56	56	58	62	64	66	72	74	80	82	88	92	96	02	11	17	27	33	37	43	49	53
CA	558	44	46	48	50	52	54	56	56	58	60	62	66	72	74	80	84	88	92	96	02	11	19	27	33	37	43	49	53
CA	559	44	46	48	50	52	54	56	56	58	60	64	68	70	74	80	84	86	92	96	02	08	19	27	33	37	43	49	53
CA	560	44	46	48	50	52	54	56	56	58	60	64	66	72	74	80	82	88	90	96	04	08	19	27	33	37	43	49	53
CA	561	46	46	48	50	52	54	54	56	58	60	62	66	70	74	561	82	86	92	96	02	11	19	27	33	37	43	49	53
CA	562	44	46	48	50	50	54	54	56	58	60	62	66	70	74	561	82	86	92	96	02	08	17	27	33	37	43	49	53
CA	563	44	46	48	48	50	52	54	56	58	60	62	66	70	74	80	82	86	92	94	02	08	17	27	33	37	43	49	53
CA	564	44	46	48	48	50	54	54	56	58	60	62	66	72	74	78	82	86	92	96	02	08	17	27	33	37	43	49	53
CA	565	44	46	48	48	50	52	54	56	58	60	62	66	70	74	78	82	86	90	96	02	08	17	27	33	37	43	49	53
CA	566	44	46	48	48	50	54	54	56	58	60	62	66	72	74	80	84	86	90	96	02	08	17	27	33	37	43	49	53
CA	567	44	46	48	48	50	52	54	56	58	60	62	66	72	74	78	82	86	92	96	02	08	17	27	33	37	43	49	53
CA	568	44	46	48	48	50	54	54	56	58	60	62	66	72	74	78	82	86	92	96	02	08	17	27	31	37	43	49	53
CA	569	44	46	48	48	50	52	54	56	58	60	62	66	70	74	78	82	86	92	96	02	08	17	27	31	37	43	49	53
CA	570	44	46	48	48	50	52	54	56	58	60	62	66	72	74	78	82	86	90	96	02	08	17	27	31	37	43	49	53
CA	571	44	46	46	48	50	52	54	56	58	60	62	66	72	74	78	82	86	90	96	98	08	17	27	31	37	43	47	53
CA	572	44	46	46	48	50	52	54	56	58	60	62	66	70	74	78	82	86	90	96	02	08	17	27	31	37	43	47	53
CA	573	44	46	46	48	50	52	54	56	58	60	62	66	70	74	78	82	86	90	94	02	08	17	25	31	37	43	47	53
AK	574	10	10	12	12	12	12	14	14	14	14	16	18	18	18	20	22	24	24	26	28	30	32	52	54	56	58	58	60
HI	575	32	36	36	36	36	38	40	40	42	44	46	48	50	52	56	58	64	64	68	72	76	78	88	92	96	04	06	06
HI	576	30	32	32	36	36	38	38	40	42	44	44	48	50	52	54	58	60	64	66	72	74	76	88	92	96	02	04	04
DC	577	46	48	50	52	52	52	54	56	56	58	60	60	64	64	66	68	72	74	74	76	78	80	86	88	92	96	96	98
DC	578	48	46	48	50	52	52	54	54	56	56	58	60	62	64	66	68	70	74	74	76	78	80	86	88	92	94	96	96
DC	579	30	48	48	48	50	52	54	54	54	56	58	60	62	64	66	68	70	72	74	76	78	80	84	88	90	94	96	96
Virgin Islands	580	28	40	48	54	62	66	72	78	82	86	92	96	98	98	98	98	98	98	98	98	98	98	02	04	06	06	08	08
Puerto Rico	581	28	40	48	52	60	68	74	78	80	86	92	96	98	98	98	98	98	98	98	98	98	98	11	19	23	41	55	63
Puerto Rico	582		40	48	52	60	66	72	76	80	86	92	98	98	98	98	98	98	98	98	98	98	98	11	17	23	41	55	61
Puerto Rico	583													07	10	22	34	46	54	64	74	84	94	11	17	23	39	55	61
Puerto Rico	584													03	10	18	34	40	50	62	74	84	92	08	17	23	39	55	61
NM	585								01	05	09	12	18	26	30	38	44	50	58	66	78	88	94	08	13	19	23	25	27

Identity, Privacy, and Personal Freedom

STATE	Area	1951	1952	1953	1954	1955	1956	1957	1958	1959	1960	1961	1962	1963	1964	1965	1966	1967	1968	1969	1970	1971	1972	1973	1974	1975	1976	1977
Guam	586						01	01	01	01	01	01	03	03	03	03	03	05	05	07	07	07	09					
Amrican Samoa							20	20	20	20	20	20	20	20	20	22	22	22	22	22	22	24	24					
Phillipine							30	30	30	30	30	30	30	30	30	30	30	30	30	30	30	30	30					
Islands							60	60	60	60	60	60	60	60	60	60	60	60	60	60	60	62	62	64	66	68	68	7
(see above)	587														05	26	46	58	74	92	98	98	98	15	19	23	27	29
RR	700	18	18	18	18	18	18	18	18	18	18	18	18	18	18	18	18	18	18	18	18	18	18	18	18	18	18	18
RR	701	18	18	18	18	18	18	18	18	18	18	18	18	18	18	18	18	18	18	18	18	18	18	18	18	18	18	18
RR	702	18	18	18	18	18	18	18	18	18	18	18	18	18	18	18	18	18	18	18	18	18	18	18	18	18	18	18
RR	703	18	18	18	18	18	18	18	18	18	18	18	18	18	18	18	18	18	18	18	18	18	18	18	18	18	18	18
RR	704	18	18	18	18	18	18	18	18	18	18	18	18	18	18	18	18	18	18	18	18	18	18	18	18	18	18	18
RR	705	18	18	18	18	18	18	18	18	18	18	18	18	18	18	18	18	18	18	18	18	18	18	18	18	18	18	18
RR	706	18	18	18	18	18	18	18	18	18	18	18	18	18	18	18	18	18	18	18	18	18	18	18	18	18	18	18
RR	707	18	18	18	18	18	18	18	18	18	18	18	18	18	18	18	18	18	18	18	18	18	18	18	18	18	18	18
RR	708	18	18	18	18	18	18	18	18	18	18	18	18	18	18	18	18	18	18	18	18	18	18	18	18	18	18	18
RR	709	18	18	18	18	18	18	18	18	18	18	18	18	18	18	18	18	18	18	18	18	18	18	18	18	18	18	18
RR	710	18	18	18	18	18	18	18	18	18	18	18	18	18	18	18	18	18	18	18	18	18	18	18	18	18	18	18
RR	711	18	18	18	18	18	18	18	18	18	18	18	18	18	18	18	18	18	18	18	18	18	18	18	18	18	18	18
RR	712	18	18	18	18	18	18	18	18	18	18	18	18	18	18	18	18	18	18	18	18	18	18	18	18	18	18	18
Railroad	713	18	18	18	18	18	18	18	18	18	18	18	18	18	18	18	18	18	18	18	18	18	18	18	18	18	18	18
Retirement	714	18	18	18	18	18	18	18	18	18	18	18	18	18	18	18	18	18	18	18	18	18	18	18	18	18	18	18
RR	715	18	18	18	18	18	18	18	18	18	18	18	18	18	18	18	18	18	18	18	18	18	18	18	18	18	18	18
RR	716	18	18	18	18	18	18	18	18	18	18	18	18	18	18	18	18	18	18	18	18	18	18	18	18	18	18	18
RR	717	18	18	18	18	18	18	18	18	18	18	18	18	18	18	18	18	18	18	18	18	18	18	18	18	18	18	18
RR	718	18	18	18	18	18	18	18	18	18	18	18	18	18	18	18	18	18	18	18	18	18	18	18	18	18	18	18
RR	719	18	18	18	18	18	18	18	18	18	18	18	18	18	18	18	18	18	18	18	18	18	18	18	18	18	18	18
RR	720	18	18	18	18	18	18	18	18	18	18	18	18	18	18	18	18	18	18	18	18	18	18	18	18	18	18	18
RR	721	18	18	18	18	18	18	18	18	18	18	18	18	18	18	18	18	18	18	18	18	18	18	18	18	18	18	18
RR	722	18	18	18	18	18	18	18	18	18	18	18	18	18	18	18	18	18	18	18	18	18	18	18	18	18	18	18
RR	723	18	18	18	18	18	18	18	18	18	18	18	18	18	18	18	18	18	18	18	18	18	18	18	18	18	18	18
RR	724	18	28	28	28	28	28	28	28	28	28	28	28	28	28	28	28	28	28	28	28	28	28	28	28	28	28	2
RR	725	18	28	18	18	18	18	18	18	18	18	18	18	18	18	18	18	18	18	18	18	18	18	18	18	18	18	18
RR	726	18	18	18	18	18	18	18	18	18	18	18	18	18	18	18	18	18	18	18	18	18	18	18	18	18	18	18
RR	727	10	10	10	10	10	10	10	10	10	10	10	10	10	10	10	10	10	10	10	10	10	10	10	10	10	10	10
RR	728	09	09	18	12	12	14	14	14	14	14	14	14	14	14	14	14	14	14	14	14	14	14	14	14	14	14	14
RR	729	09																										

THE PRINCIPALITY OF NEW UTOPIA

DEPARTMENT OF NEW CITIZEN NOMINEES

CITIZENSHIP NOMINEE INFORMATION

IMPORTANT: Read instructions carefully before completing the Nominee Form

HOW TO COMPLETE NOMINEE FORM

1. All sections of this form must be completed by all Nominees. The form should be clearly written in the nominee's own handwriting using block Capitals.

2. Additional sheets of paper may be used if the space provided on the form is insufficient. Indicate which section(s) is/are being answered on the additional sheet(s) of paper.

3. **Requirements:**

    a) Photographs. Four copies of a recent photograph of the Nominee must be included with the Nominee Form. These photographs must be taken full face without hat, and the photographs must not be mounted. The size of the photographs must be standard passport size (not be more than 2 inches x 2 inches.) The photographs must be printed on normal thin photographic paper and must not be glazed on the reverse side.

4. **Documents to be produced:**

    a) Four copies of recent photographs.

    b) Photocopy of the current passport or Nominee's birth certificate.

N.B.: All sections must be translated into English.

Mail To:	**Voice Phone:**
The Principality of New Utopia	**(918) 712-9980**
9441 East 31st. Street, Suite 160	**FAX:**
Tulsa, Oklahoma 74145 U.S.A.	**(918) 438-2611**

NOMINEE

Given Name _____

Family Name _____

Nominee's Photograph

> ### Photograph
> ### Here

NOMINEE
YOUR PERSONAL DETAILS

1. Family name
(in English)
_____

2. Given name
(in English)
_____

3. Father's name
_____

4. Mother's maiden name
_____

5. Have you been known by any other names?   (including name before marriage or an alias)

No ___   Yes ___   Name before marriage (if applicable)   _____

N.B.: For other names, enclose a note giving the required details.

6. Sex: Male ___   Female ___

7. Date of Birth   (DAY MONTH YEAR) ____ / ____ / _____   **Age** _____

8. Place of Birth   Town _____

State or Province _____

Country _____

9. Color of eyes   _____

10. Color of hair   _____

11. Height   _____

12. Distinguishing Marks   _____

CITIZENSHIP

13. Present country of Citizenship   _____

14. Do you hold any other citizenships?   _____

No ___   Yes ___   Which countries? _____

PASSPORT

15. Do you have a passport?   Passport Number   _____

No ___   Yes ___   Give details: _____

Place of issue: _____

N.B.: If you have more than one passport, enclose a note giving the required details.

Date of issue: (DAY MONTH YEAR) ____ / ____ / _____

Valid until: (DAY MONTH YEAR) ____ / ____ / _____

IDENTIFICATION NUMBERS

16. Do you have any identification numbers?(National identify card, social security card [Optional])

	Country	Type of number	Your number
No __ Yes __ Give Details:	_____	_____	_____
	_____	_____	_____
	_____	_____	_____

MARITAL STATUS

17. Show your marital status (Tick more than one if appropriate)

Never married _____	Separated _____	N.B: Enclose a note giving the
Divorced _____	Engaged _____	required details.
Widowed _____	Married _____	(See Explanatory Notes)

ADDRESSES

18. Your home address:

_____

_____

_____

19. Your postal address:
(If different than home address, above)

_____

_____

20. Your telephone numbers

Home	(Area code _____)	_____
Work	(Area code _____)	_____
Mobil Phone	(Area code _____)	_____

LANGUAGES

21. Give details of your speaking and writing ability in English and other languages.

Mark your standards of speaking and writing

Languages	Vocational	Social	Survival	Zero	Mark your main languages
English	_____	_____	_____	_____	_____
_____	_____	_____	_____	_____	_____
_____	_____	_____	_____	_____	_____
_____	_____	_____	_____	_____	_____
_____	_____	_____	_____	_____	_____

NOMINEE'S FAMILY

22. Give details of ALL NOMINEE'S family.

NOMINEE'S PARENTS

Name	Sex	Date of Birth DAY / MONTH / YEAR	
_____	__	___ / ___ / _____	_____
_____	__	___ / ___ / _____	_____

ALL NOMINEE'S CHILDREN UNDER 18

Name	Sex	Date of Birth DAY / MONTH / YEAR	
_____	__	___ / ___ / _____	_____
_____	__	___ / ___ / _____	_____
_____	__	___ / ___ / _____	_____
_____	__	___ / ___ / _____	_____
_____	__	___ / ___ / _____	_____
_____	__	___ / ___ / _____	_____

ALL NOMINEE'S OTHER DEPENDENTS & CHILDREN AGED OVER 18

Name	Sex	Date of Birth DAY / MONTH / YEAR	
_____	__	___ / ___ / _____	_____
_____	__	___ / ___ / _____	_____
_____	__	___ / ___ / _____	_____
_____	__	___ / ___ / _____	_____
_____	__	___ / ___ / _____	_____
_____	__	___ / ___ / _____	_____

HEALTH

23. Do you, or anyone in your family, suffer from: Give details below.

A serious contagious, transmissible or hereditary disease or condition.   No __   Yes __

A serious condition or disability which requires regular medical attention, hospital treatment or special care.   No __   Yes __

A physical disability or mental retardation.   No __   Yes __

Do any of the above require regular medical attention, hospital treatment or special care? No __   Yes __

Health Details:

Full Name	Nature of condition, illness or disease
_____	_____
_____	_____
_____	_____
_____	_____

CHARACTER

24. Please answer the following questions about yourself.

Convicted of a crime or offense	No __	Yes __	To be approved
Sentenced to serve a period of time in jail or in other form of detention	No __	Yes __	you are required
Placed on probation	No __	Yes __	to be of good
Charged pending trial	No __	Yes __	character.

If Yes to any question above, give details below. (If necessary, use additional sheets of paper.)

Full
Name _____

Nature of
Offense _____

Nature of
Court _____ Country _____

Date of sentencing
DAY / MONTH / YEAR

Sentence _____ ____ / ____ / _____

Full
Name _____

Nature of
Offense _____

Nature of
Court _____ Country _____

Date of sentencing
DAY / MONTH / YEAR

Sentence _____ ____ / ____ / _____

25. Have you ever served in the armed forces? No __   Yes __

Nationality _____   Date of Discharge   Rank

DAY / MONTH / YEAR

Service _____ ____ / ____ / _____ _____

Type of Discharge _____

Training or
Specialty _____

26. Have you ever been:

Deported, excluded or removed from any country?	No __	Yes __
Asked to leave a country?	No __	Yes __
Refused entry to any country?	No __	Yes __
Refused a visa (including a visa to migrate to any country)?	No __	Yes __

DECLARATION

I declare that the information supplied on this form, and any attachments, is complete, correct and up-to-date in every detail.

I understand that if I have given false or misleading information, my application may be refused.

I undertake to inform the New Utopian Government Office of any material changes to my circumstances while my application is being considered.

I declare that I have read and understood the information supplied to me and in particular the information contained in the Explanatory Notes to this application.

By signing below or otherwise permitting my nomination for citizenship, I agree to be subject to the provisions of the Constitution of the Principality of New Utopia and to abide by the laws duly passed in accordance with it.

Signature of Nominee   N.B: If Nominee is under the age of 18, his Nominee Form must be signed by his parents.

Date
DAY / MONTH / YEAR

_____ ____ / ____ / _____

REFERENCE

I certify that the Nominee has been known personally to me for years and that to the best of my knowledge and belief the facts stated on this form is correct.

Signature of Referring Person

_____

Date (DAY / MONTH / YEAR)

_____ / _____ / _____

Full Name _____

Profession _____

Address _____

_____

_____

Telephone
Number _____

Important: Nominees are warned that should any statement made in connection with this nominee form prove to be untrue, the consequences to them may be serious.

OFFICIAL USE ONLY:

1. NOMINEE FORM DELIVERED BY: _____

2. NOMINEE FORM RECEIVED BY: _____

3. NOMINEE FORM REVIEWED BY: _____

4. DOCUMENTS PRODUCED: A. _____

5. B. _____

6. C. _____

7. D. _____

8. E. _____

9. F. _____

10. G. _____

11. H. _____

12. I. _____

13. J. _____

14. K. _____

15. L. _____

16. NOTES:

_____

_____

_____

_____

_____

_____

17. NOMINEE FORM: APPROVED __   DISAPPROVED __

18. SIGNATURE: _____   TITLE: _____

The Principality of New Utopia

Department of New Citizen Nominees

Citizenship Nominee Information

Donation and Document Purchase Form

Amount Enclosed for Donation (minimum $1500)		$ _____
Amount Enclosed for Documents	Number of Applicants _____ X $24.00 US =	$ _____
Total Amount Enclosed		$ _____

Note: US $1,500 minimum donation is mandatory for citizenship nomination.

Mail To:

    The Principality of New Utopia
    9441 East 31st. Street, Suite 160
    Tulsa, Oklahoma 74145 U.S.A.

Voice Phone:

    (918) 712-9980

Fax:

    (918) 438-2611

Articles of Incorporation
of
[NAMES OF INCORPORATORS]

The undersigned, a majority of whom are citizens of the United States, desiring to form a Nonprofit Corporation under the Nonprofit Corporation Law of [YOUR STATE], do hereby certify:

First:
The name of the Corporation shall be [NAME OF CORPORATION].

Second:
The place in this state where the principal office of the Corporation is to be located is the City of [CITY], [COUNTY] County.

Third:
Said corporation is organized exclusively for charitable, religious, educational, and scientific purposes, including, for such purposes, the making of distributions to organizations that qualify as exempt organizations under section 501(c)(3) of the Internal Revenue Code, or the corresponding section of any future federal tax code.

Fourth:
The names and addresses of the persons who are the initial trustees of the corporation are as follows:
[NAME] [ADDRESS]
[NAME] [ADDRESS]

Fifth:
No part of the net earnings of the corporation shall inure to the benefit of, or be distributable to its members, trustees, officers, or other private persons, except that the corporation shall be authorized and empowered to pay reasonable compensation for services rendered and to make payments and distributions in furtherance of the purposes set forth in Article Third hereof. No substantial part of the activities of the corporation shall be the carrying on of propaganda, or otherwise attempting to

influence legislation, and the corporation shall not participate in, or intervene in (including the publishing or distribution of statements) any political campaign on behalf of or in opposition to any candidate for public office. Notwithstanding any other provision of these articles, the corporation shall not carry on any other activities not permitted to be carried on (a) by a corporation exempt from federal income tax under section 501(c)(3) of the Internal Revenue Code, or the corresponding section of any future federal tax code, or (b) by a corporation, contributions to which are deductible under section 170(c)(2) of the Internal Revenue Code, or the corresponding section of any future federal tax code.

[**NOTE:** If reference to federal law in articles of incorporation imposes a limitation that is invalid in your state, you may wish to substitute the following for the last sentence of the preceding paragraph:]

Notwithstanding any other provision of these articles, this corporation shall not, except to an insubstantial degree, engage in any activities or exercise any powers that are not in furtherance of the purposes of this corporation.

Sixth:
Upon the dissolution of the corporation, assets shall be distributed for one or more exempt purposes within the meaning of section 501(c)(3) of the Internal Revenue Code, or the corresponding section of any future federal tax code, or shall be distributed to the federal government, or to a state or local government, for a public purpose. Any such assets not so disposed of shall be disposed of by a Court of Competent Jurisdiction of the county in which the principal office of the corporation is then located, exclusively for such purposes or to such organization or organizations, as said Court shall determine, which are organized and operated exclusively for such purposes.

In witness whereof, we have hereunto subscribed our names this [DAY] day of [MONTH], [YEAR].

_____
Name

_____
Name

Declaration of Trust
of
The [NAME OF TRUST] Charitable Trust

Made this [DAY] day of [MONTH], [YEAR],

by [NAME], of [ADDRESS],

and

[NAME], of [ADDRESS],

who hereby declare and agree that they have received this day from, [name of Donor], as Donor, the sum of Ten Dollars ($10) and that they will hold and manage the same, and any additions to it, in trust, as follows:

First:
This trust shall be called The [NAME OF TRUST] Charitable Trust.

Second:
The trustees may receive and accept property, whether real, personal, or mixed, by way of gift, bequest, or devise, from any person, firm, trust, or corporation, to be held, administered, and disposed of in accordance with and pursuant to the provisions of this Declaration of Trust; but no gift, bequest or devise of any such property shall be received and accepted if it is conditioned or limited in such manner as to require the disposition of the income or its principal to any person or organization other than a charitable organization or for other than charitable purposes within the meaning of such terms as defined in Article Third of this Declaration of Trust, or as shall in the opinion of the trustees, jeopardize the federal income tax exemption of this trust pursuant to section 501(c)(3) of the Internal Revenue Code, or the corresponding section of any future federal tax code.

Third:

A. The principal and income of all property received and accepted by the trustees to be administered under this Declaration of Trust shall be held in trust by them, and the trustees may make payments or distributions from income or principal, or both, to or for the use of such charitable organizations, within the meaning of that term as defined in paragraph C, in such amounts and for such charitable purposes of the trust as the trustees shall from time to time select and determine; and the trustees may make payments or distributions from income or principal, or both, directly for such charitable purposes, within the meaning of that term as defined in paragraph D, in such amounts as the trustees shall from time to time select and determine without making use of any other charitable organization. The trustees may also make payments or distributions of all or any part of the income or principal to states, territories, or possessions of the United States, any political subdivision of any of the foregoing, or to the United States or the District of Columbia but only for charitable purposes within the meaning of that term as defined in paragraph D. Income or principal derived from contributions by corporations shall be distributed by the trustees for use solely within the United States or its possessions. No part of the net earnings of this trust shall inure or be payable to or for the benefit of any private shareholder or individual, and no substantial part of the activities of this trust shall be the carrying on of propaganda, or otherwise attempting, to influence legislation. No part of the activities of this trust shall be the participation in, or intervention in (including the publishing or distributing of statements), any political campaign on behalf of or in opposition to any candidate for public office.

B. The trust shall continue forever unless the trustees terminate it and distribute all of the principal and income, which action may be taken by the trustees in their discretion at any time. On such termination, assets shall be distributed for one or more exempt purposes within the meaning of section 501(c)(3) of the Internal Revenue Code, or the corresponding section of any future federal tax code, or shall be distributed to the federal government, or to a state or local government, for a public purpose. The donor authorizes and empowers the trustees to form and organize a nonprofit corporation limited to the uses and purposes provided for in this Declaration of Trust, such corporation to be organized under the laws of any state or under the laws of the United States as may be determined by the trustees; such corporation when organized to have power to administer and control the affairs and property and to carry out the uses, objects, and purposes of this trust. Upon the creation and organization of such corporation, the trustees are authorized and empowered to convey, transfer, and deliver to such corporation all the property and assets to which this trust may be or become entitled. The charter, bylaws, and other provisions for the organization and management of such corporation and its affairs and property shall be such as the trustees shall determine, consistent with the provisions of this paragraph.

C. In this Declaration of Trust and in any amendments to it, references to charitable organizations or charitable organization mean corporations, trusts, funds, foundations, or community chests created or organized in the United States or in any of its possessions, whether under the laws of the United States, any state or territory, the District of Columbia, or any possession of the United States, organized and operated exclusively for charitable purposes, no part of the net earnings of which inures or is payable to or for the benefit of any private shareholder or individual, and no substantial part of the activities of which is carrying on propaganda, or otherwise attempting, to influence legislation, and which do not participate in or intervene in (including the publishing or distributing of statements) any political campaign on behalf of or in opposition to any candidate for public office. It is intended that the Organization described in this paragraph C shall be entitled to exemption from federal income tax under section 501(c)(3) of the Internal Revenue Code, or the corresponding section of any future federal tax code.

D. In this Declaration of Trust and in any amendments to it, the term charitable purposes shall be limited to and shall include only religious, charitable, scientific, literary, or educational purposes within the meaning of those terms as used in section 501(c)(3) of the Internal Revenue Code, or the corresponding section of any future federal tax code, but only such purposes as also constitute public charitable purposes under the law of trusts of the State of [STATE].

Fourth:

This Declaration of Trust may be amended at any time or times by written instrument or instruments signed and sealed by the trustees, and acknowledged by any of the trustees, provided that no amendment shall authorize the trustees to conduct the affairs of this trust in any manner or for any purpose contrary to the provisions of section 501(c)(3) of the Internal Revenue Code, or the corresponding section of any future federal tax code. An amendment of the provisions of this Article Fourth (or any amendment to it) shall be valid only if and to the extent that such amendment further restricts the trustees' amending power. All instruments amending this Declaration of Trust shall be noted upon or kept attached to the executed original of this Declaration of Trust held by the trustees.

Fifth:

Any trustee under this Declaration of Trust may, by written instrument, signed and acknowledged, resign his office. The number of trustees shall be at all times not less than two, and whenever for any reason the number is reduced to one, there shall be, and at any other time there may be, appointed one or more additional trustees. Appointments shall be made by the trustee or trustees for the time in office by written instruments signed and acknowledged. Any succeeding or additional trustee shall, upon his acceptance of the office by written instrument signed and acknowledged, have the same powers, rights and duties, and the same title to the trust estate jointly with the surviving or remaining trustee or trustees as if originally appointed.

None of the trustees shall be required to furnish any bond or surety. None of them shall be responsible or liable for the acts or omissions of any other of the trustees or of any predecessor or of a custodian, agent, depositary or counsel selected with reasonable care.

The one or more trustees, whether original or successor, for the time being in office, shall have full authority to act even though one or more vacancies may exist. A trustee may, by appropriate written instrument, delegate all or any part of his powers to another or others of the trustees for such periods and subject to such conditions as such delegating trustee may determine.

The trustees serving under this Declaration of Trust are authorized to pay to themselves amounts for reasonable expenses incurred and reasonable compensation for services rendered in the administration of this trust, but in no event shall any trustee who has made a contribution to this trust ever receive any compensation thereafter.

Sixth:

In extension and not in limitation of the common law and statutory powers of trustees and other powers granted in this Declaration of Trust, the trustees shall have the following discretionary powers:

a) To invest and reinvest the principal and income of the trust in such property, real, personal, or mixed, and in such manner as they shall deem proper, and from time to time to change investments as they shall deem advisable; to invest in or retain any stocks, shares, bonds, notes, obligations, or personal or real property (including without limitation any interests in or obligations of any corporation, association, business trust, investment trust, common trust fund, or investment company) although some or all of the property so acquired or retained is of a kind or size which but for this express authority would not be considered proper and although all of the trust funds are invested in the securities of one company. No principal or income, however, shall be loaned, directly or indirectly, to any trustee or to anyone else, corporate or otherwise, who has at any time made a contribution to this trust, nor to anyone except on the basis of an adequate interest charge and with adequate security.

b) To sell, lease, or exchange any personal, mixed, or real property, at public auction or by private contract, for such consideration and on such terms as to credit or otherwise, and to make such contracts and enter into such undertakings relating to the trust property, as they consider advisable, whether or not such leases or contracts may extend beyond the duration of the trust.

c) To borrow money for such periods, at such rates of interest, and upon such terms as the trustees consider advisable, and as security for such loans to mortgage or pledge any real or personal property with or without power of sale; to acquire or hold any real or personal property, subject to any mortgage or pledge on or of property acquired or held by this trust.

d) To execute and deliver deeds, assignments, transfers, mortgages, pledges, leases, covenants, contracts, promissory notes, releases, and other instruments, sealed or unsealed, incident to any transaction in which they engage.

e) To vote, to give proxies, to participate in the reorganization, merger or consolidation of any concern, or in the sale, lease, disposition, or distribution of its assets; to join with other security holders in acting through a committee, depositary, voting trustees, or otherwise, and in this connection to delegate authority to such committee, depositary, or trustees and to deposit securities with them or transfer securities to them; to pay assessments levied on securities or to exercise subscription rights in respect of securities.

f) To employ a bank or trust company as custodian of any funds or securities and to delegate to it such powers as they deem appropriate; to hold trust property without indication of fiduciary capacity but only in the name of a registered nominee, provided the trust property is at all times identified as such on the books of the trust; to keep any or all of the trust property or funds in any place or places in the United States of America; to employ clerks, accountants, investment counsel, investment agents, and any special services, and to pay the reasonable compensation and expenses of all such services in addition to the compensation of the trustees.

Seventh:

The trustees' powers are exercisable solely in the fiduciary capacity consistent with and in furtherance of the charitable purposes of this trust as specified in Article Third and not otherwise.

Eighth:

In this Declaration of Trust and in any amendment to it, references to trustees mean the one or more trustees, whether original or successor, for the time being in office.

Ninth:

Any person may rely on a copy, certified by a notary public, of the executed original of this Declaration of Trust held by the trustees, and of any of the notations on it and writings attached to it, as fully as he might rely on the original documents themselves. Any such person may rely fully on any statements of fact certified by anyone who appears from such original documents or from such certified copy to be a trustee under this Declaration of Trust. No one dealing with the trustees need inquire concerning the validity of anything the trustees purport to do. No one dealing with the trustees need see to the application of anything paid or transferred to or upon the order of the trustees of the trust.

Tenth:

This Declaration of Trust is to be governed in all respects by the laws of the State of [STATE].

_____Trustee
_____Trustee

Below are some of the texts I consulted while working on this book. They are listed alphabetically by title.

Acquiring New ID. Ragnar Benson (Boulder, CO: Paladin Press, 1996)
Beat The Bill Collector. Max Edison (Boulder, CO: Paladin Press, 1997)
Bulletproof Privacy. Boston T. Party (Ignacio, CO: Javelin Press, 1997)
Computer Privacy Handbook. André Bacard (Berkeley, CA: Peachpit Press, 1995)
Dual Irish Citizenship Guide. (Potomac, MD: Sidhe Information Services, 1996)
Freedom Wealth & Privacy Report. Issues 19 through 23 (Channel Islands: Liberty Publishing, 1998-1999)
I Am Not a Number. Claire Wolfe (Port Townsend, WA: Loompanics Unlimited, 1998)
I.D. Checking Guide. (Redwood City, CA: Drivers License Guide Company, 1998)
Irish Citizenship Handbook. Dr. Frank Faulkner (Springfield, MA: Hungry Hill Press, 1996)
Modern Identity Changer. Sheldon Charrett (Boulder, CO: Paladin Press, 1997)
Optical Document Security. Rudolf L. van Renesse (Boston/London: Artech House Publishing, 1998)
Paper Trip III. Barry Reid (Fountain Valley, CA: Eden Press, 1998)

I used the following products to find sources and compile demographic information while working on this book:

88 Million Households Phone Book (Omaha, NE: CD USA, 1998)
Select Phone Telephone Database (Danvers, MA: Pro CD Inc, 1997)